Gus Dorais

GUS DORAIS

Gridiron Innovator,
All-American
and Hall of Fame Coach

Joe Niese
with Bob Dorais

Foreword by Roland Lazenby

McFarland & Company, Inc., Publishers
Jefferson, North Carolina

ALSO OF INTEREST: *Burleigh Grimes: Baseball's Last Legal Spitballer* by Joe Niese (2013)

LIBRARY OF CONGRESS CATALOGUING-IN-PUBLICATION DATA

Names: Niese, Joe, author. | Dorais, Bob, 1957– author.
Title: Gus Dorais : gridiron innovator, all-American and hall of fame coach / Joe Niese with Bob Dorais.
Description: Jefferson, N.C. : McFarland & Company, Inc., Publishers, 2018. | Includes bibliographical references and index.
Identifiers: LCCN 2018038350 | ISBN 9781476675244 (softcover : acid free paper) ∞
Subjects: LCSH: Dorais, Charles, 1891–1954. | Football players—United States—Biography. | Football coaches—United States—Biography. | University of Notre Dame—Football—History.
Classification: LCC GV939.D663 N54 2018 | DDC 796.332092 [B] —dc23
LC record available at https://lccn.loc.gov/2018038350

BRITISH LIBRARY CATALOGUING DATA ARE AVAILABLE

ISBN (print) 978-1-4766-7524-4
ISBN (ebook) 978-1-4766-3409-8

Front cover: Gus Dorais, captain of the University of Notre Dame football team, in 1912 (Dorais family photo collection)

Printed in the United States of America

McFarland & Company, Inc., Publishers
 Box 611, Jefferson, North Carolina 28640
  www.mcfarlandpub.com

Table of Contents

Acknowledgments

Once again I find myself indebted to the many people who supported me during the years I worked on this book.

First and foremost, I'd like to send endless love and gratitude to my loving wife, Sara, and our children: Oliver, Evelyn and Henry. You'll never know how much you have inspired me.

Special gratitude to:

My parents, Marvin and Mary, who finally relented and let me play high school football.

My brothers, Andy and Marty. I still remember those early days of playing touch football on the side of the house on Ableman Avenue.

My great in-laws and extended family—the Slatterys and Hahns. I couldn't have asked for a better group of people to call family.

The wonderful services that libraries, historical societies and museums provide. To the top-notch interlibrary loan department at the Indianhead Federated Library System—thank you, Maureen Welch and Gayle Spindler. Also, to the amazing staff at the Chippewa Falls Public Library. Thank you to: Michael D. Gibson, Archivist, Loras College; Patricia Higo, Research Librarian, University of Detroit Mercy Archives and Special Collections; Angela Kindig, Assistant Archivist, University Records, University of Notre Dame; Stephanie Plowman, Special Collections Librarian, Gonzaga University; and David Jankoski, Stanley Area Historical Society. Also to the outstanding collections at the Chippewa County Historical Society and the Chippewa County Genealogical Society Library (Chippewa Falls, Wisconsin). A final thank you to Erik Solberg at the *Spokesman-Review*.

The thriving literary community in the Chippewa Valley. Thank you to my fellow authors who provided encouragement along the way.

Gary Mitchem, Senior Acquisitions Editor at McFarland. Thanks for believing in this project.

My former teammates, coaches and the entire football program at Eau Claire Regis High School.

Bonnie Kellman, a great Notre Dame lawyer (Class of 2010) and football fan.

Bob Dorais. In my previous book efforts, I was fortunate to find that one person, whether it be a friend or family member of the subject, who helped push me along. That person was Bob, Gus' grandson. We made contact at a time when I was growing overwhelmed and frustrated with my progress. Bob openly shared his writing based on decades of research, filling in gaps where only a family member can. This book wouldn't be the same without his knowledge of the subject matter and eye for detail. I am forever thankful for the connection Bob and I made.

—Joe Niese

* * *

It's been a long journey to get this book to fruition. There are so many people I want to thank for their help and encouragement over the years. I apologize if I forget some names. To Vi Dorais, whose pride in Gus never wavered, which inspired me to start a book. To my family whom I dragged around the Midwest every year when they were young. It was necessary to visit many institutions before the internet age. Gus, Alex, Jake, Will and Molly, thank you for your patience and support. To Tom & Mary Kay Dorais, for encouraging me and helping along the way. To other friends and family members who helped: Patty Adolphs, Jim & Nancy McDonald, Amy Crudo, Dr. Tom McDonald, Bill & Helen Dorais, Bob Dilworth, Bob Mulcrone, Joan Robinson and Tom Riordan.

Many thanks to the archivists and librarians who went above and beyond to find material about Gus. Notre Dame: Peter Lysy, Charles Lamb, Susan McGonigal and Elizabeth Hogan. Pro Football Hall of Fame: Pete Fierle. CFHOF: Pat Harmon and Chris Saingas. University of Detroit: William Gould-McElhone, Caroline Roulier, Mark Engle, Sara Armstrong and Joshua Duffy. Detroit Lions: William Clay Ford, Mike Murray and Deanna Ivey. Gonzaga University: Oliver Pierce and Sharon Prendegrast. Amateur Athletic Foundation: Michael Salmon and Shirley Ito. The Indiana Album: Joan Hostetler and John Harris.

To Joe Niese, who was going to write a Gus Dorais book on his own. Thank you for reaching out and letting me collaborate on the book. I'm not a writer and could never do the Gus Dorais story justice like you have. You have put in a Herculean effort and I can't begin to tell you how much I appreciate your dedication and skill.

Finally, to Gus Dorais, whose long and amazing career in football entertained, inspired and educated. Gus loved the game of football. He never sought recognition or fame. It's long overdue that he gets a little of both. I hope those who read this book would agree.

—Bob Dorais

Foreword by Roland Lazenby

In looking back at his own career, Michael Jordan once told me, "Timing is everything."

Indeed, Jordan stepped forward with his immense talent in that moment when the game of basketball was beginning its grand evolution. Likewise, sports media itself was undergoing a similar transformation.

These two developments together brought Jordan to a global audience that so adored him it eventually made him a billionaire.

At the outset of his own grand sporting life, Gus Dorais also found himself blessed with perfect timing. He entered high school in 1906, just as the rules committee for football had adopted the forward pass in the wake of a slew of deaths in college football the previous season.

From high school in Chippewa Falls, Wisconsin, Dorais would find his way to Notre Dame, where he would gain fame as the quarterback lacing the ball to end Knute Rockne as they drove the Fighting Irish to three straight undefeated seasons and ignited the prominence that today still feeds the school's ravenous fan base.

Over his lifetime, Dorais played an immense role as an early expert and practitioner of the forward pass, as one of the pivotal, legendary figures in the school's unrivaled legacy in college football, and later as a college and pro football coach.

Despite all that, Dorais' fascinating life story has somehow managed to escape the brightest spotlight of history.

Authors Joe Niese and Bob Dorais have remedied that with this publication. It is a story researched and told lovingly, one that helps provide immense context and understanding not just of Dorais' life and competitive fire but of Notre Dame's rise as a power and the foundation of American football itself.

The game today, of course, is the forward pass.

1

With his then-unique throwing style, Gus Dorais was the pioneer who pointed the way and thus defined the pass.

His story is the game's story.

With a timing that meant everything.

Roland Lazenby has written more than 60 books, including *Michael Jordan: The Life* (2015) and *Showboat: The Life of Kobe Bryant* (2016), and contributed articles to magazines and newspapers. In 2005 he co-created Planet Blacksburg, a student organization focused on new media.

Preface

Charles Emile "Gus" Dorais was not the inventor of the forward pass. He never claimed to be. However, he did help revolutionize the play. On November 1, 1913, he and his good friend, roommate and receiving end, Knute Rockne, put on a shocking display of what an effective passing attack could do for a football team. Notre Dame defeated perennial Eastern powerhouse Army, 35–13. "We merely changed the forward pass from a weapon of emergency and final hope to one that was to be relied on to win," recalled Dorais.[1]

The misnomer of Dorais being the "Father of the Forward Pass" has been reinforced for over 40 years at, of all places, Dorais Field, in his hometown, Chippewa Falls, Wisconsin. There, a plaque tells how "Gus Dorais threw the first forward pass ever attempted in a college football game." Dorais played when the line between fact and fiction was often non-existent in the press. Add in the hundreds of banquet speeches, whether it was celebrating his current team, a former teammate or the local civic or fraternal organization, and some exaggerations can be translated into common knowledge. In writing the book, it could be difficult to separate that line, and at times a double or even triple verification from multiple sources was needed.

I played a high school football game at Dorais Field, as have hundreds of other prep players. I even scored a touchdown on a pass that would have made Dorais proud—the receiving end of a halfback option. My early knowledge of Dorais began and ended with his involvement in the evolution of the forward pass. Even when I became a resident of Chippewa Falls, I was content with the narrative I had. It wasn't until I took a closer look that I realized the impact he had beyond that one monumental game in 1913.

Researching a book can be an exhilarating and overwhelming experience all at the same time. One can get lost on the internet searching for a lead, or paging through endless books to piece it all together. Searching digitized newspapers made my quest a lot easier, but somewhat not as satisfying as unearthing a kernel of information while looking through reels of microfilm in a dark room. In writing the book, efforts were made to include quotes from Dorais whenever they fit, in hopes of giving the feeling that he was a part of the process. There might be information that will contradict previous writings. Rest assured that no assumptions were made and that tireless verification of stories and sources was made.

Gus Dorais passed away on January 3, 1954. The next day, Harry Leduc of the *Detroit News* surmised, "A detailed chronology of Gus Dorais would fill a book—and some day it may." Over six decades later, that prediction has finally come to fruition.[2]

Introduction

To tell the story of Gus Dorais, one must first address what he is known for—the forward pass. The evolution of the play is a murky one. The first recorded forward pass took place in 1879 during the Yale–Princeton game, when Yale's Walter Camp—known as "The Father of Football"—threw the ball to teammate Oliver Thompson as he was being tackled. For years the play would occasionally surface, but interpretation, specifically legality, varied. Finally, in 1906 the Rules Committee legalized the forward pass. That same fall, Dorais entered high school.

On a national level, football had been in jeopardy due to numerous deaths and countless injuries in the first few years of the 20th century. In 1905 alone, there were 18 deaths and 149 serious injuries caused by the physicality of the sport. The flying wedge was the biggest contributor to this epidemic, and seemingly no strongarm tactic was off-limits. Some universities and high schools planned on dropping their football programs altogether. Even President Theodore Roosevelt, a proponent of the game, demanded that rules be changed to make play safer.

Coaches and others heavily invested in football kept the game alive during these times. In December 1905, a group convened to enact a safer game created the precursor to the National College Athletic Association (NCAA). On January 12, 1906, a Rules Committee heard the latest proposal. Since 1903, John Heisman, head coach of Georgia Tech (and the namesake of the Heisman Trophy) had been writing to Walter Camp of the Rules Committee to consider the forward pass as a way of opening up the game. Each of Heisman's requests was denied. With the sport in danger of being dropped by more institutions, he again brought it to the Rules Committee, who this time accepted the proposition. At the larger April 1906 meeting, it was accepted along with other rules to open up the game. The committee also added a neutral zone and changed the first down yardage from five to ten yards. That had to be obtained in three downs—a fourth down was added in 1912.

Dorais had been playing football since childhood and took advantage of the zeitgeist that surrounded the forward pass in his home state, Wisconsin. Before his senior year of high school, Dorais transferred from the Catholic high school in town, Notre Dame, to Chippewa Falls High School, the public school, which had a more established football tradition. Utilizing a wide-open offensive attack, including frequent passes, Dorais led the team to a state championship and was an all-state quarterback. His coaches—both in their first year in the program—were Albion (A.G.) Findlay and Carl "Coots" Cunningham, the latter a graduate of Chippewa Falls High School. Both graduated from the University of Wisconsin–Madison, lettering in football. Findlay was a third-team All-American (Walter Camp) halfback in 1905.

Findlay and Cunningham were beneficiaries of the early interest shown in the forward pass by Eddie Cochems—an assistant coach at the University of Wisconsin–Madison in 1904, while the two played there. Cochems was a three-sport star at Madison, along with Norsky Larson and Keg Driver referred to as the "the most feared backfield trio in the middle west."[1] Cochems is often regarded as the first coach to use the overhand forward pass to its full advantage. In 1906, he guided a pass-happy St. Louis University (St. Louis, Missouri) to an undefeated 11–0 season, leading the nation in scoring with an astounding 407 points. Others who found early success with the now-legal pass were Pop Warner at Carlisle Indian Industrial School (Carlisle, Pennsylvania) and Alonzo Stagg at the University of Chicago (Chicago, Illinois).

In his landmark 1931 book, *The Forward Pass and Its Defense*, Dorais described the progression of the pass:

> The first throwers grasped the ball with one hand over the end of the ball parallel to the arm and with an underhand throw would toss it end over end down the field. The next development in passing was to lay the ball in the palm of the hand and with the same underhand throw to send it spiraling for a good distance. The next step was to lay the ball on the hand and with a side arm sweep of the arm shoulder high to throw the ball to the receiver. Many good passers were developed using this method and it is still good in throwing a wet muddy ball. The next and final step in the evolution of passing was to throw the ball gripped much as a baseball with an overhand throw which is the method that will be discussed more in detail later.[2]

In 1932, Dorais was speaking at the 11th annual American Football Coaches Association about the history of the forward pass. When comparing his behind the ear, overhand method of throwing to the way others were in those early legalization days, Dorais said: "I believe I was the first one, to my knowledge at least, ever to throw the ball in that manner."[3]

The early days of the pass made it a risk to attempt one. A pass—whether complete or incomplete—was a turnover if it was within five yards of the line of scrimmage. Passers had to drop back five yards and move at least five yards laterally to throw the ball, causing the field to be marked in a checkerboard pattern. Passes couldn't be caught more than 20 yards from the line of scrimmage, and a pass received over the goal line was a touchback, not a touchdown. An incomplete pass on first or second down was a 15-yard penalty from the spot of the pass. Those rules, and the fact that the fat, rugby-style ball was difficult to throw, made the pass an act of desperation.

Fatalities continued and rules were tinkered with to combat these occurrences. By 1912, the field was shortened to 100 yards, with end zones added. A seventh man was put on the line, and all interlocking formations were banned. The lateral rule was done away with, and passes could now be caught in the end zone for a touchdown, which was increased to six points from five.

Dorais continued to throw the ball brazenly at the University of Notre Dame (South Bend, Indiana), where he took over quarterbacking duties a few games into his freshman year. He went undefeated as a starter (22–0–3) under three coaches. His collegiate career culminated with the famous victory over the United States Military Academy, Army (West Point, New York), and All-American honors followed. The passing exhibition by Dorais and Rockne became a thing of lore. "Dorais and Rockne did not originate the forward pass any more than Tinker, Evers and Chance invented the double play," wrote longtime sportswriter Jimmy Powers. "But, their uncanny skill with the weapon in a major game linked them inseparably with the aerial attack."[4] Hyperbole aside, it was one of the most referenced sporting events of the 1900s. The frequent questions about the Army game became an inside joke between Dorais and Rockne.

Dorais' playing career extended beyond college, playing in the pre–National Football League days for the Massillon Tigers (Massillon, Ohio) and Fort Wayne Friars (Fort Wayne, Indiana), as well as during his stint in the Army during World War I. His career on the field ended on a vicious (and some might say illegal) hit by Jim Thorpe. For over three decades, Dorais brought the same quiet, confident approach that he played with to the sideline, gaining the respect of players and opponents alike. He coached multiple sports collegiately at three Catholic institutions: Dubuque College (Dubuque, Iowa), 1914–1917; Gonzaga University (Spokane, Washington), 1920–1924, and the University of Detroit (Detroit, Michigan), 1925–1942. He led the Detroit Lions for half a decade, 1943–1947. During those years he was the one of the most trusted voices, frequently serving on or heading committees that decided on rules or improvements to the game. He wrote a book and was frequently a sports columnist. He led football clinics for coaches and the public and was often a guest on the radio, describing football in layman terms. Much of that respect and acclaim can be traced back to his lineage with the forward pass.

CHAPTER 1

A River City Childhood

In the latter half of the 1800s, Chippewa Falls, Wisconsin, was at the epicenter of the lumber industry. At one point the city was home to the largest sawmill under one roof in the world—The Chippewa Lumber & Boom Sawmill. Over the years the prospects of work lured thousands of people—mostly men—to western Wisconsin for not only the steady pay that working with timber brought, but also the industries that sprang up to support the influx in population. One of those men was Antoine Dolvida Dorais.

Dorais came to the United States from Saint-Jean-Chrysostome, a small village just outside Montreal, Quebec. By the early 1880s, he was living in Chippewa Falls, working as a barkeeper at a saloon and boarding house owned by Mrs. Marceline Grandmaitre on West Central Street in downtown. The establishment was one of the oldest in the city and just a few hundred yards from the Chippewa River, a major thoroughfare for lumber.

During those years, Dorais, who went by the name "David," met a local girl, Mary Alivne Murphy (who went by "Melvina" or "Malvina"), who also had Quebec family roots. Marriage followed a brief courtship. Over the next several years the couple had four children (and at least one that died in infancy): George David Xavier, born December 14, 1886; Flora Leona, June 17, 1889; Charles Emile, July 2, 1891; and Joseph Emery, August 13, 1893.

Though the growing Dorais family moved to several locations in Chippewa Falls, they never ventured far from the town's east hill, known as "Catholic Hill," in reference to Notre Dame Catholic Church that overlooked the city. David worked a variety of jobs to support the family, including as a laborer for Chippewa Lumber and Boom. Between David's drinking and Melvina's religious fervor, home life was not easy for the Dorais children. Nor did it get any better when they attended the parochial school on Catholic Hill, Notre Dame. Charles expounded upon these times in a revealing essay entitled "Living Backward," written during his junior year at the University of Notre Dame shortly after his father's death. In it he wrote of the emotional and spiritual abuse he suffered both at home and at school: "It seemed as if all were in a contest to see who could deal out the most effective and abundant amount of punishment in a given time; and the competition was always a close one."[1]

As the end of the century neared and lumber numbers began to dwindle, David decided to chase another boom—ore. In the 1900 census, the Dorais family shows up in Silver Bow, Montana, living in the rough and tumble eighth ward of Butte, Montana, close to David's brothers, Donat, Joseph, Emery, Louiset and William. David was employed as an ore miner, as over 40 percent of the world's copper ore was mined in the Silver Bow Valley. The Dorais family struggled as David's drinking increased, and living in the bustling town was dangerous for Melvina and the children. When her parents became ill and needed full-time care, Melvina made the decision to move back to Chippewa Falls with the children. David stayed behind in Butte.

Back in Chippewa Falls, the Dorais family moved into a house on South

Dorais was a leader from the beginning. He is seated in the front row, middle, holding the football in this early 1900s photograph of the Star Football team (Chippewa County Historical Society Collection).

State Street, on Catholic Hill. Despite David still being alive in Montana, Melvina was listed as a widower in the June 1905 Wisconsin census. She provided for her family by taking on laundry from the many boarding houses in the area, as well as working as a midwife. She also took care of her father, John, who passed away in March 1904, and her mother, Millie, March 1905. The eldest Dorais child, George, worked as a barkeep in the city.

Charles helped maintain the home and property, including keeping the fire wood properly stocked and trimming the ever-growing lawn. He supplemented income for the family by doing odd jobs around the city. One of these duties was hauling items around the city for people by mule and wagon. One day, the mule was particularly stubborn. No matter what Charles did, he couldn't get the animal to budge. Needing to get his deliveries done and blocking the road, Dorais scrounged pieces of wood and anything that would burn. He piled it under the mule and lit fire to the kindling. The mule did finally move, but only a few feet to resist the fire, which was now ablaze. Now directly over the fire, the wooden wagon was quickly engulfed in flames, putting an end to that day's deliveries.[2]

Dorais found solace in any physical activity and was a frequent face on the sandlots around the city. He once made reference to Saturday activities: "a ball game, a fight, a marble game, or a swimming tournament."[3] Like most towns in the area, Chippewa Falls was baseball crazy. Dorais dreamed of playing the game professionally. It seemed that every block had a squad. Some of the city's most famous teams—including one year (1906) of being home to a minor league team—were during Dorais' formative years. When he was old enough, Dorais played for teams in Chippewa Falls and nearby towns such as Bloomer and Eau Claire. He was a strong-armed shortstop when he wasn't pitching.

In the winter, Dorais took a liking to downhill skiing. During his high school years, Chippewa Falls built a large ski hill in the town flats and had a very successful ski club—the North Star Ski Club. Among members of the club were two Norwegian immigrants—Lars and Anders Haugen— the latter of whom won a bronze medal at the 1924 Olympics. Since he couldn't afford skis, Dorais competed in ski jumping events on skis he constructed out of barrel staves.[4]

Football was also a major interest in Chippewa Falls. In addition to the two high school teams, different parts of town fielded their own amateur squads. Dorais was drawn to football at an early age and could often be found in the lots playing games with boys from the neighborhood on the Star football team. When Dorais entered Notre Dame High School in the fall of 1906, he was lucky to play a few games. At the top of the city's football hierarchy was the public school, Chippewa Falls High School. Notre Dame had fielded a team for years, but during Dorais' first few years of high school, games were seldom reported. In 1908, the program finally got some press thanks in part to the talent of Dorais, the team's quarterback and captain. He was an excellent open field runner, utilized the forward pass, was an adept tackler in the defensive backfield, and handled the squad's kicking duties. He was fearless. In an era when headgear was starting to be used, Dorais never did—a practice he continued throughout his playing career, both in college and the professional ranks.

Though overshadowed by the exploits of the undefeated Chippewa Falls High School team, Dorais led the Notre Dame team to a 4–1 record in his junior year. Notre Dame defeated the Eau Claire Union Business College, 9–6, in late October. The Chippewa Falls *Daily Independent* made note of a forward pass by Dorais that went for 25 yards. Late in the game he suffered a broken thumb and bruised finger, which hampered him when Notre Dame took the field against Chippewa Falls High School at the South Side Athletic Park two weeks later. Notre Dame lost, 10–0, in wet conditions, but the *Daily Independent* pegged Dorais as the star of the game: "Dorais, the plucky little Notre Dame quarterback, although handicapped by a heavy field, displayed both generalship and kicking ability

By the time Dorais (back row, fourth from left) entered Notre Dame High School in 1906, he was already a standout. By his sophomore year, he was the quarterback and team captain (Chippewa County Historical Society Collection).

seldom seen on any high school team."[5] Though there were rarely players over 200 pounds, throughout his playing days Dorais' size was often a point of amazement for newspapers. He was often listed at 5'7" or 5'8" and never more than 150 pounds. He was frequently referred to as "Little Napoleon" or the "Little General."

Notre Dame dedicated a new state-of-the-art school in January 1908. It was so well-equipped and the staff and curriculum were so highly thought of that graduates were granted admittance to the University of Wisconsin–Madison without examination. Despite that, Dorais had football on his mind, particularly playing for Dr. Henry Williams at the Big Nine Conference powerhouse, the University of Minnesota. With the Notre Dame team in jeopardy of playing fewer games or being cut altogether, Dorais made the decision to transfer to the public high school for his senior year. He was joining an established football team that went undefeated and unscored upon in 1908. Besides Dorais, the squad had a handful of players who went onto play collegiately: team captain Guy DeLong (left halfback) and Wilfred Smith (lineman), Carroll College (Waukesha, Wisconsin), and Robert Wiley (right end), Lawrence University (Appleton, Wisconsin). Dorais' departure from Notre Dame ultimately coincided with the end of football at the high school. There wouldn't be another team at the Catholic High School until 1927.

There were other changes to the Chippewa Falls High School team. A new coaching staff was taking over—one that would greatly benefit Dorais' progression as a quarterback. The new head coach was Albion G. Findlay, also serving as high school principal and history teacher. Findlay, known as "A.G.," had recently married a girl from Chippewa Falls, Lucy Hamacher, a relative of Dorais' mother. The relation undoubtedly had an impact on Dorais transferring schools.

Findlay grew up on a farm in Aurora, Illinois. As a youth he harnessed his agility by running down jackrabbits. He was a four-year letter winner at the University of Wisconsin–Madison, spending the first three years on the line before moving into the backfield in his senior season, 1905. He earned 3rd-team Walter Camp's All-American honors as a halfback. His shining moment during the 1905 campaign came in a 16–12 defeat of the Minnesota Gophers, when he scored two first half touchdown runs totaling 85 yards. It was the eighth game on the schedule, and these were the first points that Minnesota had given up. In the previous two years, the Gophers had surrendered 12 point in each season. The Badgers topped that in the first half. It was the only blemish of Minnesota's 12–1 season, but it cost them a share of the Big Nine Conference title.

After graduating, Findlay played professionally for the Massillon (Ohio) Tigers in 1906. It was the pinnacle of his playing days. The most historically significant games took place against the Canton Bulldogs. "I was credited with being the greatest backfield man in the game," recalled Findlay over half a century later. "Our opponents, The Canton Bulldogs, had four All-Americans in their backfield. Pardon an old man for a little boasting."[6]

Findlay spent the 1907–1908 school year at the University of Montana in Missoula, where he taught geology and mineralogy, ran the gymnasium, and coached the football team to a 4–1–1 record. In 1908 he returned to Wisconsin, working a year as principal of West Salem High School, finding success coaching the football team.

Joining Findlay on the sidelines was Carl Cunningham, a local boy who, like Findlay, starred at the University of Wisconsin. A 1905 graduate of Chippewa Falls High School, "Coots," as Cunningham was known, played several positions for the Badgers (including quarterback and place-kicker) from 1905 to 1908. In 1907, he intercepted a pass against Purdue and ran it back 105 yards for a touchdown. During Cunningham's playing days at Wisconsin, the *Wisconsin State Journal* described him as "not only a Wisconsin star, but a western star," and said that he "excels on the forward pass and the outside kick."[7]

With the addition of Dorais, several returning players and the expertise of Findlay and Cunningham, expectations were high for Chippewa Falls High School. Before the season had even begun, the *Daily Independent* spelled it out: "If the people turn out and support the team there is a strong possibility of the championship being brought to Chippewa Falls."[8] In a preview by the *Eau Claire Leader* just days before the team's opener, praise was heaped upon the coaches and the quarterback: "Dorais, the 145 pound cannon ball from Notre Dame will be a line smashing terror this year. He is the fastest and cleverest open field runner in the state."[9]

It was quickly evident that the football team was a special one. On October 2, Chippewa Falls High School obliterated a squad from nearby Stanley High School, 71–0, at the Stanley Fairgrounds. The *Daily Independent* stated that of all the plays, Dorais' 90-yard kickoff return was the "most sensational."[10] He also made 11 of 12 extra point attempts.

When the high school yearbook, the *Monocle*, came out at the end of the year (Dorais was the publication's Associate Business Manager), there was a section called "Extracts From a Senior Girl's Diary." After that first game, she wrote of Dorais: "C.D. plays football like an angel. They

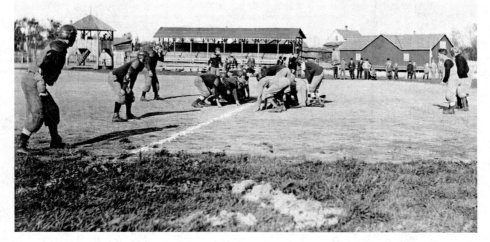

Dorais (far right, without headgear) and his teammates set the tone for the 1909 season in their opener, a 71-0 win over Stanley High School at the Stanley Fairgrounds (Stanley Historical Society).

say he has no time for girls." The next weekend she noted dancing with Dorais at a party. "C.D. danced with me twice. He dances divinely."[11]

The next week, in a drizzling rain, Chippewa Falls shut out Stevens Point Normals, 38–0. Dorais scored on a 40-yard fake punt and "made a number of spectacular runs from [sic] position and handled his team well."[12] The team followed that up by squeaking out a 6–0 win over a much larger LaCrosse High School team. Once again the elements wreaked havoc, but Dorais' foot was able to navigate strong wind gusts in what was described as a "punting duel."[13] Despite numerous fumbles, the team then easily handled Menomonie High School, 28–0. For the next month, the team only practiced as high schools from Sparta, Wisconsin, and Wabasha, Minnesota, canceled on gameday. Superior came to town, only to be unable to play due to weather conditions.

On October 30, Findlay and Cunningham took several players, including Dorais, to Greater Northrop Field in Minneapolis to watch the University of Minnesota defeat Alonzo Stagg's University of Chicago, 20–6. The Gophers were considered one of the top programs in the west over the past decade. Much of the success could be attributed to coach Dr. Henry Williams, who came to Minneapolis in August 1900 to take over as University Athletic Director, work as a member of the faculty, and practice medicine. Like many boys, Dorais dreamed of playing for Williams' team.

Almost a month after their last game, Chippewa Falls High School was finally able to return to the field of play. On November 20, Oshkosh High School came to Chippewa Falls. All week heavy snow kept the game in jeopardy, but constant attention to the playing surface allowed the teams to play as three feet of snow surrounded the nearly dry field before kickoff. Chippewa Falls battled a much larger Oshkosh line to a 0–0 tie. According to the *Chippewa Independent*, three times Dorais "shook off and evaded a half dozen tackles only to be downed by the only Oshkosh man that stood between him and the goal.[14]

Despite the abbreviated schedule, Findlay and Cunningham felt they had one of the best teams in Wisconsin. They reached out to Marinette High School, a top performer in the southern part of the state, inviting them for a game in Chippewa Falls on November 27. Marinette initially refused, but countered midweek with a proposition to play on that date in Milwaukee at Marquette University's Campus Field. They bolstered the offer by offering to pay all of Chippewa Falls' expenses, including train and accommodations at the St. Charles Hotel. Chippewa Falls High school agreed to the terms.

The only problem for Chippewa Falls was that when their initial offer to Marinette was rebuffed, the season seemed to be over. As a show of appreciation, a Thanksgiving Day exhibition game between the high school team and an alumni squad was put together. As a bonus, Findlay and Cunningham helped round out the alumni roster. The Thanksgiving game went on as planned. The teams played to a 5–5 tie. Both Dorais and DeLong suffered minor injuries, which they would feel in the game against Marinette.

Shortly before noon the next morning, the team left Union Depot on the Soo Line for Milwaukee, to play their third game in seven days. A banner hung from each train coach: "Chippewa Falls High School Team. Championship Game Milwaukee." As the group traveled south, they learned that the game was being touted as the championship of five states: Wisconsin, Michigan, Indiana, Illinois and Iowa.

The next day, a small group settled into the west bleachers of Campus Field, cheering on Chippewa Falls High School. Initially, plans had been made for a special train to follow the team to Milwaukee from Chippewa Falls, but when the funds weren't raised in time, it was canceled, leaving fans to travel on regular trains. Back in Chippewa Falls, a large crowd gathered at Herbert Bros. Smoke Shop on Bridge Street, spilling out into the street. They waited anxiously for updates from the nearby Western Union.

The seats on the opposite side of Campus Field were filled with several hundred Marinette backers. They arrived by special train, paid for by Wisconsin State Senator and Marinette resident Isaac Stephenson. He sent along a band that incessantly played "Hail! The Conquering Hero Comes."

Following a brief warm-up and a rousing pep talk from Coots Cunningham, Chippewa Falls took the field. The weather was unseasonably warm, and the field conditions were dry, favoring Dorais and his teammates. Though being significantly outsized by Marinette, Chippewa Falls was able to keep the ball in Marinette's territory for much of the first half. Chippewa Falls took advantage of a Marinette fumble and scored on a 15-yard run by DeLong, who was playing with what the *Daily Independent* reported as "one arm almost useless."[15] A Dorais extra point made the score 6–0.

It was much of the same in the second half, with most of the action in Marinette territory. Dorais added a 35-yard field goal to make the score 9–0. A few minutes later, Ed Hunt broke through the line on a cross tackle play, stiff-arming his way to a 65-yard touchdown. Dorais' kick made it 15–0.

Marinette threatened to score one time on a trick play, but Dorais thwarted the attempt when he was the only one left to make the tackle. Sensing defeat, Marinette attempted a 20-yard field goal toward the end of the game to avoid a shutout, but missed. Chippewa Falls was victorious, 15–0, claiming the title of Interscholastic Football Champions of the State.

Though kept out of the end zone, Dorais' all-around play was lauded by every outlet that reported on the game. He helped showcase a brand of play that had yet to be seen in that part of the state. As the *La Crosse Tribune* said, "It was a game in which a light team with the modern game outplayed a heavier team using the old style play."[16]

After the game, the Chippewa Falls team was treated to a banquet by Senator Stephenson. The Marinette squad and fans assembled at the St. Charles Hotel to pay their respects for the Chippewa Falls team. The group removed their caps and shouted, "The best team won!" The Chippewa Falls boys were eager to return home, where a hero's welcome awaited them. Instead of spending one more evening in Milwaukee, they engaged a special sleeper car headed back north.

Of all the games that lay ahead of him as both a player and coach, Dorais recalled that moment as one of his fondest. Just months before his death, he told Harry Leduc of the *Detroit News* how the team "returned

Dorais (middle row, fourth from right) helped the Chippewa Falls High School to the 1909 Wisconsin Interscholastic Football Championship, earning All-State honors at quarterback. A. G. Findlay and Coots Cunningham (back row, second from right and far right respectively) were his coaches (Chippewa County Historical Society Collection).

home to be met at the depot by the entire town and the welcome band, behind which we marched right up the main street." Dorais concluded, "I believe that day remains the greenest and the greatest in my memory."[17]

In the days that followed the victory, letters and telegrams of congratulations came in from all over the state. Several schools challenged Chippewa Falls to defend their championship, including Oshkosh, who wanted a rematch. Findlay finally put an end to any conversation of another game. "We have played our final game," he announced. "We would like to play Oshkosh in Ripon or Milwaukee, but the players have broken training and as we think our claim to the title cannot be disputed, no game will be played."[18]

Cunningham echoed those sentiments: "Local critics generally credited Marinette with the strongest eleven in the state and Marinette offered to play Oshkosh, Madison or Chippewa Falls a post-season game for the state championship. Chippewa Falls was the only eleven to accept the Marinette defy."[19]

Over the next month, the Chippewa Falls boys reveled in their moment of glory. They were celebrated with a banquet and dance. There was a ceremonial presentation of letters to put on their new letterman sweaters. Dorais was one of five Chippewa Falls High School players elected to an all-state team. He was, of course, the quarterback. Two decades later Findlay called Dorais "the most accurate football passer I have ever seen."[20]

Dorais participated in a few activities during the remainder of his senior year, including track and field. His football exploits were common fodder in the yearbook: "D is for Dorais our football star, He's known all over, both near and far."[21] "But sure the eye of time behold no name. So great as thine in all the rolls of fame," taken from Homer's *The Odyssey*, was the quote that accompanied Dorais' senior photo.[22]

Findlay and Cunningham encouraged Dorais to attend their alma mater, the University of Wisconsin–Madison, but he had other ideas— the University of Minnesota. Dorais was confident that he could make the Gophers' roster. "I was one of those enthusiastic kids who was setting out to conquer the world, unmindful of the pitfalls that may be ahead," Dorais said decades later.[23]

Dorais claimed that he even went to the University of Minnesota to try out for Henry Williams, only to be met with indifference. The Gophers' coach seemed to know nothing of the Western Wisconsin prep star. He was already set at quarterback with Consensus All-American John McGovern returning for his senior season. When Williams scoffed at Dorais' aspirations of a spot in the backfield, the youngster seemed surprised. Dorais asked Williams where he thought he should go. "'Boy, I don't know, but I'm sure it isn't in our backfield,'" Dorais recalled Williams saying. "You're too small. We want big fellows here at Minnesota and I'm afraid you won't do."[24]

Findlay continued to attempt to find a suitable university for Dorais. One of those, Notre Dame, was coached by a Findlay contemporary, Frank C. "Shorty" Longman, a former star fullback at Michigan, who was entering his second year at the Catholic university. He already had a standout quarterback in Don Hamilton, but Longman was intrigued by the reports he received on Dorais. Longman contacted University of Notre Dame President Father John W. Cavanaugh on Dorais' and another student-athlete's behalf, asking for financial assistance.

In March, Longman, back in Ann Arbor, Michigan, at his photograph business, received a letter from Father Cavanaugh. He requested that Dorais reach out to Mr. Francis McKeever, a Chicago-based attorney and Notre Dame alum who expressed interested in providing financial assistance to prospective students. Dorais did as asked, and McKeever obliged the request. Longman expressed his pleasure with the arrangement in a correspondence with James Hope, Notre Dame's student athletic manager, just days before Dorais would be arriving on campus.

Over the years a few stories have been bantered about how Dorais earned money that summer before heading off to college, including working in a carnival at the hamburger stand, as a barker and finally a boxer. Joseph Gantz, a friend of Dorais' while he attended Notre Dame, said that it consisted of selling ice cream and hot dogs with a traveling carnival.[25]

Dorais arrived in South Bend on the Chicago, South Bend & Northern Indiana rail. At South Shore depot he boarded the Hill Street Car, which ran to the Notre Dame campus. Already unsure if he had made the right decision, the situation wasn't made any easier when Dorais approached Coach Longman in the gymnasium. The interaction resembled the demoralizing one Dorais had with Henry Williams in Minneapolis.

"Who are you?" said the coach curtly.

"I am Charles Dorais, of Chippewa Falls," responded Dorais, expecting Longman to greet him warmly.

"What do you play?" asked the coach, unimpressed.

"I am a football player—a quarterback," replied Dorais with as much confidence as he could muster.

Longman looked Dorais up and down. "Kinda light, aren't you?" he said, turning and walking away to tend to other business.

The rude introduction to collegiate football continued when Dorais made his way over to be fitted for a uniform. He was pulled from the first line he entered because it was for varsity players only. Finally, an oversized outfit was thrown at him without consideration of size. It was so ill-fitting that he asked for another, which was met with indifference. He would have to write home for his mother to send his high school uniform.

"If I had an idea I was good, it sure was knocked out of me that afternoon in the gym," recollected Dorais decades later.[26] The treatment was something Dorais soon learned was commonplace. "And that's the ways all newcomers are treated. Past reputations mean nothing down here— you're just one of the gang until you prove yourself."[27]

One thing that Dorais did find out in the gymnasium was his living arrangement. He was assigned to a basement of Sorin Hall (better known as a subway room), where many of the athletes lived. As he exited the gymnasium, he was so shaken by the interaction with Longman that he had thoughts of fleeing. Famed sportswriter Arch Ward, who got his start as a scribe when Dorais was coaching at Dubuque College later in the decade, said Dorais was "so light, young and lonesome the day he reported for classes at Notre Dame that he packed his suitcase and decided to go home. A friend caught him as he was boarding the streetcar for downtown."[28]

When he entered his room in Sorin Hall, Dorais was met by his roommate, a 22-year-old Norwegian immigrant from Chicago. His name was Knute Rockne, and together the pair would change the game of football forever.

CHAPTER 2

Notre Dame's Little General, 1910–1912

Knute Kenneth Rockne didn't come to the University of Notre Dame to play football. He hadn't decided to venture to South Bend until just days before he was on campus. Born in Voss, Norway, on March 4, 1888, Rockne immigrated to the United States at age five. His family lived in the densely Scandinavian-populated northwest side of Chicago. His father Lars had been in the country for a few years, falling in love with the city after his one-horse carriage won a second prize at the 1891 Chicago's World Fair.

A constant throughout Rockne's childhood was athletic endeavors. He boxed, ran track, played sandlot football and wanted to be a professional baseball player like his heroes, Rube Waddell and Mordecai "Three-Finger" Brown, pitchers for the Chicago Cubs. Rockne attended high school at North West Division High School, where he ran track and played end on the football team. In 1903, he became mesmerized by a prep football player, Walter Eckersall—just two years Rockne's senior. That year, Rockne watched Eckersall quarterback Hyde Park to a 105–0 victory over Brooklyn (New York) Polytechnic for the unofficial national high school championship. Eckersall went on to a successful collegiate career as an All-American quarterback for Alonzo Stagg at the University of Chicago. Eckersall then became a storied sportswriter for the *Chicago Tribune* and a referee, including games in which Rockne played and then coached.

After graduating from high school, Rockne spent three years working at the post office to earn money to attend college. His goal was to earn $1,000 and attend the University of Illinois (Champaign, Illinois) for an education. "Athletic fame was secondary, for, to me, college players loomed as supermen to whose heights I could never aspire," he once said of his early university aspirations.[1]

Rockne reached his monetary objective and looked forward to enrolling at Illinois, until fate intervened. While at a track meet, two friends changed his mind. Johnny Devine and Johnny Plant, runners at Notre Dame, encouraged Rockne to come with them to South Bend for the Fall semester. "Why who ever heard of Notre Dame?" Rockne, a Lutheran, recalled exclaiming.[2] The allure of cheaper living and the prospects of a job intrigued him, and on a whim he decided to enroll in the Catholic university. That brought him to the first meeting with Dorais on that September day in 1910.

Dorais and Rockne were roommates all four years, though their initial meeting became clouded over the years. Depending on where one looks, the pair lived in every hall on campus during their time in South Bend. Even in Rockne's autobiography, he said that he lived in Brownson Hall his freshman year. Transcripts don't clear anything up either. Dorais' records don't mention his lodging during his freshman or junior year, and Walsh Hall and Corby Hall his sophomore and senior year, respectively. In an interview, Dorais recalled that they lived in Sorin Hall basement one year and Corby the rest. Hall directories and the Notre Dame yearbook, *The Dome*, corroborate this account.

There have been several recollections of the first meeting between Dorais and Rockne. The most thorough was written by Dorais himself, in a three-part series in *Street & Smith's Sport Story Magazine*:

> I knocked on the door, and a voice shouted, "Come on in!"
>
> So I opened the door, and saw about as tough-looking a guy as I had ever seen in my life.
>
> He was wearing a faded blue jersey and an old pair of corduroy pants, and he had a shapeless cap pulled down over one eye. Somehow, his nose had been mashed sort of flat, and he was walking up and down the room like a lion in a cage.
>
> "My name's Dorais," I said. "I've been assigned to this room."
>
> "Mine's Rockne," he told me. He took another turn and walked away from me. "Better have 'em send up your trunk," he said, with his back to me.
>
> I pushed my suitcase into the room and closed the door. "Haven't got a trunk," I said. "Everything I own is in this suitcase."
>
> He turned around again by that time, and was coming toward me. He gave me a grin that was to become known to, and be loved by, a million or so football fans all over America.
>
> "I haven't got a trunk, either," he said. "We're starting even."[3]

Sorin Hall, Notre Dame's first dormitory, opened to 50 male students in January 1889. Originally called Collegiate Hall, the name was changed on May 27 that year to honor Father Edward Sorin, the founder of Notre Dame and the University's first president. He was celebrating the golden jubilee of his ordination and laying the cornerstone of the new residence hall. Nearly half a century earlier, Sorin and seven other brothers—members of the Congregation of Holy Cross—hiked 300 miles from Vincennes, Indiana, where they had been serving as missionaries, to the 524 snow-covered acres. Sorin had plans for a college there, but they were rebuffed by the Bishop of Vincennes, who directed them to the large acreage in north-central Indiana. Inspired by the nearby lake, the French Sorin suggested the name "L'Universite de Notre Dame du Lac" or "The University of Our Lady of the Lake."

The University of Notre Dame flourished thanks to the vision of Sorin, who served as President from 1842–1865. It was much more than a college: a center for early training for those interested in taking religious vows, a grade school, a preparatory school, and a manual labor college.

Dorais in his early days as a freshman at the University of Notre Dame. There were no practice jerseys that fit him, so he sent home for his Chippewa Falls High School sweater (Dorais family photo collection).

Athletic endeavors were all over campus within a few decades. Baseball, boating and football found the most interest. Informal football games began popping up in the late 1860s, but the sport remained disorganized for the next few decades. "Frequently, a keg of cider or a barrel of apples offered inspiration to the Reds and the Blues, as the two teams were called," wrote Arthur J. Hope in *Notre Dame: One Hundred Years.*[4]

Intercollegiate football at Notre Dame began on November 23, 1887, when visiting University of Michigan shutout Notre Dame, 8–0. The next year, 1888, Michigan beat Notre Dame three consecutive times by a combined score of 43–9. It wasn't until the last game of the season that the first win in program history was secured, a 20–0 win over Harvard Prep. But for a two-year gap of no team (1890 and 1891), Notre Dame played out the remainder of the century against a variety of opponents, compiling winning records each year.

Notre Dame's first coach was hired in 1894, but he didn't stay long. James

L. Morison, a former tackle at the University of Michigan, was hired by Notre Dame on a two-week contract. After a win and tie to start the season, his contract expired, and he moved on to Hillsdale College (Hillsdale, Michigan), the team Notre Dame defeated in the opener. For the next decade and a half, Notre Dame found success (82–26–8 from 1894–1908), but couldn't keep a coach more than a few years. The longest tenure was the three-year term put in by Frank Hering, 1896–1898. A former player for Alonzo Stagg at the University of Chicago, Hering is considered by some to be the "Father of Notre Dame Football," having transitioned the program from intramural to intercollegiate. During Hering's tenure, athletics began to transform into a major interest at Notre Dame. In the fall of 1898, a Faculty Athletic Board was established. According to the *Indianapolis News*, the board made sure that the athletic department "is maintained on a strictly amateur basis, and carries out all financial obligations according to contract," adding that "No institution in the country backs up its athletes more strongly than Notre Dame, or gives a more emphatic guarantee concerning their eligibility."[5]

During Dorais' time Notre Dame had no official nickname. They were frequently referred to as the "Catholics," "Hoosiers," or "Gold and Blue." When Jesse Harper took over as coach in 1913 and took the team to far-off destinations, "Ramblers" was also a common label. By the mid-teens, the "Fighting Irish," or "Irish" moniker had taken its place.

The implementation of a Faculty Athletic Board coincided with a campus-wide assessment of athletic facilities by the University President, Father Andrew Morrissey. Two of the most glaring needs were a new gymnasium and an enclosed football field, with the former taking precedence. In March 1899, a state-of-the-art facility was dedicated, taking up a bulk of the funding (a fire destroyed much of the building in November 1900 and it had to be rebuilt, opening in February 1901).

An enclosed football field to replace the current accommodations—an open field—was still a priority. Crowds had grown in recent years, and admission fees were impossible to impose with the current set-up. In June 1899, Father Morrissey wrote to alumnus Warren Cartier (1887, Civil Engineering), a Michigan lumber baron who played on the school's first football team, for financial assistance. Cartier, the newly minted mayor of Ludington, Michigan, happily obliged, wondering why the issue hadn't been addressed earlier. He purchased ten acres of land on the east side of campus and turned over the deed to the University. Cartier then provided the lumber for the fence and grandstand. The gift went much further than the football field. The parcel of land housed a pair of football fields, a baseball diamond, a quarter-mile banked track for bike racing, and a 220-yard straightaway. Cartier Athletic Field was officially opened on May 12, 1900, with a track and field championship between Notre Dame, Purdue University and Indiana University, followed by a baseball game between Notre Dame and the University of Nebraska.

A decade after its erection, 1910, the athletic facilities at Notre Dame began to lag behind, particularly Cartier Field. Dorais described the bleachers during his four years as "ramshackle." There were no locker rooms. The players dressed in the gymnasium. Funds for equipment were also sparse. Dorais recalled how the first time he was hurt, "Doc" Maris, the football trainer and track coach, looked at him with great concern. Dorais thought the injury was severe until he "realized that what he was concerned about wasn't my twisted ankle, but the carefully wound adhesive tape he would have to use in strapping me."[6]

The athletic amenities began to deteriorate, but the Faculty Athletic Standards put in place over a decade earlier hadn't wavered. Just days before preliminary drills, the team suffered a setback—quarterback incumbent and team leader, Don Hamilton, was kicked off the team. He was ruled ineligible by the Notre Dame Faculty Athletic Board for playing baseball under the alias of "Hoffman" for the Louisville Colonels of the American Association. Initially, with Hamilton returning, Longman seemingly gave little thought to Dorais' prospects as a quarterback.

On the first day of practice at Cartier Field, the quarterback position seemed to be wide open. The *South Bend Tribune* took notice of the athleticism of Dorais, or "Doria" as they misidentified him. When he broke into the roster that first year, his nickname became "Dory." The paper mentioned his success as a prep quarterback, predicting Dorais to be the frontrunner for the position. "He will not have competition for the pivotal position," reported the paper, "but in case he losses [sic] out he will probably be seen at some other place in the back field."[7]

Longman had other ideas. Returners Robert (R.L.) Mathews and Billy Ryan, both running backs the year before, were the favorites to replace Hamilton. Ryan had been the team's quarterback in 1908 before Hamilton took the job from him. It was likely that Longman didn't feel comfortable or didn't want a freshman in the line-up, evident by the fact that no first year men started or were substitutes on the 1909 team. With only six returners, the coach would be forced to play freshmen.

There were circumstances that may have had Longman initially looking for an upperclassman under the center, even if Dorais' talents shone from the get-go. Michigan's head coach, Fielding Yost, was making more stipulations for the game on November 5. The latest was that only players with at least a sophomore standing could play—leaving Dorais on the sidelines for the biggest game of the year.

Dorais was undeterred. "I reported with the squad the first day, but wasn't given much of a tumble," he told W.W. Edgar of the *Detroit Free Press*. "I stuck around every day, attended the lectures and tried to absorb the system."[8]

When Dorais did catch the eye of Longman, it was for the wrong reason. The coach despised Dorais' overhand throwing style and tested the freshman. Dorais recounted the incident in a seminar he was giving on the "Forward Pass Technique" at the 11th annual American Football Coaches Association meeting in March 1932:

> When I left high school, throwing with this overhand grip throw, the first coach I had at Notre Dame, Shorty Longman, saw me pass one day and said, "Well, I don't like your style of passing and I think you ought to change. We throw the ball here with the flat-hand throw, because, to my mind, on a wet day, or with any mud on the ball, there is no chance of your getting it away."
> I said, "Well, Coach, I believe I can."
> He said, "I don't think you can, not with a grip throw."
> He took a ball and soaked it in the water bucket and got it good and wet. We had a demonstration and I proved to him, I think, that a wet ball can be thrown with an overhand grip throw as well as it can be with a sidearm throw. So I kept throwing that way.[9]

Even after completing seven straight passes, the drenched ball-throwing demonstration didn't change Longman's mind. The former University of Michigan fullback knew the game, and no runt freshman was going to change his views. Longman had coached previously at the University of Arkansas, 1906–1907, and the College of Wooster (Wooster, OH), 1908, before becoming the first non-eastern coach employed by Notre Dame. He gave impassioned (albeit repetitive) pregame speeches and incorporated boxing into practice. The year before, he combined a power running attack and surprisingly effective passing game, relying on the arm of Hamilton. The team finished 7–0–1, beating Longman's alma mater and mentor, Fielding Yost, 11–3, at Ferry Field in Ann Arbor, Michigan. Notre Dame was deemed the "Western Champions" by many and promptly punished schedule-wise for their success. According to author, Karen Croake Heisler, a Notre Dame official was told, "It is no glory to beat you, and it is a disgrace to be beaten by you."[10]

Ryan got most of the quarterback repetitions after Mathews went down with a hip injury in the first week of drills. When Ryan injured his ankle during a scrimmage, a healthy Mathews returned to the position.

Dorais ran the second team effectively at quarterback and did the kicking. One of his ends was Cy Williams, a future major league baseball player who was the first National Leaguer to surpass 200 home runs.

Longman had heard about Rockne's track prowess and inserted him at fullback early in practice. It was a mistake. In one drill, Rockne fumbled six out of eight carries. Exasperated, Mathews yelled to the sideline, "Hey, coach! Send us out a fullback!" Longman obliged and a dejected Rockne trudged off the field, got dressed and retreated to Sorin Hall to contemplate his future. Dorais had seen his roommate leave and wanted to go after him, but was called upon by Longman to relieve Mathews.

Dorais rushed off the field when practice ended in search of Rockne. He found him in their dorm room, pacing back and forth, suitcase on the bed, all packed. "They can't do that to me, Gus! They can't do that to me!" Rockne said frantically. "I wish I'd never come to this place. I'm going home to Chicago and get back my old job in the post office. I was happy there!"[11] Dorais was able to talk Rockne into letting him go to the train station with him to see him off. In the meantime, Dorais dispatched a hall mate to get Coach Longman to their room immediately. Dorais kept Rockne busy until Longman arrived. The coach talked his despondent player into staying, agreeing that he would remain at fullback, but would not carry the ball. Also the understanding was that he would eventually move to end, a position Rockne knew and preferred.

With Ryan's knee still on the mend, Mathews led Notre Dame to an easy 48–0 win at home over Olivet College (Olivet, Michigan). Dorais did get into the game as left halfback. Rockne started at fullback. Most of the Gold and Blue's scoring came from their tackles on end-around plays. George Philbrook scored four times. Soon to be named captain Ralph Dimmick scored twice. The win kept Notre Dame's home winning streak alive, one that would remain intact through Dorais' days and beyond. Between 1905 and 1928—93 games—no visiting team left Cartier Field victorious (90 wins and three ties).

An open spot on the schedule gave the Gold and Blue two weeks to prepare for Buchtel College (Akron, Ohio). By the second week, players were starting to wear down during unseasonably warm days. Rockne suffered a knee injury that kept him out of the Buchtel game. Longman instructed Mathews to take a few days off. Dorais was given a chance to quarterback the first team and, according to the *South Bend Tribune*, he "ran [the] team in clockwork fashion."[12]

In the dressing room prior to the game against Buchtel, Longman gave a rousing speech—at least in the eyes of the injured Rockne. It was a similar to the pep talk that Longman gave the week before, and several of the players were aware of this, including halfback Alfred Bergman and Dorais, both of whom gave subtle yawns. "What do you think of the act today?" asked Bergman.[13]

"Not so good," responded Dorais. "I thought he was better last week."

Rockne took their words to heart. Dorais was a man of few words as a player, leading by example. When Dorais did speak, his deep voice and calm demeanor demanded respect. Once he became coach, Dorais seldom gave pep talks before the game or at halftime. When he did, the words carried weight.

"One oration a season is quite enough for any football squad," wrote Rockne when recalling the scene. "Action brings reaction, and if the coach talks too much, his words lose weight."

Mathews started against Buchtel, but in the third quarter, he was ejected for fighting with the opposing quarterback, Gemis. With Ryan still not ready to play, Longman began to panic. "We haven't got a fellow left who knows the signals," he worried aloud. "What will we do?"

Dorais approached Longman. "Coach, I know the signals."

"Well, there's nothing else I can do," replied Longman. "If you know the signals, get in there."[14]

Dorais was put in the game. Though he didn't score any touchdowns, Dorais had a 50-yard run and kicked five extra points. Notre Dame won, 51–0. "The little freshman ran the team like a veteran and made many sensational plays," raved the *South Bend Tribune*.[15]

With all that has been made of Dorais' offensive skills, he was the proverbial triple threat—adept at all phases of the game—offense, defense and kicking. Often overlooked was his kicking aptitude. He was an excellent punter and kicker, with drop kicking being a particular area of expertise. Simply put, a drop kick is executed by dropping the ball on the ground and then kicking it when it bounced. Dorais had pinpoint accuracy and a very strong leg. During his sophomore season, the *South Bend Tribune* described Dorais' practice routine: "Dorais standing on the 40 and 50 yard lines, spent much time in endeavoring to boot the ball between the goal posts. His drop kicking was of the cleanest variety, and it is thought the little field general will do some tall booting in Saturday's game."[16]

The extra point wasn't the bygone conclusion that it became in later years. "It had to be made from a spot directly out from the point where the ball-carrier had crossed the goal line in scoring the touchdown," Dorais explained. "If he happened to go over near one of the side lines, the kicker had to make his effort from a difficult angle."[17] Still, Dorais rarely missed.

Dorais (front row, middle) as a member of the 1913 Corby Hall Track team. One of his coaches was his roommate, Knute Rockne (far left), who was a standout on the university track team. Dorais went on to coach Track and Field at several colleges (Dorais family photo collection).

Former Notre Dame teammate Mal Edward remembered Dorais as "one of the best drop kickers of all time and an excellent punter."[18]

On the Monday after the Buchtel game, Dorais was named quarterback for the upcoming weekend's game against Michigan Agricultural College (later Michigan State) in East Lansing, Michigan. That same day it was announced that 4–0 Wabash College (Wabash, Indiana), Notre Dame's opponent on November 12, had canceled the remainder of their schedule after the death of freshman halfback Ralph Lee Wilson. He died from a skull fracture suffered in a game against St. Louis University. His last words were said to be "Did Wabash win?"

By Thursday, Dorais was back running the second team. Mathews returned to quarterback and Ryan finally returned to the lineup, too. When the travel roster was released in the *South Bend Tribune*, Dorais' name was absent. The trip to East Lansing was a disaster. Notre Dame failed at nearly every facet of the game. Longman did bring Dorais and put him in the game, but he didn't fare much better than Mathews. The Gold and Blue lost, 17–0, the first defeat in over two years. The last came in 1908, a 12–6 loss in Ann Arbor, Michigan—the next place Notre Dame was scheduled to play.

Preparation for the University of Michigan began immediately. Longman emphasized a whole new set of signal calling after exhausting their trick plays. Four days before the game, Michigan filed an official protest, citing player eligibility. Despite playing an independent schedule after dropping out of the Big Nine Conference in 1907, Michigan still abided by conference rules, including freshmen not playing in varsity games and playing three seasons thereafter. Michigan coach Fielding Yost's focus was on Philbrook and Dimmick. He accused the two of far exceeding their eligibility, having played college ball on the West Coast before enrolling at Notre Dame. The pair claimed they attended the institution as a preparatory school. Michigan stated that Mathews should be deemed ineligible, too. Notre Dame maintained that Michigan had agreed to the roster the week before, which included all three players. They also asserted that Michigan had two ineligible players. Alas, on Friday, November 4, the game was canceled when the two sides failed to budge.

The Wolverines did more damage to themselves by canceling the game. The team played an intrasquad scrimmage instead, during which starting quarterback Shorty McMillan tore muscles in his shoulder. Yost seemed to have a vendetta against Notre Dame. He put great effort into keeping the Gold and Blue out of the Big Nine Conference and encouraged other conference teams not to play them. When Rockne took over as coach, Yost despised him, claiming that Notre Dame's shift offense was illegal. The schools would not resume play until 1942, two years after Yost retired as Michigan's athletic director. It wasn't until 1978 that the series resumed on a more consistent basis.

There was innuendo in Yost's efforts that was at times anti–Catholic in sentiment. It was a common roadblock for scheduling games at that time, and only grew when anti–Catholic feelings increased over the coming decade. By the 1920s, when Rockne was growing Notre Dame football into an institution, the second wave of the Ku Klux Klan was trying to prove that Catholicism was un–American.

After nearly a week off, practice reconvened at Cartier Field. Dorais didn't miss a beat, solidifying his position at quarterback moving forward. In haste, Notre Dame scheduled a game against Rose Polytechnic Institute, who had an open spot on their schedule. The Gold and Blue had defeated the forward pass-happy Terre Haute, Indiana, college, 60–11, in the schools' only other meeting the year before, 1909. Dorais started his first game of his college career. He mainly handed the ball off, as Dimmick scored three touchdowns. Dorais made three extra points and a field goal in the 41–3 Notre Dame win. Over the next four seasons, Notre Dame wouldn't lose another game with Dorais at quarterback. Rule changes in the coming years barred freshman from playing varsity ball, making Dorais the last quarterback to start all four years for over 70 years, until Blair Kiel in 1980.

The following week, Dorais scored his first touchdown on a long punt return at muddy Cartier Field against Ohio Northern. According to the Notre Dame student newspaper, *The Scholastic*, Dorais "grabbed the ball down near his own goal and brought it to the danger mark after much very effectual dodging and squirming." Now at left halfback, Ryan scored the game's first touchdown, a 95-yard sprint. Later, Mathews, at right half-back, scored on a 75-yarder. In the end, Notre Dame was victorious, 47–0, in the last home game of the season. It was the program's 100th victory.[19]

Five days later, on Thanksgiving Day, nearly a year to the day of his high school triumph in Milwaukee, Dorais returned to Campus Field to take on Marquette University. That was not forgotten, as it seemed that his Wisconsin roots endeared him to the Marquette fans over the next few years when Notre Dame played in Milwaukee. The game was delayed for sawdust to be applied to the wet, mud-caked field. The game ended in a 5–5 tie. Marquette's touchdown was scored by Joe Brennan, Notre Dame's backup center in 1909. The Gold and Blue's score came on a recovery fumble by Bill Martin. Dorais further cemented himself as a team leader, demonstrating what *The Scholastic* called "natural ability when it comes to handling the destinies of a football team." The school newspaper added that his punting "outclassed that of Voelkel, the veteran Marquette man," and Dorais' punt-returning was the "feature of the game."[20]

In early December, Dorais was in attendance at the Notre Dame Football banquet at the swank Oliver Hotel in downtown South Bend. The Gold and Blue celebrated their third straight Indiana State Championship, elected a captain for 1911 (guard, Luke Kelly) and awarded monograms (Dorais received one). In the season review, *The Scholastic* said of Dorais: "'Dory' has a cool head and is a determined player at all times. His work in running the team was almost faultless, and he is the equal of any man playing football when it comes to returning punts."[21]

Dorais' foray into athletics didn't end with football. He participated in Notre Dame's long-standing tradition of inter-hall athletics. Both he and Rockne played on Sorin Hall's baseball team. Dorais was also a member of Sorin Hall's Inter-Hall Track Meet Champions, which Rockne coached. Rockne excelled on the University's intercollegiate track and field team, earning a monogram all four years. He was a standout at the pole vault—his 12-foot jump in 1912 stood as the Cartier Field record for years. He also participated in the quarter- and half-mile, and, according to

Dorais, despite Rockne's lighter frame (around 165 pounds), "his exceptionally fine coordination made him a useful performer with the sixteen-pound shot."[22]

Academically, Dorais had his sights set on architecture, before switching to law the next year. In one of his freshman classes, the History of Architecture, the nickname "Gus" was born. During their studies, the class came across a French artist, Gustave Dore, a painter and book illustrator (*Dante's Inferno, Paradise Lost* and *Don Quixote*). Dore was pronounced the same as Dorais (Door-A), giving a classmate fodder for a nickname. "Dory," his nickname during the football season, was soon replaced with "Gus." Dorais explained, "So as a sort of a gag, since the painter's name and mine are pronounced alike, they began calling me Gustave and then cut it to Gus. The nickname caught on so quickly that I'm sure not more than half a dozen fellows I went to college with could have told you my right name."[23]

Socially, Dorais and Rockne settled into the college life. The roommates became popular rather quickly. Dorais was the quarterback, ever confident. Rockne was extremely likable, so much so that Dorais said that his roommate's personality "drew everyone who didn't have anything in particular to do to our room, which became the most popular hang-out in Sorin Hall."[24] Rockne didn't arrive on campus the larger-than-life figure he became during his coaching days. He was quiet, had occasional bouts of depression, and in those early days rarely divulged too much to people. Dorais was one of the few he did confide in. Rockne was especially sensitive about his prematurely balding hair, to which he would apply a putrid smelling concoction each night before bed. According to Dorais, Rockne would awake each morning and optimistically ask, "You can feel a little fuzz coming up, can't you, Gus?"[25]

The roommates found other ways to make money. Their freshman year included candlelight poker games in their room, with candles stolen from the Grotto. The guilt of taking the candles never left Dorais. When he was visiting his son Tom on campus in 1941, Gus sought out penance. "We went over to the Grotto and he took out 10 dollars and put it in the offering—didn't even light a candle."[26]

When Tom asked his father why, Gus responded, "I still don't know how much money I owe for those candles."[27]

It became a Dorais family ritual to stop by the Grotto and continue to make reparations for the candles.

Rockne earned a stipend playing flute in the band and orchestra. In coming years he and Dorais became more resourceful—and their schemes more daring. "Rock was always doping out new ways to fatten our slim treasury," Dorais recalled in his *Associated Press* tribute to his roommate following Rockne's death in 1931.[28] When they moved to Corby Hall their sophomore year, they had a corner room on ground level with a perfect view of St. Mary's Lake. They rigged the screen so that it could be opened, but appear as though it was barred. For two years they collected a fee for hallmates wanting to use the secret exit for skiving, or sneaking off campus—an activity that Dorais and Rockne occasionally partook in. Dorais explained to W.W. Edgar of the *Detroit Free Press* years later:

> It was always tough to get out at night and go downtown. So "Rock" and myself conceived the idea of breaking open the window. We arranged it so the window could be raised and we used that as an exit. When the rest of the gang learned about it they all wanted the privilege of making it their exit and their avenue of entrance when they returned.
>
> It was a great stunt and "Rock" and myself made a little pin money in that room. We rented the use of the window and naturally that room was a great hangout for the gang.[29]

Dorais failed to mention that it wasn't a very popular levy. Eventually, his and Rockne's hall mates grew tired of paying the fee and enacted some revenge. One evening upon returning, a group piled up lanterns, ladders and tools from a nearby construction site outside the pair's window. When their room was inspected early the next morning by Hall rector Father John Farley—a former Notre Dame football captain (1900) and winner of nine varsity monogram letters—they were found in violation of Hall rules. As a result, they were sent to live in Brownson Hall—known amongst students as "Siberia"—for two weeks.

Their junior year, Dorais concocted a plan to barge in on freshmen at Walsh Hall and inquire if their (nonexistent) radiator rent had been paid. It never was, and so he called on Rockne, dressed in overalls and carrying a large pipe wrench, who would come in and begin dismantling the radiator until the students paid. They ran the Corby Hall pool room for two years and fielded a baseball team—the Gutter Snipes—that played offcampus opponents. Yet another scheme was Dorais being a corner man for Rockne in out-of-town boxing matches. Playing semi-pro football on Sundays was commonplace for members of Notre Dame, Rockne included. Surprisingly, there are no accounts of Dorais partaking.

Over the next few years, Dorais was involved in many legitimate university activities, too. He was an editor for *The Scholastic*. His interest in dancing continued from his high school days, and he was on the senior ball committee. He was a member of the Players Club, which put on plays on campus. He was cast in "What's Next" during his senior year. He was on the Law committee, serving as vice-president of the Senior Law committee. His fellow law classmates even made a prediction that Dorais would one day coach Notre Dame: "In 1935, when the Gold and Blue, representing the West, in the national Championship, shall line up against the leader of the East, a diminutive Dorais will lead our team...."[30]

As the 1911 spring semester was coming to a close, Dorais and Rockne went looking for summer employment. "It was a more serious problem to us than it was to the more plutocratic undergraduates, who only had to decide which summer resort would be more pleasant," recalled Dorais over three decades later. "We had to find a place where we could earn our keep and a little something over."[31] The pair found such a spot at Cedar Point, then a small resort on a Lake Erie peninsula in Sandusky, Ohio. For the next three summers they found employment there. Working at Cedar Point was a tradition for Notre Dame students, and during Dorais' summers there around 40–50 students worked on what he called "our postgraduate work."[32]

Notre Dame students flocked to Cedar Point for summer employment. It was here that Dorais (right) and Rockne honed their passing connection. They weren't alone, as other teammates, such as Joe Pliska (left) was there practicing the forward pass plays (Dorais family photo collection).

Cedar Point would one day become a spot of legend, but for Dorais and Rockne it was a summer job, a way to earn money and fraternize— or at least for Dorais, who worked as a lifeguard. Rockne was still incredibly shy. He worked as a checker and cashier in the grill room of the posh Hotel Breakers. This gave him access to as much food as he could eat, especially steak, his favorite. He even turned down another job and higher salary in his second year to remain in the grill room by the food. In their spare time, Dorais, Rockne, and others, including Joe Pliska, spent their afternoons on the beach, often tossing the football around. "That summer at Cedar Point, Rock began developing the first of several innovations for which football is indebted to him," said Dorais of that first summer.[33]

Those new methods included Rockne catching the ball with his relaxed hands, rather than against the body, then the norm. He also worked on his pass routes, which was uncommon, particularly over-running the pass, stopping and coming back to the ball. As the dog days of summer ended, news reached Cedar Point that a coaching change was in the works back in South Bend. In August 1911, Longman abruptly resigned as coach, leaving the Notre Dame administration scrambling to find a replacement.

Jack Marks, a former star back at Dartmouth, took over for Longman. The year before, Marks coached at St. Viator, a Catholic college in Bourbonnais, Illinois. At the early practices, Marks began implementing a new-style offense—the shift—eventually morphing into the famed Notre Dame Box system furthered by Jesse Harper and then Rockne. Initially, Marks taught it academically, with night classes, signal drills and blackboard explanations of the plays. It wasn't a particularly popular decision with the players. Dorais gave an interview a decade-and-a-half later, explaining the team's initial reaction to Marks and the foreign offensive scheme: "We had never seen a shift before, hardly ever heard of one, and we backs bucked strenuously at what we thought was sheer foolishness—the hopping back and forth did not appeal to any of us 'wise' players, I can tell you, and we said so."[34,35]

The shift formation had gained popularity over the last several seasons. Alonzo Stagg first used the shift in 1902, introducing a backfield shift by the end of the decade. The "Heisman Shift," the precursor to the T formation, had come into vogue at Georgia Tech under John Heisman the year before. Minnesota was running the "Minnesota Shift" before the pass was made legal in 1906. Yale, the alma mater of Gophers' coach, Henry Williams, turned to his strategy in 1910 after early season struggles. In a few years, Jesse Harper would build on Marks' work at Notre Dame, before Rockne created the famed Notre Dame Box.

Knute Rockne called Dorais (carrying the ball) one of the best open-field runners he ever saw. Here he is applying a stiff-arm to reach the open field in a game against Marquette University, November 28, 1912, at Comiskey Park, Chicago (University of Notre Dame Archives).

Marks was assisted by the once exiled Don Hamilton, who coached the backfield. Last year's star tackle, George Philbrook, along with Noel Dunbar, a former center from Yale, instructed the line (Philbrook would eventually play in a few games). The group had some decisions to make. Only four monogram men returned: Dorais, quarterback; Luke Kelly, captain and tackle; Charley Crowley, end, and Torgus Oass, guard. This left seven starting spots to be filled. A few reports of a quarterback competition arose, but there wasn't likely any doubt of Dorais' place on the depth chart. A good description of his offensive play was given by Billy Morice, a former University of Pennsylvania football star and current football official, writing for the *Philadelphia Evening Bulletin*. Though written during Dorais' All-American 1913 season, he was already playing this type of game in his 1911 sophomore campaign:

> He's the best quarterback in the country. I go all over the country officiating, and I will say that he is the king of them all this season. He can toss that pass like a baseball. He throws it, he flings it right at the man; he does not lob it so that while a fellow is waiting to get it, someone else comes along and nails him. He runs with the ball in front of him like Fred Geig, the Swathmore coach did when he played. That enables him to shift either arm, and use the other arm to straight-arm off a tackler. He is a great open-field runner, and, above all other things, he is a great field general.[36]

Rockne earned a starting spot at end. He came to be known for his deceptive speed, sure hands and precise routes. The roommates and good friends had a fruitful on-field relationship, one that lasted beyond their scholastic days and into the pre–NFL professional game. Together, they played on the Massillon (Ohio) Tigers and Fort Wayne (Indiana) Friars. Six decades later, Ike Roy Martin, a Friars teammate, recalled that Dorais made Rockne the player he was. Martin said Rockne was "only an average end," explaining that Rockne "wouldn't have been a good end if he hadn't had a man like Dorais throwing the ball to him."[37]

Dorais felt differently of his compatriot, calling Rockne "the surest catcher of forward passes yet produced."[38]

Rockne's confidence in the passing game came from Dorais, evident from this quote: "Without his encouragement and execution, I would never have been able to carry out the forward pass idea."[39]

Rockne's growing confidence in his own play allowed him to drop the at times crippling shyness that he displayed off the field. Dorais said his roommate's "wisecracks did a lot to keep the boys in good humor and going at top speed."[40]

Notre Dame won the first four contests of the 1911 season (all at Cartier Field) by a total of 182–6. The highlight was an 80–0 thrashing of Loyola of Chicago, setting a school record for points in a game. Dorais threw his first collegiate touchdown pass to Alfred Bergman, the only man to earn 11 varsity letters at Notre Dame. Speedy backup halfback Art Smith scored a school record seven rushing touchdowns.

Dorais injured his knee in the second game of the season, a 43–0 drubbing of Marks' former team, St. Viator. The injury lingered for a few weeks, causing him to miss practices and the intense intrasquad scrimmages. It limited his mobility greatly, somewhat hindering Marks' fast game plan. Still, the team held secret practices indoors, where timing of passes on a split-second count were perfected. According to Jim Beach and Daniel Moore, authors of *Army vs. Notre Dame: The Big Game, 1913–1947*, "chalk marks were traced on the gym floor and the exact timing of the pass and the turn of the intended receiver to grab the ball were reduced almost to habit."[41] Though the Dorais-Rockne combination changed the game forever in 1913, due to a soon-to-be changed rule about the length a pass could go (20 yards), it was the short passes, lobbed over the line to first-year player Joe Pliska, that were central to Notre Dame's passing game success starting in 1911.

Other first-year players making an impact were two halfbacks, Alvin Berger and Alfred Bergman, and lineman Albert Feeney. The standout of the group was 195-pound fullback Ray Eichenlaub—the heaviest player on the team (he would reach 210 pounds by his senior season). The pounding style of "Iron Eich" was instrumental in the progression of Notre Dame's growing passing game. The Columbus, Ohio native would gain All-American honors each year from 1912–1914.

On October 22, during Notre Dame's early-season success, the program was rocked by the death of 1910 captain Ralph Dimmick. He had returned west to practice law in Portland, Oregon, and coach football at the city's Columbia University. The week before, he played for the alumni team for Pacific University from nearby Forest Grove. He also suited up for the Multnomah Amateur Athletic Club team in Portland. Stories are conflicting. Some say he had pneumonia, while others say that he had a punctured lung or blood poisoning. He may have even suffered a concussion. He was acting unpredictably, became delirious and jumped to his death from the second-story window of the hospital.

The first test of the season for Marks' open offense took place on November 4 at Forbes Field in Pittsburgh against the University of Pittsburgh. They were coached by Joseph Thompson, a future College Football Hall of Famer. Fresh on the mind of many was the 6–0 Notre Dame victory in 1909 that clinched them the label of "Western Champs." Pittsburgh went undefeated (9–0) and unscored upon (282–0) in 1910. In an article for *Collier's* magazine in 1930, Rockne recalled that press in South Bend had spoken too much about the guile of the fully recovered Dorais in the days leading up to the Pittsburgh game. Newspapers had kicked around nicknames for Dorais and of late had taken to calling him "Will-o'-the-Wisp." Rockne couldn't fault them, saying that Dorais had "the best open-field legs in football."[42]

Thompson's defensive game plan for dealing with the elusive Dorais was led by Pittsburgh's most athletic player, Hube Wagner, who planned to key on the Notre Dame quarterback. Wagner was to take a different approach to tackling Dorais, going high, at the neck, rather than diving at his legs.

During the game, Dorais tried to incorporate what Rockne called "new and smart stuff." He dropped the signal calls and played the halfbacks based on which side the punts were aimed. Dorais worked out the plan prior to the game with the line. A surprise play around end was planned. The first time Dorais attempted this, Pittsburgh was caught off guard, but the moment was lost when the center, Keith Jones, who moved to the line from fullback earlier in the week, didn't snap the ball. Finally, Dorais told him to snap the ball. "All right," the center yelled back. "What's the signal?" Dorais called a routine play, but when the team convened in a huddle, he berated the center for not following the directive. There, Jones informed Dorais that he was half-deaf.[43]

The two teams played to a scoreless tie in the first half. Notre Dame scored first, when Dorais (some sources say Eichenlaub) surprised Pitt with an onside kick to start the second half. The ball was recovered by Rockne, who picked it up and ran for a touchdown—the first of his collegiate career. The play was called back by referee Frederic A. Godcharles, a member of the Pennsylvania state senate. He claimed that he had never blown the whistle to start the half, making Notre Dame off-sides. Later in the half, Pittsburgh had two touchdowns of their own called back, including one on an off-sides penalty.

Field conditions kept both teams at bay. Still out of shape, Philbrook's presence meant little on the line. He did have an impact at receiver, with a 20-yard gain on a pass from Dorais that brought the ball down to the Pitt 20-yard line. Objections from Pittsburgh on the referee's ruling on the play moved the ball up to the 15-yard line. Notre Dame looked like they were going to score, but Bergman was thrown for an eight-yard loss. Dorais then went back for a drop kick, which missed by a matter of feet. The rest of the game was a punting match, ending in a 0–0 tie. A gimpy Dorais had stopped two certain Pittsburgh touchdowns.

Marks kept many of his starters out against St. Bonaventure (Olean, New York), including Dorais, who continued to favor his knee. The backups had little trouble in a 34–0 thumping. Dorais' back-up, Jay Lee, a transfer from Albion College (Albion, Michigan) impressed with his play. His performance led to a half-hearted discussion of a quarterback competition between the two during the week leading up to an intrastate matchup in Crawfordsville, against Jesse Harper's unbeaten, pass-heavy Wabash College, the "Little Giants." Harper played college ball under Amos Alonzo Stagg at the University of Chicago. Harper learned early incarnations of the shift offense and motions, as well as an inklings of the forward pass. He played in the Maroons' backfield behind three-time Walter Camp All-American Walter Eckersall—Rockne's teen idol—before finding a place at end his senior season, 1905.

The most notable victory in Wabash College's history came in 1905, a 5–0 win over Notre Dame in South Bend—Notre Dame's only home field loss between 1899 and 1928, a 125-game span. In 1909, Harper's Little Giants beat Big Nine member and larger in-state school Purdue and started the 1911 season by dispatching the Boilermakers, 3–0. At 3–1–1, Wabash was poised for a program-defining win. Dorais retained his starting role and helped pull out a 6–3 Notre Dame win. It took a field-long

Dorais and his Hall mates were known for "smashing the rules," as Fr. Cavanaugh put it. Dorais (far right) and Rockne (seated, second from left) relaxed across the lake from St. Mary's College (Dorais family photo collection).

drive and a two-yard touchdown run by Berger late in the game to salvage a game that could have easily gone to Wabash College. Dorais was out-played by the Little Giants' heady quarterback, Kent "Skeet" Lambert. Lambert threw a perfect pass to his end, Brooks Howard, but it was called back by one of the passing restrictions of the day—throwing it more than 20 yards. This was one of the rules that was changed for the 1912 season. Lambert exploited a few loopholes in the rules. The Wabash College quarterback took 20- to 25-yard drops before throwing the ball away when no one became open. There were no rules prohibiting Lambert from doing this time after time, with the ball returning to the original line of scrimmage without the loss of down. Rather than punting, he simply threw the ball out of bounds. The ball automatically went to the other team at the spot it went out. Dorais added both plays to his repertoire.

Three days later, on November 23, Dorais' mother, Malvina received a telegram that Gus' father, David had passed away in the early morning hours in Butte, Montana. The contents of that message are unknown, but the *Anaconda Standard*, Butte's major newspaper, gave a disturbing account of the senior Dorais' final hours. Though his death certificate lists syphilis as the cause of death, there is no doubt that alcohol ultimately played a role in his death at the Lafayette rooming house:

Dorais had been drinking heavily for some time and Wednesday morning the proprietor of the Steele Block, 316 North Wyoming Street, saw that Dorais was apparently in a dying condition. Appeal was made at a hospital that he be given attention, but he was refused, as no provision was made there for taking care of men with Dorais' affliction. He was taken to the emergency hospital and an appeal was made to relatives to care for the man and a brother procured the room in the Lafayette block and a physician. He died at 4 o'clock yesterday morning.[44]

Notre Dame had one more game—a November 30 clash in Milwaukee against Marquette at Campus Field. Dorais' mental state just a week after his father's passing is unknown. There were conflicting accounts of his status in the week leading up to the game. One day the *South Bend Tribune* had him listed as being confined to the University infirmary with tonsillitis. The next day he was missing the game due to injury, with Lee starting in his place. There was no public mention of David's death. Dorais did start the game. The Gold and Blue's offense came out looking like it was going to blow out the Godlen Avalanche, but after Notre Dame fumbled on the Marquette three-yard line in the first quarter, a kicking battle ensued. Dorais played both goat and hero. He had three chances to drop kick a field goal but missed all three. However, on defense he saved the game twice, tackling the runner as the last person between him and the end zone—the game ending in a 0–0 draw.

Just a few weeks after his father's passing, the annual football banquet was held at the Oliver Hotel. The team celebrated a fourth straight state championship and gave out monograms. Dorais was chosen the 19th captain in the program's 23-year history. Crowley was given the vice captaincy.

Late in the spring semester, Rockne received the devastating news that his father, Lars, had passed away unexpectedly at the age of 54. Knute returned to Chicago with no intention of being back at Notre Dame next fall. He would return to the post office and take up his father's role as provider for his mother and two teenage sisters. His older sister, Annie, helped change his mind, encouraging him to follow his dream of entering the medical field. Rockne and Dorais returned to Cedar Point in the summer. They picked up their routine of work, tossing the football around at the beach and fraternizing after hours. A major point of interest was the Olympics going on in Stockholm, Sweden. The contingent, including Dorais and Rockne, cheered on Notre Dame alumnus George Philbrook who was participating in the decathlon. He lost out to Jim Thorpe, the star of the games who also won gold in the pentathlon. Thorpe, a former star under Pop Warner at Carlisle Indian Industrial School (Carlisle, PA) would one day end Dorais' football playing career.

In the annals of football history, the summer of 1912 at Cedar Point doesn't have the same acclaim that the next would, but it could be when the plan to play Army was conceived. In *Army vs. Notre Dame: The Big Game, 1913–1947*, Beach and Moore say that Dorais and Bill Cotter, student manager of athletics, were looking for a way to garner attention for the program. "It was then that the idea was hatched: try to arrange a game with Army," said the authors.[45] Although nothing came of the thought that year, it planted the seed for the following year.

The 1912 football season was met by several rule changes that would benefit burgeoning wide-open offensive styles, including Notre Dame's. The 20-yard limit on passes was lifted, allowing the ball to be thrown beyond the line of scrimmage for any distance. Another advantage for the Gold and Blue's offense was adding a fourth down to obtain a first down. Other alterations to the rules included: the field of play was reduced from 110 yards to 100, and end zones were added behind the goal line; until this point, passes caught over the goal line were touchbacks, now they were touchdowns; kickoffs were from the 40-yard line, rather than the 55, and for the first time since 1897, touchdowns were increased, from five points to six.

Dorais returned to South Bend with a renewed purpose on the football field. "Having been elected captain of the 1912 team, I naturally took football even more seriously than I ever had taken it before," he recalled.[46]

Marks' veteran team took immediate advantage of the rule changes, decimating St. Viator, 116–7, eclipsing the school record of 80 points put up against Loyola the year before. Berger scored five touchdowns and Eichenlaub three. Backfield backups Paul Nowers and Eddie Duggan

Notre Dame's passing game wouldn't have been as successful had it not been for the bruising running game provided by Ray Eichenlaub (left) and Dorais (right) (University of Notre Dame Archives).

scored four and three times, respectively. Notre Dame's defense allowed just one first down, St. Viator's touchdown coming on a fumble recovery. In the second half, Marks opened up the passing game, testing out the new series of plays that he implemented to take advantage of Dorais' skills.

Notre Dame and Dorais didn't let up, defeating Adrian (Adrian, MI), 74–7, and Morris Harvey College (Charleston, WV), 39–0, before an October 26 game against Wabash to decide the Indiana State title. There was an added incentive for the Blue and Gold players. South Bend clothing merchants promised Notre Dame players cloth prizes for touchdowns. For a person who came from a meager background, Dorais was intrigued by the prospect. He recalled the promotion to Frank Graham of the *New York Sun* over three decades later, when Dorais was coaching the University of Detroit and was in New York for the winter coaches meeting: "Ho! All those things for touchdowns—and I'm calling the signals! I'm going to be a well-dressed man."[47]

The two quarterbacks, Dorais for Notre Dame and Lambert for Wabash, were slated to be the feature of the game, as the label of best quarterback in the state was at stake. Dorais had his early season successes, but so did Lambert, who a few weeks earlier scored five touchdowns and kicked as many extra points in a 62–0 win over DePauw (Greencastle, IN). Nearly 4,000 spectators, thought to be a Cartier Field record, showed up for the game. There was little resemblance to the slippery conditions in the 6–3 Notre Dame victory in Crawfordsville last year. The Gold and Blue overcame early fumbles to outplay a grossly overmatched Wabash squad, winning 41–6. Several Notre Dame players crossed the goal line, procuring wardrobe improvements. In his chat with Graham, Dorais claimed he crossed the goal line first, under humorous circumstances.

"The ball came back to me—and just as I passed it to Eichenlaub I happened to think of all that merchandise." recounted Dorais. "As he tore by me I tackled him from behind and threw him on the one-yard line."

"Hey! What's the idea," yelled Eichenlaub.

"Are you going to split with me on that merchandise," Dorais asked.

"No," replied the big fullback.

"All, right," said Dorais, who on the next play took it over for the touchdown.[48]

Eichenlaub wouldn't leave empty-handed, scoring two touchdowns. Dorais ended Notre Dame's scoring with a long touchdown pass to Dolan.

Both Dorais and Lambert lived up to their billing. Following the game, the Notre Dame students entertained both schools with a snake dance and bonfire. According to the *South Bend Tribune*, there were "insistent calls for Dorais and Lambert," which drew short speeches from the two quarterbacks.[49]

Notre Dame's sights were set on a Western title, beginning with a showdown with the University of Pittsburgh at Forbes Field. In the week leading up to the game, Notre Dame announced that the Thanksgiving Day game against Marquette was going to be moved to Chicago's Comiskey Park. Game day conditions turned out to be brutal in Pittsburgh. "There haven't been many football games played under worse weather conditions than that one was played under," Dorais recounted. "It was a bitter cold day, it snowed all through the game. But in spite of the vile weather, there were ten thousand shivering spectators in the wooden stands."[50]

Over the years, Dorais crafted a tale about a pregame incident. It was likely a combination of several occurrences throughout his Notre Dame years. On the morning of the Pittsburgh game, Dorais complained of a stomach ache to Crowley. "Why fellow, I'll see that you get well," responded the senior end.[51]

Crowley was one of the players Dorais looked up to. "Chuck Crowley attended Harvard, was immensely more sophisticated than I, and completely idolized by me," said Dorais years later. The two walked to a nearby bar, where Dorais ended up drinking five glasses of kummel, a liqueur flavored with caraway seed, cumin and fennel. It seemed to cure his stomach ailment, but left him intoxicated. In the locker room prior to the game, he bent over to tie his shoes and fell down. Marks stormed over and demanded to smell Dorais' breath. When Marks caught a whiff of the alcohol, he roared: "When we get back to South Bend, Dorais, I'll fire you off the team."[52]

Dorais quickly sobered up in the stiff wind and raging snow. Neither team could do much on offense. The blizzard-like conditions caused numerous turnovers and penalties over the first three-and-a-half quarters. A surprise pass on fourth and short from Dorais to Rockne netted 33 yards to keep a drive alive. Three plays failed to gain any yardage, setting up another fourth down, with just a few minutes to play. "I dropped back to the thirty-yard line," recounted Dorais. "It was snowing so hard that I scarcely could see the goal posts, but somehow, I managed to dropkick the ball between them and over the crossbar for a field goal that gave us a 3–0 victory."[53]

As the team ran off the field, Marks ran up to him and patted him on the back. "Great kick, Dorais, great kick. Just forget what I said before the game. We all make mistakes," said his giddy coach.[54]

After three consecutive ties against Marquette, Notre Dame traveled the 95 miles to Chicago on Thanksgiving Day. Field conditions at Comiskey Park were suspect as a crowd of 7,000 looked on. The most noticeable was an obstacle that J.J. Delany of the *Milwaukee Sentinel* called a "miniature Panama canal."[55] A foot deep and covered with straw, the ditch was used as drainage for the field. A few players either suffered injuries from the trench or were stopped from advancing further. Dorais and Eichenlaub had no problem. When the final whistle blew, Notre Dame had demolished Marquette, 69–0. Walter Eckersall, who was pulling double duty in both refereeing and covering the game for the *Chicago Daily Tribune*, described Notre Dame as "coached to the height of football perfection."[56]

Dorais had one of his best games of the season. He gave Notre Dame an early lead, perfectly executing a fake that sucked the front four to the line. He broke tackle attempts from the remaining seven defenders on his way to an 80-yard touchdown. He scored two touchdowns on the day, kicked a field goal, and added six extra points. Eichenlaub scored four touchdown of his own, which propelled him to a spot on Eckersall's all-Western eleven. "It would be a hard proposition to find a player the equal of this warrior," said the *Tribune* scribe of the Gold and Blue fullback.

Though he would be snubbed by the Indiana All-State team put out by Jack Velock, sports editor of the *Indianapolis Sun*, Dorais' performance against Marquette clinched the quarterback spot and captaincy on Eckersall's second team (University of Wisconsin's Eddie Gillette earned first team honors). Eckersall said of Dorais: "He used rare judgement in directing his team and his gentlemanly conduct on the field was one of commendable features of his work."[57]

The win marked Notre Dame's first full-schedule unbeaten team—the inaugural 1889 team won its only game and the 1893 team went 4–0 against lesser competition. The 1912 team captained by Dorais still holds an interesting claim that no other Notre Dame team has come close to. Of all the Notre Dame undefeated teams, the 1912 squad has the largest scoring differential, +51.72. The 1912 team outscored opponents, 389 to 27. Spirits were high at the December football banquet at the Oliver, where Rockne was named captain for the 1913 season. Eichenlaub was named vice captain. Only one player would be leaving—senior end Crowley. All seemed in place for the veteran team, but a few days later it was announced that Marks was being replaced by a familiar face—Jesse Harper, the 29-year-old athletic director and head football coach at Wabash College. He would take on those duties at Notre Dame in the fall of 1913, becoming Notre Dame's first full-time athletic director at a salary of $5,000.

CHAPTER 3

A National Stage, 1913

The decision to bring Jesse Harper to Notre Dame was not made in haste by Father Cavanaugh. The athletic program had been losing money for years, and while Marks was a successful on-field coach, the program was in the red financially, with a deficit of $2,800 over the past two seasons. Confounded by the situation, Cavanaugh was in Crawfordsville, Indiana, during the fall discussing the matter with Notre Dame alumni when they suggested hiring Wabash's Harper. One of the many attributes that impressed Cavanaugh was the fiscal view that Harper had—the football program should, at the very least, be able to finance itself. Cavanaugh also looked to broaden the scope of opponents, which the baseball team had done the previous few seasons by traveling east to play schools in Pennsylvania and New York. Under Harper's guidance, the football program did both.

Jesse Harper was born in Paw Paw, Illinois, and attended Morgan Park at the University of Chicago. He was part of the preparatory school's direct pipeline to the University of Chicago, where he came under the tutelage of Alonzo Stagg. The Maroons were named Western Champions in Harper's senior year, 1905. They snapped Fielding Yost's University of Michigan "Point-A-Minute" team's winning streak at 56 games with a 2–0 win in Chicago at Marshall Field on the University campus. Following graduation, Harper took over the athletic department duties and taught history at Alma College in Alma, Michigan, at age 22, thanks to his mentor, Stagg. Implementing his coach's progressive offense, in Harper's second season the Scots football team went 5–1–1 and won the small Michigan College State Championship. He left for a year upon the insistence of his father, but farming and cattle ranching in Iowa held little interest to Harper. Once again, Stagg put out a good word for him, this time landing him the job of running the athletic department and serving as Instructor of Physical Culture at Wabash College in Wabash, Indiana. Harper found

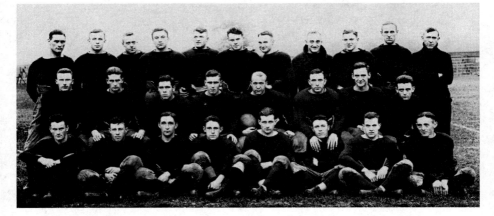

The storied 1913 Notre Dame football team, coached by Jesse Harper (back row, far right) and captained by Knute Rockne (middle row, fourth from right). Dorais (middle row, far right) credited Harper as the first coach to have the vision and courage to use the forward pass as a principal offensive weapon (University of Notre Dame Archives).

success in 1909, winning state titles in basketball and baseball, but it was his football mind that drew the interest of Notre Dame.

Even though Harper wasn't set to take up his athletic director duties until the next fall, by March he had most of the 1913 football season scheduled. He also set up Notre Dame's first spring practice. He eventually employed Howard Edwards, a former Notre Dame Captain (1909), as an assistant, but with no one to head the practices, Harper had Captain Rockne running daily drills for the veterans and new men. In the spring, Dorais took part in intra-hall athletics before he and Rockne headed to Ohio to work the summer at Cedar Point Beach. This, their last summer working at the resort, was the one that would live in infamy. For Rockne this was also the summer he met his future wife, Bonnie Skiles, who worked as a waitress in Cedar Point's Grill Room, a restaurant in the Grand Pavilion that Rockne and Dorais frequented. On the beach, Dorais, Rockne and others continued their workouts. Dorais recalled that summer in a tribute to Rockne, "Rock and I," after Rockne's death on March 31, 1931:

> That summer of 1913 at Cedar Point, Rock and I practiced more than we ever had practiced before. Rock perfected his method of catching passes without tenseness in finger, wrists or arms, and with hands giving with the ball, just as a baseball should be caught.
>
> He also continued to develop his deceptive, stop-and-go style of going down the field for a pass, a style still used by nearly all good pass receivers. I worked hard to increase both the accuracy and the length of my passes.[1]

Dorais returned to Chippewa Falls, Wisconsin, for a few weeks in August and early September to visit with his mother and sister. They had moved from Catholic Hill and were now living on the Victoria Block of Bridge Street, in downtown, close to Chippewa Falls High School. His older brother, George, moved back out west, eventually landing in Carson City, Nevada, where he spent much of the rest of his life working as a card dealer and bartender at casinos. Dorais' younger brother, Joe, was living with relatives in Minnesota. While back home, Gus Dorais helped his former high school coach, A.G. Findlay, run through early drills, even earning a coaching credit in the yearbook. Dorais and several alumni scrimmaged the high school. Besides Dorais, the other notable alum was Lorin Solon, a 1912 graduate. Solon came to Chippewa Falls from East Side High of Minneapolis in the fall of 1910, the year after Dorais graduated. Now playing at the University of Minnesota, Solon gained All-American accolades as an end in both 1913 and 1914.

Expectations intensified during the summer. Before Rockne and Dorais even arrived back in South Bend, Harper was predicting big things for the football program. He had the team playing Big Eight conference rules, which included fielding a freshman team. He found difficulties scheduling members of the Big Eight, saying "they know Notre Dame is a strong aggregation and do not wish to waste their strength on outside teams."[2] The schedule Harper assembled was undoubtedly one of the most ambitious undertaken in the school's history. After three games at home, the Gold and Blue were to embark on an ambitious five-game, over-5,000-mile road trip, against top-rate competition. Four of the games were out of state: Army, West Point, New York; Penn State, University Park, Pennsylvania; Christian Brothers, St. Louis, Missouri, and University of Texas, Austin, Texas. The lone instate game was in Crawfordsville against Harper's former team, Wabash College. One writer coined this series of road games "The Dorais Express."[3]

Harper's offensive installation consisted of three formations: an open punt, close punt and shift. Though Marks had used the shift in the two previous seasons, Harper became synonymous with laying the groundwork for the Notre Dame Box. A strong passing game was a central theme, a tactic Marks used occasionally, but not as a feature. "The first such team I know of that had a coach with nerve and daring enough to use the pass as the principal weapon of offense was the Notre Dame team of 1913 with Jesse Harper as its coach," Dorais said in his 1931 book, *The Forward Pass and Its Defense.*[4]

A 10-man shift was used to start the season. The center was on the line, with six linemen a yard back. The backfield were aligned in a T formation. After signal, the linemen shifted into an unbalanced line—four and two. The backs went to a box formation. Charles Bachman, a future All-American guard and coaching adversary of Dorais, was a freshman on the team, remembered the shift not being the weapon it would become in subsequent years, because of the senior quarterback's skill set. "Harper had in Charlie Dorais an ideal triple threat man—a dangerous runner, a fine punter and drop kicker and one of the most accurate and deceptive passers the game has known."[5]

Notre Dame easily beat Ohio Northern in the October 4 opener, 87–0. Dorais scored a touchdown and kicked seven extra points. Rockne suffered a substantial rib injury, leaving him on the sideline for the next few weeks. He had some time to recover, as the team had two full weeks to prepare for a game against a talented University of South Dakota team. Reverend James Henderson's 1912 team had gone 5–1, including a 10–0 win over the University of Minnesota. The team's only loss was a 7–6 contest against the University of Michigan.

Injuries mounted, including Dorais, who suffered a scare when he dislocated the index finger on his left hand during a scrimmage. After breaking through the line for a 50-yard run, he was tackled by an opposing player. Eichenlaub, who was blocking for him, stepped on his hand. Dorais was back to practice within a few days, inspiring his teammates and only complaining of stiffness in the knuckle.[6] With Rockne still too injured to play, Dorais served as captain for the South Dakota game. Fred Gushurst filled in for Rockne and emerged as another receiving threat. Dorais led the injury-plagued Notre Dame team to a 20–7 victory, drop kicking balls from 25 and 18 yards out, and making both extra points following touchdowns by Eichenlaub. Dorais also had to tackle one of his own teammates, Keith "Deac"Jones, to keep him from scoring for South Dakota. According to Dorais, Jones had "received a severe blow on the head. The next play he recovered the ball in deep Dakota territory and began to run the other way. We shouted at him but he continued, heedless of our yells. I ran after Jones and finally brought him down just five yards from the N.D. goal line."[7]

A 62–0 drubbing of Alma College, where Harper began his coaching career, followed. Joe Pliska scored three touchdowns. Eichenlaub notched two. Dorais returned a punt 65 yards for a touchdown and was successful on all eight of his extra points. The victory was the last home game of the season for Notre Dame. Ahead for the Gold and Blue was the most ambitious road schedule ever assembled by the University, starting with the undefeated United States Military Academy, better known as Army, in West Point, New York. The game marked the farthest east the football program had played and the most lucrative—the Army Athletic Council gave Notre Dame $1,000 for the game.

After a five-day break, Harper began an intense practice regimen, with drills twice a day. In the morning they went through repetitions in the gymnasium, training at Cartier Field in the evening. With the emergence of Pliska as an outside running threat, Harper tweaked the shift he had put in at the beginning of the season. Rather than a shift in the line, the ends moved to flank the tackles, to provide more blocking for Pliska around the edge and an extra push for Eichenlaub in between the tackles. Still, it was the shotgun formation that many of the big passing plays were made from.

On the morning of the team's departure for the East Coast, Dorais' performance was foreshadowed by the *South Bend News-Times*. "Quarterback Dorais was flawless," it was reported of the team's public practice at Cartier and the private signal drill in the gym. "The little general is working like a splendid machine and his coolness in times of trial is almost uncanny. With men coming in on all sides yesterday, he skillfully pegged pass after pass true to the hands of his waiting backs and ends."[8]

Shortly before 1pm on October 30, a large crowd saw off the 19 men. Harper was confident as he and the team left campus. "We are going for victory, but of course I'm not going to make any forecast of the result.

University of Notre Dame football team on the way to play the storied Army game on November 1, 1913. Dorais (far left) and his teammates stopped in Kingston, New York, to switch trains when this picture was taken (University of Notre Dame Archives).

Chances seem about even, but with chances even, Notre Dame always wins. I consider this the hardest game on our schedule and the men are going to fight a battle of their lives."[9]

The team rode a day coach to Buffalo, New York, eating sandwiches made in the campus refectory to save money. From there, they had sleeper berths en route to Army's campus in upstate New York. Upon arrival at West Point, Notre Dame went through a light workout and then retreated to their accommodation at Cullum Hall, where they were given open access to the Officers' Club. There, the two teams dined together the night before the game. A story came from the meal that Dorais and Rockne liked to tell during their banquet speaking days. This was Rockne's version:

> The waiter came around and asked the first Army tackle what he he would like.
> Glancing at Dorais, the first Army tackle replied in a voice like a file being rasped across rough iron, "Give me a steak and make it rar-r-e!"
> The waiter then asked the second Army tackle what he wished.
> The second Army tackle fixed Dorais with a savage look and replied in an even tougher voice, "Give me a steak and make it ra-a-a-w!"
> The waiter then turned to Dorais and asked patronizingly, "And what would you like?"
> Dorais looked from one huge and scowling Army tackle to the other and then told the waiter fairly, "Oh, just drive in that steer and I'll gnaw off what I want."[10]

Army had great respect for Notre Dame. The Cadets were undefeated at 4–0, but their last two victories were close—a 7–6 win over Colgate and 2–0 against Tufts. First-year coach Charles Daley brought in extra coaches to provide advice and former players to scrimmage the Cadets. There were, of course, numerous East Coast newspapers that thought little of Notre Dame, viewing them as a pushover, an unknown. Dorais recalled the team seeing this sentiment in print the night before the game. "That made us so mad, we decided to show em' something," he recalled two decades later.[11]

There was no stadium on the West Point campus. A field was marked out on the Plains, the Cadets' parade grounds. A small wooden grandstand could only accommodate a fraction of the 5,000 spectators, the rest of whom stood on the sidelines. Among them was the Notre Dame Club from New York City, which had chartered a special train to West Point to cheer on their alma mater. The alumni planned to entertain the Notre Dame varsity squad after the game. Adding to the historical significance of the game were a few of the Cadets in uniform. Halfback Leland S. Hobbs would go on to command the 30th Infantry Division, known as "Old Hickory" during World War II. Future General Omar Bradley was a substitute. Finally, future President of the United States Dwight Eisenhower watched from the sideline, out with a knee injury.

Notre Dame found little success in the first quarter. They tried to establish a running game against an Army line that outweighed them by at least 10 to 15 pounds per man. Dorais fumbled on his own 27-yard line, but the Cadets were unable to capitalize. They, too, struggled on the ground. The first 15 minutes were spent between the 40-yard lines. Early in the second quarter, after another failed run, Dorais gave a simple directive: "Let's open up!"[12]

Dorais began to methodically pick apart Army's defense. He completed a pass to Pliska for first down. On the play, Rockne was noticeably limping down the field. Just minutes earlier, he had put a hard tackle on the Cadets' big All-American end, Louis Merrilat. He was laid out for a few minutes, and Rockne was shaken. To Army's backs, it looked like Rockne would simply be a decoy, so they decided to focus elsewhere. On the next play, Dorais dropped back ten yards to pass. With Pliska sprinting out of the backfield and Rockne limping up the sideline, Army's backs converged on Pliska. Dorais let go a long toss towards Rockne, who lost his limp and broke into a full-out sprint, leaving his defender flat-footed. The Notre Dame end caught the ball in stride and went into the end zone untouched. Dorais kicked the point after for a 7–0 lead.

Army countered with their own aerial game. Quarterback Vernon Prichard moved the Cadets down the field with passes on consecutive drives. Both were capped off by short runs. A missed extra point after the second touchdown gave Army a 13–7 advantage—their last lead of the game. The Cadets chose to kick to Notre Dame. After Rockne was tackled on the 15-yard line, Dorais went to work. Following a five-yard sneak, he passed to Pliska for 30 yards and then to Rockne for 35—the longest play of the game—bringing the entire crowd to its feet. A quick five-yarder to Rockne was followed by a short yardage plunge through the line by Pliska for a touchdown. Dorais' kick followed, giving Notre Dame a 14–13 lead.

"Our passing attack had the Army players bewildered, so we gave them the works," said Dorais, "forward passes, lateral passes, lateral passes that turned into forward passes."[13]

Notre Dame almost scored again just before the end of the first half. With the ball on the Army 45-yard line, Dorais called for a spread play. Both ends and all of the backs except for Dorais sprinted to the opposite side of the field. He took the snap from center, calmly dropping back with Cadets defenders rushing after him. He let go what seemed to be a perfect pass across the field to Rockne, but just as it was landing in the Notre Dame end's hands, Army's Prichard leapt over him and caught the ball.

Halftime adjustments by Army made the third quarter a struggle for both teams. Neither could put any sort of significant drive together. At one point, Dorais attempted a drop kick from midfield that failed. The Cadets' backfield subsequently rammed the ball down to Notre Dame's 15-yard line. A holding penalty by the Gold and Blue put the ball down to their two-yard line. What transpired was Notre Dame's best defensive stand of the game, if not the season. Army fullback Paul Hodgson (Eisenhower's roommate) tried to run around end on Rockne, but the Gold and Blue captain picked Hodgson up and tossed him back to the five-yard line. Hobbs, was thrown for a loss, too. Finally, Prichard attempted a pass to Merillat that was intercepted by Dorais in the end zone.

Now with the ball, Notre Dame returned to the ground attack, while the Cadets continued to focus on the passing game. Dorais handed the ball off to Finegan, who broke off a 25-yard run around Merillat and into Army territory. After a few pass attempts to keep the Cadets guessing, Eichenlaub ground out yardage on several carries before he battered his way across the goal line. The Gold and Blue led, 21–13, after Dorais' kick.

Army could do little with the ball and punted. On the ensuing drive, Dorais gave the signal for a drop kick. The Cadets dropped back into their punt formation, only to see Dorais throw a 30-yard completion to Rockne. Notre Dame drove down to the Army 5-yard-line and Dorais called his own number, crossing the goal and then kicking the extra point. Again in possession of the ball, Dorais completed a 35-yarder to Finegan, followed by a 15-yard penalty against the Cadets. Eichenlaub scored on a line plunge. Dorais kicked the extra point, and the 35–13 score was how the game ended.

The aerial display put on by Notre Dame was shocking, as was their dominating physical play. All facets of Dorais' game were flawless, including catching all of the punts in the high, blue sky that gave Army difficulties. The Gold and Blue used but one substitute and took only one timeout—when Pliska's shoelace broke. "Notre Dame's Open Play Amazes Army," was Harry Cross's headline in the *New York Times*. He wrote that Dorais was "as agile as a cat and as restless as a jumping-jack," and that he "got around as if on springs and was as cool as a cucumber on ice when shooting the forward pass."[14]

According to Arch Ward, Dorais and Rockne were asked to stay on at West Point for a few days to teach Army the intricacies of the pass. If so, the invitation was turned down for a brief visit to Niagara Falls on the trip back to South Bend. Harper was eager to prepare for a trip back east the following week to University Park, Pennsylvania, to play Penn State. It would be the first meeting between the schools. The Gold and Blue returned to Indiana in a scene reminiscent of Dorais' homecoming after winning the high school state championship. "When we got out of our day coach at the South Bend railroad station, we found most of the town waiting for us. There was a parade with several bands and plenty of red fire," he said.[15]

The win over Army thrust Notre Dame and Dorais into the national headlines. It was rumored on the South Bend campus that a high-profile magazine had contacted University officials to obtain both a headshot and action photo of Dorais. In the minds of most it was *Collier's Weekly*, where Walter Camp's prestigious All-American team was published each December. Understandably, excitement spread as the next game approached, especially since the opponent was Penn State, led by quarterback Gene "Shorty" Miller. A month earlier, Miller—who was on several All-American ballots the year before—ran for over 250 yards and five touchdowns in the season opener, a 49–0 win over Carnegie Tech (Pittsburgh, PA). A theory pushed by newspapers was that if either quarterback had a standout performance, it could help propel him towards a spot on Camp's vaunted annual team. "One would have thought the game was a personal affair between 'Shorty' and myself, instead of a meeting between two football teams," Dorais said decades later.[16]

Though Penn State had been shut out their last three games—all on the road—the 2–3 Nittany Lions were returning to New Beaver Field, where they held a 20-game winning streak, dating back to the field's 1909 opening. Until the three-game slide, Penn State was 18–0–1 in games since the beginning of the 1911 season, outscoring opponents, 549–21. That same year Bill Hollenback, a three-time All-American fullback (1906–1908) at Pennsylvania University, began his second stint in Happy Valley, having coached them in 1909 before spending the 1910 season at the University of Missouri.

Notre Dame lore has the team spending the night in a cold, drafty Penn State dorm, where much of the team was up all night with food poisoning. If that was the case, the team showed no ill effects of the eventful night. The teams played a scoreless first quarter, trading punts and poor field position in sloppy field conditions. In the second quarter, the Gold and Blue took advantage of a botched field goal try, intercepting an errant pass from the Penn State kicker, Punk Berryman. Dorais capitalized on the turnover, needing just three plays to go the length of the field. He completed a short pass to Pliska that went 45 yards. Dorais ran around end for 35 more and then threw a short touchdown pass to Rockne. Dorais made the kick after for the 7–0 Notre Dame lead.

In the third quarter. Notre Dame scored another touchdown on a long run around end by Eichenlaub, followed by a Dorais kick, putting the Gold and Blue up, 14–0. Penn State scored on a pass from Miller to Levi Lamb and Miller kicked the extra point, cutting the lead to 14–7. Eichenlaub, Pliska and Finegan churned out short yardage, but Penn State got the ball back late in the game. Miller drove his team down the field and completed a touchdown pass that was called back by a penalty. A final Miller pass attempt failed, and Notre Dame ran out the clock, handing Penn State their first loss at New Beaver Field.

Dorais performed well in all aspects of the game, despite penalties and interference negating a few big pass plays. He had an outstanding game returning kicks, too, regularly returning them 20 to 35 yards at a time. Late in the game he broke one for 70 yards, only to be called back when officials said he stepped out of bounds when catching it. His national reputation was growing. Billy Maurice of the *Philadelphia Evening Bulletin* was wowed by the performance: "There is nothing in the East as good as Dorais, and while a few of the critics will not see him play, and they may miss him in their selection, I'll take him as my selection."[17]

The Penn State game was also famous for the origin of what became known as the Button Hook Pass. In the muddy conditions, Rockne was having trouble gaining separation from the defensive back. On one play, he went about 20 yards downfield and fell in the mud. The defender had trouble recovering, leaving Rockne alone when he quickly returned to his feet. Dorais saw this transpire and hit him with a pass. Rockne excitedly returned to the huddle to share what he had discovered. The pair used the play to much effect during the rest of the season and throughout their playing days.

After two emotionally exhausting games in the East, Harper's team returned to South Bend in ragged condition. In what turned out to be a stroke of luck for Notre Dame, the game with Wabash was canceled due to heavy snowfall. Harper gave the team a much-needed five-day reprieve from practice. They had over two weeks to prepare for the Christian Brothers College (CBC) of St. Louis, a college preparatory school that hadn't lost a game in two seasons. Rather than return to South Bend, the Gold and Blue would travel onto Austin, Texas, to play the University of Texas five days later.

Notre Dame's perfect season was momentarily in jeopardy when Dorais suffered a knee injury on November 17 during a scrimmage. Six days later, with a gimpy knee, Dorais led Notre Dame to a 20–7 win over CBC. Harper played his reserves for much of the first half under adverse weather conditions, but when CBC led 7–0 at halftime, he put in his regulars. Eichenlaub scored and Dorais kicked the point after to tie the game at 7–7 going into the fourth quarter. Sloppy conditions led Dorais to tossing a few interceptions, but his legs proved to be the difference in the game. He returned a punt 50 yards for a touchdown, eluding several of the Christian Brothers players. He missed the extra point—his first of the season—his streak ending at 27 straight. Dorais finished the scoring with a 40-yard run around end and kicked the point after. The *St. Louis Globe-Democrat* was another in a line of newspapers to extol Dorais' skills, calling him "one of the greatest Western quarterbacks since the days of the famous Walter Eckersall."[18]

Notre Dame moved on to their next opponent, the undefeated (and winners of 12 straight) University of Texas, in Austin, Texas, over 800 miles away. Harper's men arrived in town three days early, lodging at St. Edwards, a Catholic University in Austin that was established by Reverend Edwin Sorin, the founder of Notre Dame. On game day, Thanksgiving, over 7,000 fans withstood temperatures in the 90s. On the field it was even hotter, before rains set in, muddying the field. The playing surface was bare of grass and covered in fine alkali dust. "It hung over us in clouds and it got in your throat and mouth so you could hardly breathe," Dorais recollected nearly four decades later.[19]

The teams traded punts to start the game, before the Gold and Blue went on a 93-yard touchdown drive capped off by a 15-yard run by Dorais, who froze the Texas defense by faking a pass. He kicked the extra point for the 7–0 lead. Texas answered with a 60-yard lateral a minute into the

Another part of Dorais' arsenal was his kicking ability. Here he demonstrates a dropkick. He was arguably the best drop kicker of his era in college and the pros (Dorais family photo collection).

second quarter, but Dorais made one of two drop kicks, making the score 10–7, Notre Dame at halftime.

In the second half, the Gold and Blue took to the ground game, with Eichenlaub, Several drives stalled near the Texas goal line as the elements began to take effect. Dorais would call a player's name for a run and he would "check" it, meaning he would say he didn't want the ball.

"What's the matter with you guys?" asked a perplexed Dorais. "I keep calling your plays and you keep checking me. What's wrong with you anyway?"

Dorais recalled the scene to Lyall Smith of the *Detroit Free Press*. "They're standing there with their tongues hanging out and Rock tells me it's the darned alkali dust that's killing them so bad they can't even breathe. 'Why don't you try a drop-kick' Rockne pants. 'That's the simplest way I can think of to score."[20] Dorais did just that, making one of two field goals. With Notre Dame clinging to a 13–7 lead going into the fourth quarter, the Texas defense was finally worn down by the Gold and Blue's mixed game plan. Notre Dame finished strong, scoring two touchdowns and one more field goal by Dorais for a 29–7 Notre Dame win. On the day, the Gold and Blue rushed 77 times for 248 yards. Dorais was 10-for-21 passing for 200 yards and 3-for-7 on field goals. The attempted kicks was a school record that lasted for 58 years. He provided great field position on punt returns and once again excelled in the defensive backfield.

All-American teams were named in December. Dorais, Rockne and Eichenlaub were listed on multiple squads. Dorais was voted a Consensus All-American, the first ever from Notre Dame, He was also on several All-Western teams: *International News Service* (Frank Menke), *Chicago Tribune* (Walter Eckersall), *Chicago Inter-Ocean* (Matt Foley) and *Chicago Record Herald*. He finally earned an All-Indiana Eleven nod from the *Indianapolis Sun*, as did Rockne, Jones, Feeney, Pliska and Eichenlaub. A parody playbill appeared in the 1914 *Dome* for a fictitious play titled "Recognition, starring Miss Notre Dame and Charles Dorais, a Masterpiece by Jesse Harper with an All-Star cast." Likely a hommage to the fantastic football season and several members of the team being selected on various All-American elevens.

Conde Nast's new magazine, *Dress & Vanity Fair*, put forth what they advertised as "The First Real All-American Team," deviating from the common practice of not looking beyond the East Coast (although they did include an "All Eastern" and "All-Western Team). Dorais was both the "All-Western" and "All-American" quarterback and met the magazine's criteria of "one sure catcher of punts." *Vanity Fair* lauded Dorais' all-around game: Beyond his punt returning skills, they wrote that he was a

Notre Dame lined up in a modern-day shotgun formation, then referred to as "punt formation," Dorais at quarterback, Rockne at left end (at far left of photograph in dark jersey). This is the Texas game, where Gus attempted seven field goals, making three (University of Notre Dame Archives).

"sure tackler in open field." He was the only Notre Dame player on the "All-American" team. Rockne and Eichenlaub placed on the All-Western Team, though Dorais remained somewhat of an unknown as the magazine printed a photo that wasn't him.[21]

When *Collier's Weekly* finally arrived in South Bend, Notre Dame was recognized, but Dorais' name was absent. Rockne was on the third team; Eichenlaub, second. Instead of Dorais, Camp chose, from first to third team: Ellery Huntington, Colgate; Alexander Wilson, Yale, and Shorty Miller, Penn State.

"I think that was the greatest disappointment I ever experienced as a football player," Dorais said of the omission. "But it taught me never to build air castles."[22]

As the accolades came in for Dorais and his teammates, so did several coaching offers from schools in the Midwest and on the East Coast. Dorais had different plans. He was intent on heading west. One of the more intriguing offers came from Portland, Oregon, where the city's Multnomah Amateur Athletic Club (MAAC) was trying to persuade him to extend his playing days. The Club had tried to schedule a game against Notre Dame in 1913, and at the time of the Dorais courtship, Portland's *Morning Oregonian* called the city "the Mecca for the Notre Dame football stars of recent years."[23] Founded in 1891, the MAAC often played an ambitious schedule against any takers: high schools, club teams, universities and military squads. Several Olympians played for the team over the years.

Dorais seemed interested, hoping that he could also find a coaching job and work in the legal field. One day, he hoped to live back home. "Eventually I will hang out my shingle in my home town of Chippewa Falls, Wisconsin," he said in early December.[24] A few weeks later he was in Chippewa Falls for Christmas break. Around that time a rumor, thick with irony, was floating around Minneapolis. It was fraught with errors, though, but an amusing one to say the least. According to Frank E. Force of the *Minneapolis Sunday Tribune*, Dorais (referred to as "Frank Dorais") was, despite his eligibility elapsing, contemplating joining the University of Minnesota football team—the school that shunned him because of his size.

It was the third consecutive undefeated season for Notre Dame and second without a tie. In spite of the success the Gold and Blue found, there were still those who thought the forward pass was a risky maneuver, most notably Percy Houghton, head coach of the back-to-back national champion, Harvard. Many teams on the East Coast had tried to incorporate it, but made the mistake of throwing every down, rather than mixing in running plays. Dorais defended the pass to the naysayers. "The play should be more versatile and a number of check formations learned to give the quarterback a chance to pick out his receiver," he said.[25]

During the spring semester, Dorais was a part of the Senior Ball committee. In the senior play, *What's Next*, a farce comedy, he was Moses Madder, a heady businessman. Of his performance, the *Scholastic* said that his football instincts "equipped him with almost more savoire faire than some of the situations demanded."[26] He also played interhall baseball and ran spring football sessions with Rockne and Jones.

With the semester winding down, Harper received authorization to hire an assistant coach for the following season. Both Dorais and Rockne relished the thought of staying at their alma mater. However, the salary for the position was meager. Rockne's wedding was coming in July and he wanted to attend medical school. He needed something a little more substantial to support himself and his wife, as well as pay for school. Dorais had bigger ambitions than to be an assistant coach. He had been courted with coaching positions already and wanted to practice law as well. Still, both men kept their options open as Harper's assistant. Harper in turn agreed to hold the position until the semester was finished, leaving it up to the roommates to work out which one would fill the opening.

In late spring, 1914, Father Cavanaugh was contacted by Reverend

This is a parody playbill giving "recognition" for Notre Dame's perfect season of 1913 to Gus Dorais and Jesse Harper (University of Notre Dame Archives).

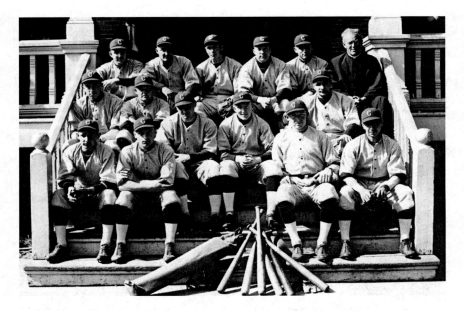

The last team the famous roommates would play together on at Notre Dame: the 1914 Corby Hall Baseball team. Dorais (top row, second from right), Rockne (top row, third from right) (University of Notre Dame Archives).

Thomas Collins, the athletic director at St. Joseph's College in Dubuque, Iowa. Reverend Collins was looking for a recommendation for a head football coach. Cavanaugh consulted Harper for possible candidates from his senior players. A much repeated falsehood arose from this request. In the story, both Rockne and Dorais showed interest in the position when approached by Harper. The trio decided the only way the quandary could be settled was with a coin flip. Harper flipped and Dorais won. He would be the next coach of St. Joseph's and Rockne would stay on as an unpaid assistant. Another version often repeated has the two flipping a coin for the Notre Dame position. There was no coin flip.

A decade and a half later, when there was no coach as popular as Rockne, a sportswriter named Feg Murray put forth a bold theory about the now infamous, non-existent coin flip that landed Dorais in Iowa and kept Rockne in South Bend. According to the *The Notre Dame Alumnus*, Murray, "in a safely speculative mood, based on many sound things, adds that Gus' records since then at Gonzaga and Detroit indicate that Notre Dame would have won, whichever way the coin could have fallen."[27]

Dorais, the natural leader, was the clear candidate for the job in Dubuque. He had intimate knowledge and experience in directing the powerful Notre Dame offense the last four years. Though the prospects in Portland beckoned, he favored the job in Dubuque for a few reasons. Not only was he offered the head coaching job for all the varsity athletics, but he was offered a position on the faculty as well as enrollment in the Master's program. Another factor was Iowa's proximity to Wisconsin, where his mother and older sister still lived, and whom he supported.

There was also the fact that Rockne had other aspirations. When the job came across Harper's desk, Rockne was in the middle of working on his application to medical school at the University of St. Louis and obtaining a high school football coaching job in the St. Louis metro area. In the meantime, Dorais verbally accepted the St. Joseph's College overture, but kept the Notre Dame option open as a fallback. Rockne's application to medical school was then rejected. Now he was faced with the prospect of no job and a wedding quickly approaching.

Dorais commented on what transpired in a 1931 interview following Rockne's death.

> What happened was this. Harper needed an assistant and he told "Rock" and myself that he would like to have us both but the school could afford to hire only one man. He left it to us to decide which it should be. We did not decide immediately but waited until school closed in June. Perhaps we would have settled it by tossing a coin if "Rock" hadn't married.[28]

It was an easy decision for Dorais to decline the Notre Dame position once and for all. He had a great opportunity at St. Joseph's. More than that, his best friend and roommate would now have a job to support himself and his wife. Rockne accepted the offer from Harper to be his assistant football coach. Harper was able to convince the university to do more for Rockne. He was also named to head the track and field program and given a position as a chemistry instructor at the preparatory school associated with Notre Dame.

At commencement, Dorais delivered a speech entitled "The Man" before receiving his diploma of Law. The next day he was named head coach of all major sports—most notably football—and faculty chair of commercial law at St. Joseph's College, which was transiting into a new name—Dubuque College. He would also be pursuing a Master's in Liberal Arts. Jesse Harper endorsed the signing. "Dorais is the most wonderful quarterback I have ever known," said the Notre Dame coach. "He knows the science of the game and will make a peach of a coach."[29]

Dorais looked forward to what lay ahead for him. "I have always desired to go west and have selected Dubuque College because of its beautiful location and because of its bright future."[30]

CHAPTER 4

Teacher, Coach and Player, 1914–1917

A week after graduating from Notre Dame, Dorais traveled to Dubuque, Iowa, to finalize his contract with Dubuque College. The institution was Iowa's first college and the second oldest Catholic University west of the Mississippi River (St. Louis University, 1818). Founded in 1839 by Bishop Mathias Loras, two years after the city of Dubuque was chartered, Dubuque College had gone through several name changes through the years: St. Raphael's Seminary, Saint Ralph's Academy, Mount St. Bernard's College and Seminary, St. Joseph's College, and the recent switch to Dubuque College. It would later be called Columbia College, before adopting Loras College during the school's centennial in 1939.

In the decade leading up to Dorais' appointment, Dubuque College saw some of the school's greatest growth, as enrollment soared and the campus expanded. All of this was done under the guidance of college president Monsignor Daniel M. Gorman, a former student at what was then St. Joseph's College. Gorman served as a faculty member at the school for a decade before taking over his presidential duties in 1904. He had a magnetic personality and was a riveting speaker. He was also a huge proponent of athletics, and not surprisingly, the college's athletic program was expanded during the infancy of his leadership. An official football team was fielded in 1907 (sporadic games were played previously). Basketball and track and field were added in 1909. Dorais would coach all three as a member of the Hawkeye Intercollegiate Athletic Conference and share some minor athletic director duties with Reverend Thomas Collins. Though the athletic teams had no official nickname at the time, they were often referred to as the "Purple and Gold."

Dubuque College's period of expansion spilled over into the next decade, both in size and academic standard. The Academy Gymnasium was constructed in 1912, and Loras Hall (where Dorais lived during his years at the college) came along in 1914, as did St. Francis Hall and the Power Plant. In 1916 Science Hall and Keane Oaks were built. All of this led to admittance into the North Central Association of Colleges, an educational accreditation organization, in March 1917. With this growth came the need for an endowment fund, which the college lacked. Plans were put in place, and with the blessing of the Archbishop of Dubuque, James John Keane, the campaign began in April 1917, the same month that the United States entered World War I. What seemed like a risky move was not; quite the opposite. According to Catholic historian Reverend Mathias Martin Hoffmann, "This was the pioneer campaign of any Catholic college for such a fund in this section of the country, and despite the innovative nature of the plan and of the inauspicious times and of the great sum striven for,—one million dollars,—the campaign was a complete and astounding success."[1]

During Dorais' first visit to the Dubuque College campus located on Fourteenth St., Father Gorman enthusiastically showed Dorais around. Gorman introduced the new coach and faculty member to whoever crossed their path. One of those faces was 17-year-old Archie Ward, a prep student at St. Joseph's Academy, located on the Dubuque College campus. Dorais and Ward would become lifelong friends. Ward and his younger brother, Tom, who had lost both of their parents, were under the legal guardianship of Father Gorman. Ward's diligence and way with words caught the eye of Dorais over the next few years. Ward eventually followed Dorais back to Notre Dame, becoming the school's first sports information director. From there, Ward became a sports reporter for the *South Bend Tribune*. He then found fame as the longtime sports editor for the *Chicago Tribune* and created, among other events: the Golden Gloves amateur boxing tournament (1923), the Major League Baseball All-Star Game (1933), the College All-Star Football Classic (1934), and the All-America Football Conference (1944).

Dorais remained in Dubuque for a few weeks before heading back east. On July 15, 1914, he served as best man at the wedding of Knute Rockne and Bonnie Skiles in the rectory of St. Peter and Paul Catholic Church in downtown Sandusky, Ohio. Dorais then returned to Chippewa Falls for a visit with family. His younger brother, Joe, would soon be leaving for college, following in Gus' footsteps to Notre Dame. Joe, too, was a quarterback. For unknown reasons, he spent his high school years in Minnesota with relatives. Built similar to Gus, Joe didn't have the same abilities as his older brother. He saw little action on the field, spending a year on the Gold and Blue freshman team before backing up Jimmie Phelan.

By early September, Dorais was a permanent fixture on the Dubuque College campus. His teaching load included: History, English and Commercial Law, on which he eventually served as chair. He took up residence at the newly constructed Loras Hall, located on a hill overlooking Dubuque and the Mississippi River. Built in a late Victorian interpretation of the Craftsman style, with a touch of Romanesque influence, the five-story building housed both professors and students. The amenities included: offices, classrooms, a library, study halls, meeting rooms, billiards and a gymnasium. It also had the luxury of modern plumbing.

Twenty-five candidates, including seven letter winners, showed up at Clark Field for the first day of practice. Besides assessing his roster, Dorais was making a decision on where to play games. Clark Field, less than a decade old, was named after Father Arthur Clark, a former librarian at the college and later a major benefactor. The on-campus field was deemed suitable for practice, but Dorais thought playing games off-campus would be of the greatest benefit to the college. His options were Nutwood Park, once heavily used for horse racing and, for a brief time, the Tri-State Fair, or the newly built Dubuque Athletic Field. Dedicated in April 1914, Dubuque Athletic Field, located downtown on the Fourth Street Extension, was near the high bridge connecting to East Dubuque, Illinois. The area was once the site of what was described by the *Dubuque Telegram Herald* as "one of the eye-sore sections of the city."[2]

Most recently the tract had been the site of Standard Lumber Company, which had burned to the ground. The reclamation was financed by Fred Leiser, a local businessman and rabid baseball fan. The park's main purpose was for use by the Dubuque Dubs, part of the Three-I League, but other entities, such as football teams, could, too. Dorais felt that the proximity to downtown was essential. "The grounds are in excellent shape and with a downtown park, I am sure that more interest will be aroused in the game and more interest means more money at the gate." Though the Athletic Park was Dorais' venue of choice, the team ultimately split time between there and Nutwood Park.[3]

It was quickly evident that the 23-year-old Dorais had his work cut out for him in assembling a roster and implementing an abbreviated version of the Notre Dame offense. Over the years, he would modify it and make it his own, adding his own twists and taking from others, creating the "Dorais System." A quarterback in his playing days, Dorais' offensive scheme, heavy on shifts, centered around a halfback who could either run or throw the ball. A decade later when he took over at the University of Detroit, Dorais explained his philosophy of not wanting to be tied to one system of play. "It is possible to adopt the whole set of of plays of one coaching school or another and still play a 'system' altogether foreign to that of the originator of these plays."[4]

A few weeks into drills, the letter winner number dropped to three, due to injury and parental objections. Gone were Dorais' potential quarterback, fullback and guard. However, he still had Oscar Heuser at halfback. For years, Heuser was regarded as the best all-around athlete to come out of Dubuque College. In 1913, serving as team captain (he was given the title again in 1914), he scored five touchdowns in a game—a record that still stands over a century later. He started on the basketball team, ran track and was a standout pitcher and captain of the baseball team. He even pitched minor league ball in 1913 without consequence for Muscatine of the Central Association. Heuser would leave school at the end of the 1915 school year to play a season of minor league ball.

With small numbers, Dorais suited up and participated in practice— something he did for years, especially when he himself was playing on the weekends. Later in life, when he was giving dozens of banquet talks a year, Dorais had crafted a tale of his first year at Dubuque College, when he inserted himself into the lineup under a fictitious name, swapping his trench coat and hat for a second-stringers' uniform and nearly leading the team to victory.

Dorais was also dealing with comparisons to and the style of play of his predecessor, John Chalmers, a lawyer in Dubuque. Chalmers preferred the conservative eastern methodology, opposed to the wide-open, aggressive version that Dorais was attempting to implement. Adding to the difficulty was that Chalmers was still coaching in Dubuque, having moved just a mile to the Dubuque German College and Seminary, a Presbyterian institution, dubbed "Dubuque German."

A native of Downsville, New York, Chalmers was one of the most decorated athletes to come out of Lafayette College (Easton, Pennsylvania). In 1903, two years after leading the Dubuque High School football team to a state title, Chalmers was hired as Alden Knipe's replacement at the University of Iowa, a member of the Big Nine Conference. In his first season he led the Hawkeyes to a 9–2 mark. The nine wins stood as a school record for 82 years. Iowa went 7–4 and 8–3 over the next two years, respectively. Despite his success, Chalmers viewed coaching as a hobby and was planning his exit, to set up a law practice in Dubuque. He was talked into staying one more year (1906), working with his successor, Mark Catlin, a disciple of Alonzo Stagg. Rule changes by the Big Nine and conflicting styles of play by Chalmers and Catlin led to a disappointing 2–3 record. The next year, 1907, Chalmers took over the newly formed Dubuque College program. In seven seasons he amassed a 28–16–4 record.

Dubuque opened up the season and Dorais' coaching career against Plateville Normal (Plateville, Wisconsin) at Nutwood Park on Saturday, October 3, at 2pm. In the schools' last meeting (1912), Dubuque won, 82–0. The teams, who played one another at Dubuque's inaugural game in 1907, skipped the 1913 game, due to Plateville joining the Inter-Normal Athletic Conference of Wisconsin. It looked like it was going to be an easy win for Dubuque, when the Purple and Gold's quarterback, Walter Martin, crossed the goal line on a 20-yard run just three minutes into the game. The extra point made it 7–0 in favor of the home team. In the second quarter, Plateville scored on a long drive, tying the game, 7–7. Dubuque responded with a short run by O'Brien. The extra point was missed, making it 13–7. The second half was played mainly around midfield, the game ending 13–7 in favor of Purple and Gold.

Dorais earned his first coaching victory, but was not satisfied with the play of his team, particularly a line that was having difficulty adjusting to the up-tempo offense. He spent the following Monday lecturing and demonstrating proper technique to linemen in preparation for Ripon College (Ripon, Wisconsin). Though improved, Dubuque was plagued by fumbles, losing, 32–6. The small roster (in both numbers and stature) couldn't seem to meet Dorais' demands, but he pressed on as injuries mounted. From the start, the calm, confident on-field demeanor he had displayed as a player carried over onto the sideline. As Arthur Dussault, a halfback from Dorais' tenure at Gonzaga in the early 1920s said, "Dorais wasn't the tongue-lashing kind of coach. He'd always correct you in a kindly, considerate manner. He wasn't much for theatrics at halftime, or before the game."[5]

Nearly two decades later, Dorais explained to Arch Ward his views on pep talks and addressing players during games.

> I assume that they have the right spirit and that they are going to try to win. My talks deal with scientific aspects of the game, the details of what I expect them to do rather than with the importance of upholding the honor of the university. I would like to have them go on the field believing that every game is just another hard scrimmage with a crowd in the stands instead of worrying about the tremendous importance of their individual efforts.[6]

During Dorais' trying first fall in Dubuque, he gained a positive reputation not only amongst players, but also faculty. He was described as a "very modest, quiet, mild-mannered gentleman," by Professor G.W. Heitkamp, who became a close acquaintance of Dorais. Added the professor of Dorais: "He had a fine sense of humor, and always seemed to take things in stride. He was not a driver-type coach, I guess you might say he was more of a phlegmatic type."[7]

Dubuque tied the State Teacher's College out of Cedar Rapids, 6–6, in the first Hawkeye Conference game on October 17 and then lost a tough 7–0 match to Chalmers' Dubuque German team on a late touchdown. That was followed up by a 28–0 blowout at the hands of Ellsworth from Iowa Falls. After a month, the Purple and Gold finally returned to the win column in Chicago with a 21–7 win over previously unbeaten DePaul University. The forward pass was a key component of the game, so Dorais declared that it would be featured in the next game against Upper Iowa in Dubuque. The pass was heavily utilized, but with little success—a third quarter touchdown—in the 32–6 loss.

The Purple and Gold were favored in the season finale, a Thanksgiving Day match game against Buena Vista College. Dorais was disappointed when the administration for the Presbyterian College from Storm Lake, Iowa, canceled due to injuries and ineptitude. Dubuque College ended the season 2–4–1, the first of only two losing seasons of Dorais' collegiate football coaching career. In the *Dubuque Football Review*, Arch Ward's cousin, Maurice Sheehy, wrote that "however disappointing the season of '14 was, we are inclined to call it a fortunate one for Dubuque, because it gave us a coach, a player, and a student of the game, than whom no better can be found today in the Western college circles."[8]

In late November 1914, speculation arose that Dorais had applied for coaching jobs at the University of Wisconsin–Madison and Iowa State in Ames. He was also mentioned as a candidate to help start and run a semi-pro team in Duluth, Minnesota. Dorais was adamant that he was perfectly satisfied with his position at Dubuque, but the Madison hearsay persisted into the New Year. Rumors of seeking better coaching situations followed Dorais throughout his coaching career. In a few years, as he built a strong football team at Dubuque College, Dorais' alma mater, Notre Dame, would be asking him to come back to coach under Jesse Harper, and alongside his friend Knute Rockne.

Dorais had only a few days to prepare the Dubuque College basketball team after winter break. A major obstacle was implementing rule changes that had been instituted in late November by the Collegiate Basketball Rules Committee, several which amended John Naismith's original 13 rules for the game. Dorais' task was aided by several players from the football team who transitioned over to the basketball squad, including Martin and Heuser. The star was center John Connell, the team captain.

Though he never played organized basketball, Dorais instituted statistical analyses rarely used at the time and led the Purple and Gold to multiple Hawkeye League titles (Dorais family photo collection).

Dorais didn't play basketball in high school or college, but it was obvious that he knew the game. He began using statistical analysis in practices, keeping track of all baskets and free throws, posting the totals at the end of each week. He also gave points for team work, floor work, passing and dribbling, and posted the averages. His approach worked, as the Purple and Gold won the Hawkeye Conference championship. He also coached the track team to a conference championship, the first of multiple titles for the Dorais-led spring sport.

Despite the 2–4–1 football record, and being outscored 50–119, Dorais' reputation was drawing some serious talent to Dubuque. He found an ally in the new athletic director, Reverend Edward Bendlage, an alumni and former player from the sport's first year of existence at the college. The *Dubuque Times-Herald* reported that Father Bendlage "was a back on the Dubuque College in thirty-two games and was never out of any one game for a minute."[9] The two worked closely together over the next few years.

Summer school pushed back the beginning of classes in fall, 1915, and thus the start of football practice. Dorais had just four returning starters report, but he saw plenty of talent when practice commenced.

Three players from Janesville, Wisconsin played major roles: Ray McCaffery, lineman; Joe Ryan, punter and halfback; and Maurice "Mugsy" Dalton, fullback. A transfer from Carroll College in Waukesha, Wisconsin, Dalton was described as short, speedy and muscular. He became a mainstay in the Dubuque backfield over the next few seasons. A prep star, he helped Janesville High School to state championships in football and basketball. Later, after serving with a machine battalion in the 6th Division during World War I, he played semipro football for several teams and eventually fullback for the Racine Legion (1922) in the National Football League.

Dorais knew who he wanted his quarterback to be—sophomore Dick Cantillon. Dorais saw a lot of himself in Cantillon, whom the *Dubuque Telegram-Herald* labeled as "the smallest player ever to don a uniform at the college."[10] Labels like that left Cantillon doubting himself as a starter, but Dorais knew first-hand that lack of size could be made up for with ability.

Dubuque started out with a 4–0 record, posting shutout wins over Plateville Normal (38–0), De Paul (1–0, due to DePaul failing to substitute after a player was ejected for fighting, with the Purple and Gold were leading, 26–0, when the game was called) and close contests against the State Teachers College (13–10) and Buena Vista (12–6). Early in the week following the Buena Vista game, a prospective player showed up at Dorais' door at Loras Hall. Just days earlier, Harold "Big Chief" Porlier, an Oneida Indian from De Pere, Wisconsin, was captain of the Carroll College team and one of the top collegiate players in Wisconsin, regardless of conference. He abruptly left school after an ugly incident over the weekend in Milwaukee against Marquette University. There was tension between the two schools, dating back to the year before, when Porlier led Carroll to the first win over Marquette in several years, scoring all the points in the 16–0 win. Porlier and a Marquette player (Meyer) were kicked out of the game due to continued fighting. Meyer went peacefully, but Porlier protested for nearly a half-hour before walking off the field with the whole team in tow. The angry Marquette crowd descended upon the Carroll dressing room, only to be held at bay by police. This meant little to Dorais, who immediately put Porlier on the roster. Dorais finally had a back who fit his scheme. Porlier quickly found his way into the Dubuque backfield, his arm often superseding Cantillon's from the halfback position. According to Sheehy, Porlier "would shoot a pass thirty, forty, or fifty yards, and Ray Sweeney or Meyer or someone else would chase down the field, tuck the pigskin under his arm, and register a score."[11]

Dorais was not only juggling his duties at Dubuque, but also being courted by top professional football teams of the day. The most persistent was the newly reformed Massillon Tigers of the Ohio League. It had been nearly a decade since Massillon had fielded a team. The organization folded in 1907, but the big blow came the year before in 1906 (the year Dorais' high school coach, A.G. Findlay, was in the backfield), when a major scandal tarnished the reputation of both the Tigers and their rival, the Canton Bulldogs. The two clubs—located just eight miles apart in Northeast Ohio's Stark County—were accused of fixing the two-game series, with each one winning a game, in hopes of setting up a financially lucrative third game. A deciding contest was never played, marking the end of football in Massillon, which had become too much of a financial burden. The Bulldogs were defunct for several years until current owner Jack Cusack resurrected the team in 1911.

Professional football returned to Massillon in 1915 thanks in part to a board of directors known as the "Tigers Football Association." They were headed by Jack Whalen, Superintendent of the Massillon Coal Mining Company. The board was creative in raising the revenue required for financing team operations. They accomplished this by offering season tickets at $10 each and investing substantial amounts of their own money as well. This was in many parts due to the peacetime prosperity that the country was enjoying, while much of Europe was at war. The needs of countries at war boosted economies all over the United States. "Moreover, the increased chauvinism of Americans for their clever, peace-loving country seeped down to a similar pride in city, town, village or hamlet, bringing rampant boosterism," said the Professional Football Research Association. "Many a local businessman believed it his civic duty to use a few of his new dollars to bring 'the championship'—whether city, county or state— to his hometown. Translated, that meant paying more for better players— importing ringers."[12]

Both Canton and Massillon cooperated in raiding the rosters of other teams in the state. When early rosters were announced, Rockne and several of his teammates from the previous year's Akron Indians were listed as Tigers. Homer Davidson, a past Massillon star and veteran of the Ohio League, was signed to start the season as the Tigers' quarterback, but the board of directors had their sights on Dorais. A player of his ilk earned anywhere from $50–75 per game plus travel expenses. The *Massillon Evening Independent* reported his signing by Massillon for the Tigers' game against the Columbus Panhandles on Sunday, October 31. He would be joining several Notre Dame alumni.

By all accounts, Dorais hadn't played an official football game since his last start at Notre Dame, the 30–7 triumph in Austin over the University of Texas. Dorais opted not to play for Massillon, but continued practicing with Dubuque College, promising to be ready when the Tigers met the Canton Bulldogs on November 14. He was considered a "weekend player" for Massillon, missing practices during the week and showing up for the game on the weekend. But for a few instances of being able to make a Saturday practice the day after a Friday game he coached, Dorais remained a weekend player. He didn't go unprepared, though. "I had the plays and studied them all week," he recalled. "I knew what I was going to call, and it was up to the other fellows to be on the alert."[13]

A healthy Dubuque squad decimated an undersized Ellsworth, 42–0, the next weekend. Dalton scored three touchdowns, including an interception return. Porlier entered the game at halfback in the third quarter and had several long runs. He also kicked four extra points. Narrow wins against St. Ambrose (6–3) and Upper Iowa (24–7) followed, but Dubuque College didn't come out unscathed. There were several key injuries, including Porlier, who seriously hurt his right, throwing shoulder. The team had nearly two weeks to heal and prepare for a showdown with the undefeated Dubuque German College and Seminary on Thanksgiving Day, 1915.

Much had been made of the rivalry in the year since the schools last played. While it looked like Dubuque College had the stronger all-around roster, John Chalmers and the Germans had one of the best athletes in the state, if not the Midwest—Sol Butler. An African-American born in Oklahoma to a former slave father and a free mother, Butler was a prep star, first in Hutchinson, Kansas, and then Rock Island, Illinois. At Rock Island he was selected all-state quarterback in 1913 and 1914. As good as he was at football, Butler was even better at track and field, breaking the National Interscholastic record for the 60-yard dash. He was an Olympic hopeful in the long jump in 1920 (only to see a tendon injury derail his chances), played for several teams in the early days of the NFL (1923–1926) and had a brief stint with the Kansas City Monarchs of the Negro National League (1925). At Dubuque German College, his extreme athletic gifts led to rumors that he wasn't attending school and was simply being paid to play.

Shortly after the Upper Iowa game, Dorais boarded a train and headed towards Massillon, Ohio, some 566 miles away. He was finally going to be joining the Tigers for Sunday's game against the Bulldogs as promised. Along the way Dorais met up with Rockne. When the pair walked into the Hotel Conrad the morning of the game, their appearance didn't seem to impress the fan base. "What, those two little guys, football players?" hissed a Tigers fan. "Why they'll never beat Canton with Thorpe in the game."[14]

Thorpe was Jim Thorpe, who starred for Pop Warner's Carlisle Indian Industrial School team. Thorpe could do it all on the football field, but his athletic prowess went well beyond running, throwing and tackling. He won gold medals in the Decathlon and Pentathlon at the 1912 Olympics in Stockholm, Sweden, only to have them stripped because he had been paid a meager sum ($2 a game) to play baseball in the Eastern Carolina League in 1909 and 1910, thus negating his status as an amateur athlete. Recently, he had finished his third season of professional baseball, seeing limited time as a light-hitting outfielder for the New York Giants. Canton had signed him just a few days earlier. This would be his first professional football game, too.

Dorais and Rockne met most of their teammates for the first time at the Driving Park. Red Fleming, Massillon's halfback, came up to Dorais before they started running through the plays. "Gus, don't ever call my signal," Fleming told Dorais. "I don't carry the ball. I just block."[15]

It was apparent that the Tigers' offense was meant to revolve around Dorais. In front of 6,000 fans, Dorais outplayed Thorpe and Canton quarterback Don Hamilton, whom Dorais had replaced at Notre Dame in 1910. Dorais booted three drop kicks from the 33, 42 and 40-yard lines, all from different angles. He caught Thorpe on an open field tackle on what was a sure touchdown and completed pass after pass to Rockne, including a 50-yarder to set up a short touchdown run of his own. For the game, Dorais had 23 yards on 10 carries and completed seven of 19 passes for 119 yards. He was intercepted twice. The Tigers won, 16–0.

The next week Massillon played the Toledo Maroons and Dorais' former Notre Dame teammate, fullback Ray Eichenlaub. The mud was nearly ankle-deep at Toledo's Armory Field. In the second half, the field began to freeze over. In the fourth quarter, Dorais made a drop kick from a seemingly impossible angle—on the 28-yard line, just feet from the sideline—calling it the greatest drop kick of his career. It was the difference in the game, giving Massillon a 3–0 win.

After the game, Dorais turned his mind back to coaching and the upcoming game with Dubuque German. Returning with him for the long train ride back to Iowa was Rockne, who volunteered to instruct the Purple and Gold linemen. Together, they prepared the team for the clash. With an undefeated season in the balance, Dubuque College was favored. The *Dubuque Telegram Herald* ran daily stories on injuries, Chalmers' private practices guarded by Dubuque German students, and accusations of ineligibility. Betting was rampant around town, with thousands of dollars on the line.

On Thanksgiving Day, November 25, 1915, game day festivities started shortly after noon. Each school's band, including some players, led a parade of students and alumni towards Athletic Park. The two converged, and together they marched together to the park, where pandemonium existed. The box office was deluged with those looking for tickets to the already sold out event (3,552 purchased entry). The temporary bleachers that were set up to accommodate 300 held nearly three times that many. Dozens of cars lined Fourth Street. Hundreds of fans peered through or over the fence. Some were even brash enough to climb over for standing room only accommodations. Minutes before the game, as a blanket of straw that had covered the field for over a week was removed, nearly 6,500 spectators let their voices be heard. It was the largest crowd to attend a game in the Park's brief history.

At 2pm, Porlier kicked off for Dubuque College. The teams traded early turnovers before Dubuque German took advantage of a botched Purple and Gold punt. The Germans scored on a short run by fullback Arends and were successful on the extra point. Porlier had a 30-yard touchdown run and kicked the point after to make it 7–7 at the half. After a scoreless third quarter, the Germans plodded towards the goal line in the fourth quarter, aided by Butler runs, before Arends again scored on a short run. The point after was unsuccessful. Dorais' Purple and Gold tried to counter with their passing attack, but the now-muddied field and Butler's pass defense hindered those efforts. The Dubuque German College and Seminary won, 13–7.

Leon Meyer, a member of Dubuque College's squad, recalled the outcome decades later. "Chalmers had his men plow and plow right through our line; much to my horror and the horror of other thousands," he said. "We were beaten much more badly than the score indicated."[16]

There were some in the crowd that thought Dorais and his players had squandered several opportunities. As the throng poured onto the field after the game, Dorais and Rockne were approached by one of the angry Dubuque College backers. According to Clark Kalvelage of the *Dubuque Telegram Herald*, "Unfortunately for this irate fellow, he made his remarks in Rockne's presence. 'Rocke' gave him a punch on the snout."[17]

The game was the last played between the two schools. "About that same time the two schools became involved in a long litigation about who owned the name Dubuque College," explained Meyer. "I supposed both schools should have seen the opportunity to have a big game like that every year. Gate receipts would have been fabulous at that time. However relations were very much strained and the games were stopped."[18]

Overall, the 1915 season was a great success. At 7–1, the Purple and Gold outscored their opponents, 168–39. Several Dubuque College players made the Hawkeye Conference All-Star squad. On the first team were: Ray Sweeney, left end; Flaherty, left tackle; Kipp, right tackle; Porlier, right halfback; and Dalton, fullback. On the second were: Weber, left guard; Matthews, right end; and Ryan, left halfback. At the post-season banquet, Dalton was named captain for the 1916 season.

Dorais wasn't done with the football season just yet. On November 29, three days after the loss to Dubuque German College, he was in Canton, Ohio, at League Field for a rematch between the Tigers and Bulldogs. It had been two weeks since the last game between the clubs. Canton had an open date the week before and bolstered their roster with three tackles, including two All-Americans: Robert Burke (Wisconsin) and E.C. Able (Cornell). The other was the Michigan Aggies' (now Michigan State) Gideon "Charlie" Smith, one of collegiate and professional football's first African-American players. Thorpe was named Captain.

The second meeting between Canton and Massillon was one of the most controversial professional games played to that point. There was no sign of security or law enforcement at over-capacity League Field, where standing room tickets were sold for the end zone. According to Jack Cusack, the two teams adopted ground rules before the game calling for "any player crossing the goal line into the crowd must be in possession of the ball when he emerged from the crowd."[19]

Early in the game, the rowdy throng spilled onto the field, halting play multiple times. At least twice the Tigers were interfered with by the horde on would-be touchdown passes. Dorais repeatedly asked the officials to manage the crowd that was closing in on the playing field. Despite the hostile environment, Dorais and Massillon outplayed Canton, containing Thorpe to a longest run of 20 yards, a first quarter drop kick from the 18-yard line, and a third quarter place kick from the 45, for a 6–0 Bulldogs lead. Dorais was 10-for-15 on passes for 163 yards, the bulk of it to Rockne, who caught three passes for 101 yards.

In the fourth quarter, Dorais began to pick apart Canton's defense, completing pass after pass. With the ball on the Bulldogs 17-yard line, he dropped back for what looked like a drop kick, only to dump the ball off to his halfback, Briggs. He tucked the ball under his arm and had a clear path to the end zone. As he dove across the goal line, he was swallowed up by the mob blocking his path. Suddenly, Smith of Canton, who had subbed late in the game, emerged from the end zone with the ball. Upon seeing this, Head Referee Ed Connor whistled the play dead, recalling the ground rule established before the game. Briggs stormed out of the pack, screaming that a uniformed police officer had kicked the ball out of his hands. When told there weren't any officers at the game, he claimed he had recognized the brass buttons commonly worn by police. For nearly 20 minutes the referees converged, surrounded by both players and fans arguing their side. Despite there being eight minutes left in the fourth period, the debate had gone on too long. The game was called by Connor due to darkness. He said he'd confer with the other two officials—both of whom had said they saw Briggs in possession of the ball as he crossed the goal line—later that evening at the Courtland Hotel. Despite their claims, Connor ruled the game in favor of the Bulldogs, leaving the results in a sealed envelope, not to be opened until 12:30 the next day, when he had left town.

Years later, Cusack claimed he found out the truth on a trip back to Canton. While riding a street car he struck up a conversation with the conductor, who wore a uniform coat adorned with large brass buttons. The subject turned to old football days. The conductor said that he was in the end zone that day and when Briggs fell at his feet he instinctively kicked the ball, directly into Smith's hands.

"Why on earth did you do a thing like that?" asked a shocked Cusack.

"Well," replied the conductor, "it was like this—I had thirty dollars bet on that game, and, at my salary, I couldn't afford to lose that much money."[20]

The Tigers Football Association demanded a third game to decide the championship. Massillon backers put up a $10,000 wager, but Canton's owner declined, saying it would sully the sport for next year. Both teams claimed the mythical state and world championship titles for 1915. The best thing that came of the controversy was the publicity that the rivalry garnered. With all the stars on both teams and the crowds the games drew, other owners took notice. In the coming years, salaries for top players increased and the crowds grew larger. In turn, so did the gate receipts, making the professional game a viable business in many towns. The season had also benefited Dorais, despite playing in only three games. The legend of Rockne and Dorais as players grew and boosted their bargaining power for coming seasons.

As 1915 came to a close, there was reflection on the triumphs of the Dubuque College athletic program. There were the late winter and spring conference championships for basketball and track and the strong record of the football team in the fall. Even the baseball team, which hadn't put a contender on the field in several seasons (since future Hall of Famer Red Faber was pitching for St. Joseph's in 1909), met victory often in 1915. Much of the credit was given to Dorais. He continued into the next year, coaching another successful basketball season in 1915–1916, taking second in the Hawkeye Conference to the State Teachers College. A memorable moment for Dorais, personally, was a return to South Bend to play Notre Dame. According to the *Waterloo Evening Courier*, upon entering the arena, Dorais was "carried around the gymnasium on the shoulders of football men followed by the military band and the entire student body."[21]

As busy as Dorais was with all of his college activities in Iowa and commitments to professional teams in other states, he was, after all, a young single man in his 20s, and as such, had an active social life. One activity that he still enjoyed very much was dancing. Known as a talented ballroom dancer in high school and college, Dorais found time to partake in the pastime whenever possible. On one occasion, he attended a dance at Clarke College, a Catholic all-girls school in Dubuque. There, he was introduced to a young sophomore, Viola Fettgather. Viola, or "Vi," was the youngest of Ferdinand and Elizabeth Fetthgather's five children. The family ran the first general store and post office in Lore, part of the township of Center in Dubuque County. Ferdinand was also a farmer, and at one point ran a saloon in Lore.

Dorais' courtship of Vi began shortly thereafter. The only problem was that the Fettgathers lived several miles outside of Dubuque. Dorais knew little about operating an automobile. He called on his friend and fellow faculty member, G.W. Heitkamp, who chauffeured Dorais around in his chain-drive Studebaker. "The road wasn't paved, and Gus didn't know much about cars. So I'd drive out there with him and wait out in the yard while he was courting Viola," Heitkamp recalled with a laugh.[22]

It seemed unlikely that Dorais and Dubuque College could top the 1915 football season, especially with the ambitious schedule Dorais had compiled, playing the likes of Creighton University (Omaha, Nebraska) and the University of St. Thomas (St. Paul, Minnesota). With numerous returnees and a few new faces, that's exactly what the Purple and Gold did in 1916. Led by captain Maurice "Mugsy" Dalton, Dubuque won the Hawkeye Conference and was the only undefeated team in Iowa with a 7–0–1 record, scoring 164 points and allowing just 33. The biggest roster addition for Dubuque College was Jerry Jones, who transferred from Notre Dame. At 6'1", 205 pounds, the future NFL lineman dominated, opening holes for the Janesville, Wisconsin, backfield tandem of Dalton and Tommy Cronin, future NFL players themselves. Jones would one day coach football, basketball and track at Dubuque College, known as Columbia College during his coaching tenure. Dubuque eventually got the nickname of "Little Notre Dame," as several of the first 13 football coaches either played or coached at Notre Dame. Dorais started the trend. Others included Dr. Eddie Anderson, Vince Dowd, Wally Fromhart, Jerry Jones, Elmer Layden and John Niemiec.

The Purple and Gold began the 1916 season with convincing wins at home against William & Vashti College and on the road in Iowa Falls against Ellsworth—both shutouts—32–0 and 34–0, respectively. Dubuque College then met a highly touted Creighton at Nutwood Park on October 21. Though greatly outsized, the Purple and Gold line dominated. In the second quarter, Jones blocked a punt and Kipp scooped it up and ran it into the end zone. Dalton, filling in at kicker, missed the point after, but Dubuque led 6–0 well into the third quarter, when Creighton competed a short touchdown pass. Their point after missed, and the game was tied at 6–6. Neither team made any headway in the final quarter, the game ending in a tie. The draw was the only blemish on the Purple and Gold's record. The next week, Dubuque College tallied a 26–7 win over the State Teachers college in Cedar Falls, highlighted by Cronin returning the opening kickoff for a touchdown. Narrow wins against St. Ambrose (13–3) and Upper Iowa (13–2) set up a clash against the University of St. Thomas, a small school Catholic powerhouse in St. Paul, Minnesota. It was also a military school, deemed so by the U.S. War Department in 1906.

Dorais continued to play professionally. In early September, he signed a season-long contract to play Sundays for the Fort Wayne Friars (Fort Wayne, Indiana) at $125 per game—a $50 increase from his Massillon salary in 1915. The Friars were organized in 1909 and for the next few years were made up of local athletes. In 1915, management began to hire professionals, thanks in part to a $2,000 investment from William Griffin of the Wayne Pump Company. Former and current collegiate players (many playing under assumed names) suited up for the Friars, including players from Notre Dame, Purdue and Indiana University. The club finished the 1915 season 7–1–1, losing to the Evanston (Illinois) North Ends, 16–0, and tying Wabash Athletic Association, 6–6.

In 1916, Friars business manager Carl Suedhoff reached out to Dorais, offering him $75 a game and his expenses to and from Iowa. Dorais accepted, despite having verbally committed to playing for Massillon in certain games, specifically against Canton. There were several other Notre

Dubuque College's 1916 team went undefeated (7-0-1), dominating the Hawkeye Conference (courtesy Loras College Archives).

Dame alum on Fort Wayne—Al Berger (halfback), Al Feeney (center), Freeman Fitzgerald (guard), Keith Jones (tackle), Pepper O'Donnell (center), Cap Edwards (lineman) and Joe Pliska (halfback). They were also trying to lure Rockne for Dorais to throw to. The situation eventually came back to bite Dorais, who played for whichever team—the Friars or Tigers—had the better competition, meaning a bigger payday. This was a common practice in the pre–NFL days, but Dorais' high profile made his actions more egregious to financial backers and fans. It would turn into an embarrassing debacle that found Dorais receiving a rare dose of bad publicity.

Dorais traveled to Fort Wayne—on the Indiana-Ohio border, some 350 miles from Dubuque—on the weekend before the Friars' first game. He went through a morning and afternoon workout at League Park, located on the northern part of downtown known as Jail Flats. By the end of the day, he was running the offense at full speed, much to the relief of the team's investors. The fluidity of the Notre Dame alumni-heavy team showed in the opener on Sunday, October 1. The Friars demolished the outmanned Dayton Cadets (Dayton, Ohio), an astounding 101–0, behind six touchdowns from Pliska. Dorais and the Friars had a much more difficult the following week against the Hammond Clabby Athletic Association. He reportedly suffered a major charley horse during the 9–0 Friars victory.

The alleged injury allowed Dorais a reason to wire Friars management that he would not be in Fort Wayne the following Sunday for a game against a team from Detroit made up of former players for Carlisle. Instead, he was in Ohio, leading Massillon to an easy 54–0 win over a Carlisle Indian team from Altoona, Pennsylvania. He didn't show up in Fort Wayne the week after that, letting them know the Monday after he played for the Tigers that he was still unable to suit up. By now, Friars management and fans had heard the whispers that Dorais was playing for Massillon.

Heading into the second half of Fort Wayne's schedule, Suedhoff looked to solidify his roster in hopes of winning the Independent Football Championship. Locking down the services of Dorais was a top priority. Suedhoff did this in early November by offering Dorais a larger per game salary and naming him team captain. Dorais accepted, but quietly kept his agreement to play with Massillon when the game against Canton came around. In his first game as captain, Dorais led the Friars to a 7–0 win over the Pine Village—just the second loss in 13 years for the defending state champions. Dorais handled all the scoring with a short run and the extra point. He was absent the following week, though, reportedly hospitalized with tonsillitis.

Dubuque newspapers made no mention of Dorais' illness. Instead, the talk was of the high challenge that lay ahead for the Purple and Gold. The team left Thursday evening for the Friday afternoon game in St. Paul. A small cheering section of alumni attending a nearby seminary gathered in the concrete stands. Athletic Director Father Bendlage sat among them. Around them, St. Paul men debated the eligibility of the Dubuque roster, in particular that the Purple and Gold had former players from Notre Dame—besides Jones—who were beyond their qualification for playing. When one said he sat next to Flaherty in classes for two years at Notre Dame, Father Bendlage jumped to his feet and wagered the men $5,000 to prove their claims.[23]

The Purple and Gold's task didn't get any easier on the field. During the game, Dubuque was assessed 105 yards in penalties to St. Thomas' 15, by a hometown referee crew. Three of the penalties were called on the opening drive of the game, bringing St. Thomas down to the Dubuque five-yard line, where the halfback, Ward, ran the ball around end for a touchdown. The extra point was missed. After the Purple and Gold squandered a first and goal from the St. Thomas 3-yard line, the teams went into halftime, 6–0 in favor of the home team. In the third quarter, Dubuque quarterback, McGuire carried the ball over the goal line from five yards out. Cronin missed the kick, leaving the game tied at 6–6. In the final quarter, Dorais took the offense to the air. Two passes from McDonald to Meyer gained 40 yards. From just outside the St. Thomas 20, McDonald lofted a ball to a streaking Cronin. The halfback out-jumped three defenders, landed and leapt into the end zone for a touchdown. A Meyer kick made the score 13–6. St. Thomas tried to make things happen via the pass, but after two incompletions, Cronin intercepted a desperation heave to preserve the win.

The once-raucous crowd left the stadium quickly. The Purple and Gold changed clothes at a nearby school building, as the Dubuque College alumni in attendance cheered for them outside. Back in Dubuque over 100 fans, including the college band, celebrated downtown outside the *Dubuque Telegram-Herald* office, where they had applauded every update from the staff correspondent. The team boarded street cars and headed back to downtown St. Paul to their hotel—the Ryan—for a celebratory dinner. The following day, Father Bendlage and the Dubuque players watched from the University of Minnesota cheering section as the Gophers routed the University of Wisconsin, 54–0. Dorais was absent, on his way to Fort Wayne, Indiana, for a Friars game against the Wabash Athletic Association.

More than 5,200 fans crowded into Fort Wayne's League Park, in what was billed as the largest crowd to see a pro game in northern Indiana. Dorais' second quarter touchdown run around right end was set up by a long pass play from Dorais to Rockne. Dorais threw the ball from the Friars' 40-yard line across the field all the way down to the Wabash 10, where Rockne, surrounded by defenders, leapt up and caught the ball at its highest peak. Dorais' point after attempt ricocheted off the goal post for a miss. Wabash took advantage of a fumble in the third quarter, scoring and kicking the extra point for the 7–6 lead. The Athletic Association squad kept Fort Wayne pinned in their territory until late in the fourth quarter, when Dorais ushered an 80-yard drive, keyed by an acrobatic catch by another one of his Notre Dame receivers, Mal Elward. Pliska's short run and a Dorais point after made the score 13–7. Wabash threatened late, but the Friars held on for the win. Dorais was given a $50 bonus to ensure he would be in Wabash for the rematch the following Sunday.

Dorais found himself in a conundrum. He was captain of a team that was expecting him to be in the lineup for a rematch with the Wabash Athletic Association the next weekend in Wabash. The game was the same day the Massillon Tigers played the Canton Bulldogs. Canton stood undefeated at 8–0, outscoring opponents, 234–7. Thorpe led the way for the Bulldogs, but was helped by new quarterback Milt Ghee, an All-American from Dartmouth. Dorais, Rockne and Elward opted for the big game in Ohio, not only risking good standing with the Friars' players and management, but also to their reputation and that of Notre Dame.

Thousands of fans from Canton showed up wearing Bulldogs colors—red and white—led by a 40-piece brass band and what Massillon's *Evening Independent* called "confidence enough to choke a horse."[24] Nearly 10,000 spectators packed into the Massillon Driving Park. An unpredictable, gusty wind blew in from the south. The warm sun thawed the ground, making for slippery field conditions. The game was dominated by the home team, but it ended in a 0–0 tie. The Tigers had six first downs to the Bulldogs' one. Canton never got inside the Massillon 30-yard line, and Thorpe was shut down, the slick field taking away his speed game. The Bulldogs' only scoring attempt was a badly missed Thorpe place kick in the second quarter. Dorais and Massillon moved the ball, but he had two drop kicks of his own that missed, the wind wreaking havoc by pushing both wide of the goal. One was a 24-yarder on the first play of the second quarter. The second, from 19, went askew, too. Despite those misses and completing just two of his nine passes for 11 yards and an interception, he impressed. "Dorais was the same as always," said the *Evening Independ-*

ent. "Cool and collected he directed the Tiger attack in such a manner that it brought telling results."[25]

In Wabash, the Athletic Association beat a depleted Fort Wayne club, 3–0. In addition to the absence of Dorais, Rockne and Elward, the Friars were also missing Pliska to injury. The papers in Fort Wayne immediately picked up reports of the game in Massillon and who was playing. Of those missing, Dorais was the only contracted player. He was openly chastised in the local press for his actions. Dorais wrote a letter of contrition to the Fort Wayne management explaining his situation, reprinted in the *Fort Wayne Journal Gazette*:

> Your letter of a few days ago requesting my side of the story at hand and contents noted. It was a mistake pure and simple and I sincerely regret it. For that reason, I have not put on a suit since although I had several offers to play in games with Massillon [sic] and Columbus.
>
> I cannot justify myself although there are several extenuating circumstances which might interest you. Season before this when I played with Massillon, I promised them that I would be back this year to play in the game against Canton no matter what team I was with, or where I might be located. The people there remembered that promise and [since] I had been instrumental in beating Thorpe's Canton team a year ago they bet considerable money this time expecting me to

1916 Fort Wayne Friars. All the players in this photograph are Notre Dame men. From left to right: Al Feeney, Joe Pliska, Keith Jones, Howard Edwards, Gus Dorais, Alvin Berger and Hugh O'Donnell (Dorais family photo collection).

make good my promise and be on hand. I absolutely was honor bound to help them out. I swear that money played no part in my move as I did not know what I would find when I went there.

Also, Canton fans sent me an anonymous letter declaring that I had better stay away if I thought anything of my health. Of course that got me up in the air more than ever and helped me make the wrong choice. Also in making my decision I was practically sure that For Wayne did not need me to beat Wabash and I cannot realize now how that team beat the Friars.

This business hurt me more because I liked all of the fellows there immensely and after the excellent manner in which Suedhoff and the others treated me I am sure my ingratitude hurt them too. I don't think I will ever play again unless to fill a promise I recently made to Suedhoff that I would play the Wabash game next year without pay. I thank you for your note and I hope you will try to impress a few others with the fact that we are all human and liable to err. With best wishes.

Yours truly,

C.E. DORAIS[26]

Dorais did not play a game the rest of the season, including a Massillon and Canton rematch, won easily by the Bulldogs, 24–0. On Thanksgiving Day, Dubuque College tallied a 27–9 win at the Dubuque Athletic Field over St. Viator College. The Purple and Gold were the Hawkeye Conference champions and the only undefeated team in Iowa at 7–0–1. According to Athletic Director Father Bendlage, the team claimed the title of Western Catholic Colleges by victories over St. Ambrose, St. Viator and St. Thomas.

The 1916 Dubuque College team was considered the strongest in the program's decade of existence. Once again, several players made the All-Star Hawkeye Conference team: Leon Meyer, right end; George, right guard; Jones, left guard; Kipp, right tackle; and Dalton, fullback, graced the first team. McCarthy, left guard; Sweeney, left end; Cronin, right halfback; and Fulton, fullback, were on the second. A 1916 "All Western Catholics Eleven" was put forth by the *Milwaukee Sentinel*. A first team included: Jerry Jones, voted offensive captain at right guard; Leon Meyer, left end; and Dalton, fullback. The second team included: Flaherty, defensive captain at right tackle; Kipp, left tackle; and Sweeney, left end.

In January 1917, the *Dubuque Football Review* was released by the University of Dubuque. A compendium of pieces about the history of football at the school, Dorais' teams were featured prominently throughout the text. At the end, Dorais wrote a brief piece entitled "A Winning Team." Over the next half a century, Dorais would give countless talks and write numerous essays about the making of a solid football player and successful team. This looks to be one of the first:

For eleven years I have been connected with football either as a player or coach, and during this time I have been interested both in the amateur and the professional phases of the game. Experience, therefore, has given me some opportunity to observe teams closely, to analyze their make-up, and study the factors that chiefly bring success. So much for my authority to speak on the subject.

The winning teams I have known were all endowed with the same essential qualities. They all were composed of genuine football material. The real player has a head; he is apt to grasp the fine points of the game, and quick to read the opposition and sense the right play at the right time. He has a heart; he loves the sport. Love of the game makes him stick to it, overcome his defects, and develop all his power. He is conscientious in his training. He never misses a practice, and works every minute as if on his individual efforts depended the team's success.

Inspiration, confidence, harmony, teamwork, are largely the results of leadership. To secure these results is the principal business of the coach. The captain should be a shining example upon the field, he must inspire his men by his own aggressiveness, and by intelligent, cool-headed direction in the heat of play.

Winning teams do not often have a complex assortment of plays. Too many are a handicap. The execution, not the play, is the important consideration. A few well-selected plays skillfully executed, have made the greatest football history. Harvard is a notable case in point.

These are the usual, fundamental elements, which most successful teams have in common; but there is another quality, the lack of which may spell failure for an otherwise formidable combination. It is a certain indefinable spirit that pervades the very atmosphere of training quarters in which winners are produced. The spirit is composite of good will, confidence, harmony, congeniality, and we-can't-lose, never-say-die feeling, which is present wherever a championship team is found. It is a spirit hard to acquire, but once acquired by a team, that team will be hard to defeat by any aggregation, impossible to defeat by a team without this spirit though with equal mechanical ability.[27]

The early months of 1917 brought a change to the complexion of Dubuque College. In January, a Reserve Officer Training Corp was established on campus as World War I raged on and the prospect of the United States getting involved increased. Finally, on April 6, the United States declared war against Germany and entered the conflict in Europe. In the spring, Dorais, who had recently led the basketball team to a Hawkeye Conference title behind three all-conference players, including Dalton, decided to cancel the remainder of the track and field season as students left campus to enlist in the military. On May 18, the Military Draft Act was enacted. A week later, Dorais registered at Loras Hall for military service. Within a year he would be a lieutenant in the Army Reserves, serving in Waco, Texas.

CHAPTER 5

A Brief Reunion, 1918–1919

As students vacated university campuses all over the country, administration began trimming or dropping athletic programs altogether. Dubuque College did not. Though many able-bodied men of college age enlisted, the United States attitude towards athletics during World War I was very positive. No higher endorsement of continuing college sports was given than that of President Woodrow Wilson:

> I would be sincerely sorry to see the men and boys in our colleges and schools give up their athletic sports and I hope most sincerely that the normal course of college sports will be continued so far as possible, not to afford a diversion to the American people in the days to come when we shall no doubt have our share of mental depression, but as a real contribution to the national defense, for our young men must be made physically fit in order they later that may take the place of those who are now of military age and exhibit the vigor and alternates which we are proud to believe to be characteristic of our young men.[1]

The 1917 Dubuque College football roster was hit hard by graduation, military enrollment and raging influenza. There were no starters amongst the returnees, but Dorais was expecting big things out of McGuire and McDonald, who played prominent roles in the backfield late in the 1916 season. Within the first week of drills, both suffered injuries that kept them out of play for the entire season. A saving grace for Dorais was the emergence of freshman quarterback and kicker William Sheeley, an all-state player from Dorais' hometown, Chippewa Falls, Wisconsin. Sheeley helped the Purple and Gold to wins at home over Wisconsin's Plateville Normal and a Hawkeye Conference opponent, Ellsworth College. The third game was a much-anticipated rematch against Creighton University in Omaha, Nebraska—the longest road trip in the football program's history. The trip, the first of three games away from Dubuque, was a disaster and the beginning of the season's downfall.

The venture west to Nebraska began fine, until the boys became hungry before they had made it out of Iowa. The train had no dining car, but

Dorais had thought ahead. He brought a dollar for each of the players to find a meal at a long layover before crossing the state line. The boys rushed into town, piling into the first restaurant they saw, quickly filling the capacity of 15. The others, many of them starters, moved on to another eatery. With a time crunch, one of the players kept watch for the train. They finished their meal and even had dessert with the cars still at the depot. As the players returned to the station, they were horrified to find that the train they were watching was not theirs, but rather one on a siding track. Dorais had pleaded with the engineer to wait for the tardy group, but he refused.

Dorais quickly made plans as he and the remaining 15 players rode toward their destination. He wired the panicked group behind them at the next stop, letting them know that cabs would be awaiting with their jerseys when they pulled into Omaha. Dorais put together a makeshift lineup. According to Lewis Walter of the *Detroit Free* Press, Creighton jumped out to an early lead before "a shrieking of sirens outside and a shrieking of brakes, then a roar as the rest of the Dubuque team, piling out of their cabs, came rushing down into the natural bowl that is Creighton's stadium. Right down the aisles the players came galloping right down to the Dubuque bench. And Coach Dorais, standing there, sent them into the game as fast as they got to him."[2]

The fast start by Creighton was too much for the Purple and Gold to overcome, losing 21–0. The loss in Omaha started a four-game slide for Dubuque. Injuries mounted during defeats in Davenport to St. Ambrose and at Fayette to Upper Iowa University. The fourth loss, 19–0 to Morningside College, was a moral victory. The private institution from Sioux City, Iowa, had hung close to Notre Dame the week before in a 13–0 loss. The Purple and Gold finished with a 19–6 victory over St. Viator's on Thanksgiving Day to finish 3–4. In the season review for the *Dubuque Telegram-Herald*, Arch Ward wrote, "It is an indisputable fact that no football mentor in the state was confronted with such a discouraging outlook this season as the Purple and Gold tutor, and a wealth of respect is due to the Notre Dame idol for the machine he constructed this fall."[3]

After the way things ended for Dorais in the professional ranks in 1916, it was unclear where he would end up in 1917. It seemed that any animosity that remained in Fort Wayne had dissipated, when the *Fort Wayne Journal-Gazette* reported that Dorais would be in the Friars' backfield when they opened the season at home against Camp Custer (Battle Creek, Michigan) to "satisfy a popular demand."[4] No contract was agreed upon with the game just a few days away, but Fort Wayne management made it clear that all efforts to solidify an agreement after the game would be made. Without a practice, Dorais and the Friars were disjointed in a 9–0 loss against the team of military officers, many of them former college players.

The Massillon Tigers were once again vying for Dorais' services, too. An overture by the club had been reported a few days prior to the Fort Wayne offer. Part of the Friars' deal likely included a guarantee that Dorais wouldn't play for the Tigers at all. Massillon wanted him to join the team for the season, or at least play in the big games, specifically against Canton. Dorais gave no indication which way he was leaning until things were decided one way or the other. With a favorable deal signed shortly after the Fort Wayne opener, he now needed to let Massillon know that he couldn't play for them. With World War I looming and all able-bodied American men required to register for service, including Dorais, he had the perfect alibi. He verbally agreed with the Tigers under the stipulation that his claim for military exemption be accepted. In a letter to Massillon's management, he broke the news that it had been rejected by a district board in Iowa. "I had hoped to be with the Tigers this fall and regret very much that I will be unable to do so as I wanted to help Massillon win back the world's championship from Canton—something it never should have lost."[5]

The Friars, who played all but one of their 1917 games at home (League Park) obliterated the Detroit Ex-Carlisle Indians the next week, 56–0. Dorais didn't enter the already-decided game until the second half, tacking on a touchdown with a long run around end. From there forward, Dorais, named captain, played in every game for Fort Wayne. Even with him and his former Notre Dame teammates Pliska and Rockne (who didn't come aboard until the seventh game), the successes of previous years eluded the Friars. After starting 2–2, they compiled three impressive wins in a row over the Toledo Maroons, 45–7, Racine Regulars, 28–0, and Columbus Panhandles, 13–0. However, the final two weeks were a disappointment against intrastate rivals. Fort Wayne tied Wabash Athletic Association, 7–7, in the annual clash, and suffered a shocking 28–0 loss at the hands of the Hammond Clabbys. The Friars finished with a mediocre 5–3–1 record. Worse yet was the financial loss suffered. It was a blow that Fort Wayne would never recover from. The club estimated a loss of $3,000 and saw a slight profit in only one game. Much of that was due to paid attendance, less than half of seasons past.

Before the New Year, Dubuque College finally suspended all intercollegiate athletics. Dorais enlisted in the Army on December 29, 1917, and arrived at Camp Dodge near Des Moines on January 5, 1918. His college degree earned him an immediate rank of Sergeant, assigned to the 351st Infantry, Company L. Quickly, steps were made to make him an officer, honorably discharging him as Sergeant to get his officer commission started. He was put in the Camp's Third Officers' Training Camp, Company Two.

The day after completing officer training, Dorais married 20-year-old Viola. Their courtship had accelerated in recent months, and when Dorais finally proposed, Vi accepted. When she went to her father to ask permission to marry, her father told her she was too young. Circumstances changed, specifically Dorais' enlistment, leading to their eventual marriage. After guard duty the day before and into the early morning hours of April 20, Dorais traveled to Des Moines, unbeknownst to his fellow soldiers. At 5 a.m., the couple was married by Father Conroy of Dubuque College in front of a few friends, including Rockne. Dorais rushed back to Camp Dodge for his last day of training without telling anyone about the union. He then returned to Des Moines for a ten-day furlough. The newlyweds spent much of their honeymoon in Chicago before returning to Dubuque to surprise friends.

Dorais was commissioned as a Second Lieutenant in the infantry on June 5, 1918. Soon after, the couple boarded a train to Camp MacArthur, a military training base in Waco, Texas, where he served in the Provost Marshal office. The newly married couple used the train ride down as a second honeymoon. Camp MacArthur, a cantonment camp, was often a last stop for soldiers before going overseas. Within a few months, he was appointed director of athletics. He took part in daily expositions at the Cotton Palace Athletic Field, giving demonstrations of modern warfare to onlookers. He was part of a three-man crew that gave exhibitions of boxing, wrestling and other hand-to-hand techniques.

In the late summer, Dorais faced the prospect of not being around football—and he didn't like it. Notre Dame was on his mind. Rockne had spent the summer as athletic director at Fort Sheridan, a military base north of Chicago. He was beginning his first year as athletic director and head football coach at their alma mater. Rockne took over for Jesse Harper, who resigned from his duties at the end of the 1918 school year and returned to his Kansas ranch. Harper lobbied for Rockne to take over the position, but Father Cavanaugh initially looked elsewhere, corresponding with outside candidates. When Harper finally told Cavanaugh that he had promised Rockne the position, the priest acquiesced.

Harper would not be easy to replace. The *Scholastic* wrote that developing winning teams wasn't his only contribution, but rather, "His gentlemanly qualities, his true sportsmanship, and—what is so rare in coaches—his appreciation of the proper position of athletics in the life of the college man, have endeared him unforgettably to everyone at the University."[6]

In early September, Dorais wrote to Father Cavanaugh, who had some authority in assigning on-campus positions for the Army. Dorais hoped that his old mentor could get him transferred to South Bend to serve as military instructor on the Notre Dame campus. Father Cavanaugh couldn't order the transfer, but he could petition on Dorais' behalf to be reassigned. Father Cavanaugh wrote Dorais back two weeks later, informing his former pupil that he had written the War Department, but had not heard anything as of yet. That was the last correspondence regarding the transfer. The course of the war was changing, and a big push was on to end the conflict. More troops were being readied for overseas fighting, and Dorais was needed in Waco—where he started a football team at Camp MacArthur. "They think a great deal of our Notre Dame down this way," he wrote.[7]

In addition to coaching the team, Dorais quarterbacked, despite the protests of Vi. The games were even rougher than the brand of football that Dorais was used to. "Army football in those days was plenty tough. Every outfit had its quota of former college stars and it being war times, not too much attention was paid to the niceties of the rules," explained Edward A. Batchelor, Sr., of the *Detroit News*. "A guy who was handy with his fists was as much in demand as one who could carry the ball. The idea was that the men were training to kill people in battle, they might as well get a little practice on the football field."[8]

Reports on the success of the Camp MacArthur football team vary. Some say they were a perfect 7–0, but a handful of wins, a loss and a tie have been confirmed. A definitive record may never be known. The team was absent from the 1919 *Spalding Football Guide*, containing most of the service team records. On Thanksgiving Day 1918, Camp MacArthur defeated previously undefeated Camp Pike (Little Rock, Arkansas), 6–3, in front of 5,000 fans. Dorais ran the offense and made several touchdown-saving tackles on the muddy field. Some deemed Camp MacArthur National Army Champions with the victory. Ever the Dorais advocate, Arch Ward wrote that Lieutenant Dorais, "the sensational great big little man of all-American fame, is without a peer when it comes to running a football machine."[9]

When his transfer to Notre Dame fell through, Dorais was certain he would be assigned for overseas duty. In a letter to Father Cavanaugh dated

October 21, 1918, Dorais seemed excited at the prospect of going abroad and taking a more active role in the war. Little did he know when he wrote that the war would end in three weeks and he would be honorably discharged five months later.

The couple returned to Iowa to assess their future. They stopped first in Davenport to visit Vi's only sister, Irene, for a few days, before moving on to Dubuque. When they stopped by the Dubuque College campus, Dorais was met in the Loras Hall dining hall with a long standing ovation. It was unlikely that Dorais would return to his former position as athletic director and coach at the college, although there were a few allusions to such an agreement. The college canceled most of its athletic activities due to the war. The football team only played one game in 1918, and the athletic department was all but non-existent at the end of 1919 school year. There was another option for Dorais—a return to South Bend to assist his friend, Knute Rockne.

Rockne and Notre Dame, now referred to as the "Fighting Irish," struggled through the 1918 football season, finishing 3–1–2. Between military enlistment, the Great Pandemic raging through Indiana from September 1918 to February 1919, and bad weather, Notre Dame was lucky to play the six games they did (all of their October games were canceled). Rockne realized the importance of a qualified assistant to help him with the athletic department, one who could step in without any grooming. He needed to look no further than Dorais, who now was in Chippewa Falls, Wisconsin, celebrating the holiday with family. It could be assumed that there was a standing offer for Dorais whenever he got out of the Army, considering that he went from thinking he was going overseas when he was in Texas to walking into the Notre Dame gymnasium in a matter of weeks.

On the evening of December 28, 1918, the Reverend John Cavanaugh announced that Dorais would be returning to Notre Dame as an Instructor of Physical Education and coach of athletics. Eventually, he would unofficially share Athletic Director duties with Rockne, but for now, Dorais was to be head coach of the upcoming basketball season and baseball in the spring. Rockne was to serve as his assistant when needed. In the fall, Dorais was tabbed to assist Rockne with the football team. The timing couldn't have been better for Rockne, whose contempt for basketball was described by Dorais as "so intense it was absolutely bitter."[10]

The proclamation of Dorais' homecoming set off a small celebration by those remaining on campus during the winter break. The headline in the next day's edition of the *South Bend News-Times* read, "Man Who Put

N.D. on Eastern Map Is Rockne's New Mate." The article referred to Dorais as "one of the most popular men ever graduated from the university," and a perfect complement to the excitable Rockne. "With Rockne's force and Dorais' persuasive methods the gold and blue will have a pair of coaches who are unbeatable."[11]

The time was right for Dorais to return to Notre Dame—at least temporarily. He was given a salary of roughly $2,000 to serve in the assistant capacity. Rockne made at least twice that. Gus and Vi temporarily stayed with the Rocknes before finding a place of their own. The coaching experience would be invaluable for Dorais, leading to his next job, just 18 months away in Spokane, Washington, at Gonzaga University. There was excitement to have the former All-American back on campus. The feeling was mutual. "You can say for me," said Dorais, "that they are not half as glad to have me with them as I am to be back among them."[12]

Dorais didn't have much time to be nostalgic. A few days later, he was on the basketball court, instituting the statistical analysis he used at Dubuque College. Dorais' presence brought interest to the sport, but the results were not good. The Gold and Blue went 2–10 in 1919 and 5–13 in 1920. The only good thing to come of the 1919 basketball season was that Dorais was able to establish a rapport with a few of the players he would be coaching in the backfield next fall, including quarterback and captain Leonard Bahan and the talented, yet trying sophomore halfback, George Gipp.

Shortly after signing his contract, Dorais and Rockne sat down to talk about the returning roster for the 1919 football season. They had strong returners, most notably: Bahan, Ed Anderson (end), Hartley Anderson (guard) and Clipper Smith (guard). Edward "Slip" Madigan (center) and Dutch Bergman (halfback and Gipp's roommate) were returning from serving in World War I. All became successful college coaches. Sophomore Bernie Kirk provided a threat at end, opposite Ed Anderson. From his left end spot, Kirk caught many passes from Gipp's left halfback position.

Gipp's off-field behavior was by far the coaches' biggest concern. Dorais and Rockne themselves had occasionally sneaked out of their dorm after curfew to take in the nightlife of downtown South Bend, but Gipp was making it a nightly venture. He was a card and pool shark and quickly became an established member of the night poker games at the Oliver Hotel, where he eventually took up residence to keep up his nocturnal schedule. Gipp frequently shot pool across the street at Hullie and Mike's poolroom and restaurant, playing some of the best shots from Chicago for $100 a game. Dorais called the lithe left halfback "a combination of an iron-willed individualist and an irresponsible kid."[13]

"On the field, I was to try to improve Gipp's passing, which already was fair," said Dorais of the player he ranked behind Jim Thorpe as the best he ever saw. "Off the field, I was to keep an eye on him, and use my powers of persuasion in trying to get him to behave in the way a football player is supposed to behave during the season."[14]

Dorais' task wasn't made any easier by the loose way that Rockne dealt with Gipp, letting his star skip class and practice without retribution. Dorais said that Rockne "quickly recognized the fact that Gipper was a natural-born nonconformist, and let him do pretty much as he pleased."[15]

Born in Lauriem, Michigan, Gipp came to Notre Dame as a 22-year-old high school dropout. The tale goes that he planned on playing baseball for the Irish, but in the fall of his freshman year, Rockne, then an assistant coach under Harper, noticed Gipp casually kicking the football around with booming results. Although he had played semi-pro football at home in the Calumet area, Gipp had no interest in playing college ball. He had a change of heart and was a man among boys on the freshman team. Over a three-year career on the varsity squad he proved to be a triple-threat back, garnering numerous personal accolades. For his career he amassed 2,341 yards rushing, a record that lasted a half-century, until Jerome Heavens broke it in 1978. Gipp also passed for 1,789 yards, scored 21 touchdowns and intercepted five passes. His 4,410 total yards eclipsed Jim Thorpe's mark of 3,946.

Gipp trounced through the first several weeks of the 1920 season, but in November he was hampered by a sore shoulder. A perpetual cough (he was a chain-smoker) worsened, and he developed a sore throat. His last time on the football field was November 20 in Evanston, Illinois, against Northwestern University. Rockne wasn't going to play Gipp, whose illness was worsening, but with a big lead in the final quarter the crowd began a "We want Gipp!" chant. Shortly thereafter, Gipp was admitted to St. Joseph's Hospital in South Bend. The strep throat progressed into pneumonia, and the outlook seemed grim. A blood transfusion from Hunk Anderson seemed to help. Within days Gipp began to recover, but suddenly he worsened and died in the early morning hours of December 14, at the age of 25. He had just finished his career at Notre Dame by being named the school's first Walter Camp All-American and second consensus All-American—Dorais being the first.

Gipp's on-field accomplishments have long been overshadowed by a deathbed conversation he supposedly had with Rockne. In 1928, Notre Dame was in the midst of what would be the worst season in the Rockne regime (they would finish 5–4). Playing against Army in front of 78,000 at Yankee Stadium, the teams went into halftime tied, 6–6. Rockne, at the height of his motivational prowess, summoned a speech for the ages, telling his outmanned team that on his deathbed, Gipp requested that one day, when the Irish needed it, that they win a game in his memory. Inspired, Notre Dame pulled off a 12–6 victory, thanks to a juggling, late-fourth quarter touchdown catch by reserve end Johnny O'Brien, and a defensive goal line stand preserved the win. The interaction between Rockne and Gipp was mythologized in the 1940 movie, *Knute Rockne, All American*. In the film, Gipp, played by Ronald Reagan, tells Rockne (Pat O'Brien) to "win just one for the Gipper."

After basketball, Dorais jumped to the baseball diamond in the spring of 1919. He found more success than on the hardwood, but was shocked at the paltry turnout. What was once the school's most popular sport had a sparse candidate group of 20. Dorais relayed his thoughts to Charles D. Grimes of the *South Bend News-Times*, wondering aloud if the war had turned college students into bookworms. "A few years ago, in fact until just before the war started, when first call for baseball candidates was sounded so many responded it was next to impossible for them all to get any more than elbow room in the gym," said Dorais, "This afternoon you could run 40-yard dashes between them and maybe not touch all."[16] The team flourished under Dorais, anchored by the pitching of Pat Murray, who turned down an offer from the Pirates to stay in school and would pitch two games for the Philadelphia Phillies later that year. The Gold and Blue won the western title in 1919 over Big Ten Conference Champions, Michigan, finishing 10–4–1.

Rockne and Dorais continued to share many of the Athletic Director duties. In the summer, Dorais mapped out the ever-competitive inter-hall football schedule. He also addressed the athletic department's need for a publicity director—something that Rockne and Father Cavanaugh had been pushing for. Dorais knew exactly whom to go after. While vacationing back in Iowa, Dorais dropped in on former acquaintances. Among them was 22-year-old Arch Ward, now a student at Dubuque College and sports editor for the *Dubuque Telegraph-Herald*. Dorais was a frequent subject in Ward's *Shrapnel* column, and the young sportswriter regularly sent him the clippings. Dorais asked if Ward was interested in becoming Notre Dame's first sports publicity director. He could also finish his education in South Bend. The next day, Ward mentioned Dorais' presence in Dubuque and bid farewell to his readers. Ward became known as Rockne's "official news correspondent," preparing pregame stories for the *South Bend News-Times* and *South Bend Tribune*. When outside papers wanted information about the Irish for an upcoming game, Rockne directed them to Ward.

The 1919 Notre Dame football opener was on October 4 at Cartier Field against Kalamazoo College (Kalamazoo, MI). The game was deemed an easy win, so Rockne skipped the contest, opting to travel to Iowa City to scout the University of Nebraska, the Irish's opponent in two weeks. Dorais acted as head coach, leading the Fighting Irish to a 14–0 win. Gipp, who was slowed by injuries in 1918, once again pulled up lame, but still managed to rush for what ultimately was a season-high 148 yards on 11 carries. He also had two long touchdown runs called back. After the second one was canceled by the penalty, Gipp said to the official: "Next time give me one whistle to stop or two to keep going."[17]

Rockne returned to his head coaching duties, but in many regards he and Dorais were co-head coaches during the 1919 season. Rockne coached the line, Dorais the backfield. Together, the good friends ran practice, sometimes from motorcycles. Ward wrote of the pair's symbiotic connection: "The two Gold and Blue coaches work in perfect harmony and are considered the most brainy brace of gridiron colonels in America."[18]

During the 1918 season, Rockne was hesitant to change much of anything from the Harper regime, including the playbook on either side of the ball. Dorais pushed Rockne to integrate some of the wrinkles that he added during his time in Dubuque, ones that eventually became major concepts of the famed Notre Dame Box. Though neither Rockne nor Dorais ever spoke of Dorais' involvement in the evolution of "the Box," Ward wrote that Notre Dame's offensive success during 1919 and the coming seasons "lay in its bewildering style of open play, a system devised principally by Dorais."[19]

One thing that Dorais and Rockne never saw eye to eye on was how to defend the pass. "It is a known fact, of course, that Rock favored the man-to-man defense strictly," Dorais told the American Football Coaches Association, while giving a lecture called "Forward Pass Technique" in 1932. "My impression was that it wasn't able to cope with the style of passing which was then in vogue."[20]

Dorais' services as a coach were wanted elsewhere in the city for the 1919 season. Initially he was set to coach the South Bend Athletic Association team, winners of recent Northern Indiana and Southern Michigan Independent Championships. Instead, he led the South Bend Arrows, assisted by Notre Dame senior center, Slip Madigan. Sponsored by the Kann & Schellinger Brewing Company, the Arrows were, in theory, a professional team, as players were paid and all expenses (uniforms, travel,

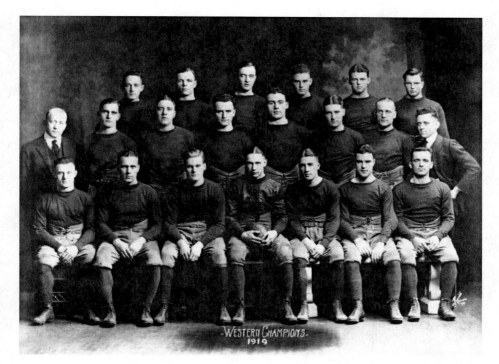

The 1919 Notre Dame team was the first of five undefeated Rockne-coached teams. Dorais (middle row, far right) would coach against several of his former players, including Hunk Anderson (back row, second from left). Also pictured is Dorais' star backfield pupil, George Gipp (back row, third from left) (Dorais family photo collection).

meals and hotels) were covered. Practices were held at night, except for Monday afternoons when the coaches were available due to Rockne giving his regulars the day off. Most home games were played at Springbrook Park, often in front of crowds in excess of 4,000, on a few occasions outdrawing Notre Dame. Game records were sparse, but the Arrows claimed several victories, and a few losses, one of them a disputed game against intracity rival Koehler and Schaefer. The point of contention was a call made by a referee that should have been made by the head linesman.[21]

Dorais returned to playing for the Massillon Tigers in 1919. It was the last season for the Ohio League before the ushering in of the American Professional Football Association. Like many professional teams, the Tigers didn't field a squad in 1918 due to various wartime circumstances, including government sanctions on train travel. It was a long year for Massillon's backers, Jack Donahue and Jack Whalen, who lost $4,700 on the

1917 team, even more than the $3,000 initially reported. The pair hadn't gone public on fielding a team until a July 1919 meeting at the Cortland Hotel in Canton. League managers looked to reassemble the Ohio League, but with certain stipulations. The most pressing was raiding other team's rosters and limiting a player's salary. In a surprising move, Donahue said what managers paid players was their own business.

Dorais stayed in shape by quarterbacking the Notre Dame freshman team against the varsity during the week. The day after coaching the Irish to a win over Kalamazoo College, Dorais was quarterbacking the Tigers—adorned in new black and orange uniforms—to an easy 27–0 victory over the Youngstown Patricians. He wouldn't be the team star during the 1919 season, but Dorais aptly led Massillon, playing all but one game on the road. The standout label belonged to a former Notre Dame Captain, Stan Cofall. A fullback, he was a freshman during Dorais' senior season, 1913.

The Canton Bulldogs still had the face of their franchise, Jim Thorpe. Like Dorais, Thorpe was on the back end of his career, beset by his dependence on alcohol. Off the field, Canton underwent a change in ownership. When the 1918 Ohio League season was officially canceled, Bulldogs owner Jack Cusack moved to Oklahoma to work in the oil business. He was contacted the following spring by a Canton businessman and Bulldogs fan, Ralph Hay. Regarded as one of Ohio's top salesman of Jordan Hupmobiles and Pierce-Arrows, Hay hoped that acquiring the Bulldogs would increase exposure for his business. Keeping much of Cusack's roster, including Thorpe, Hay and Canton found success. Hay famously organized a meeting in September 1920, which led to the formation of the American Professional Football League, which turned into the National Football League in 1922.

Dorais was beginning to lose a step on the field, but was still able to guide Massillon to a 5–0 start before losing 3–0 in Cleveland to the Cleveland Indians on November 11, Armistice Day. Five days later, the Tigers were at League Field in Canton to play the 5–0–1 Bulldogs. Canton was coming off a November 9, 3–3 tie with the Hammond All-Stars (Hammond, Indiana) at Cubs Field in Chicago. Thorpe had been in pre-war form in recent weeks, and the match-up against Massillon in front of over 10,000 onlookers added even more incentive. He rushed for 85 yards and a touchdown on 16 carries, and completed two passes, one of them a touchdown to his Carlisle teammate, halfback, Joe Guyon. Thorpe also punted 11 times for an average of 43 yards. Dorais struggled, completing four of 12 passes for 28 yards. He was intercepted twice. Rockne caught just one pass for 19 yards.

Towards the end of the 23–0 Canton win, Dorais suffered an injury at the hands of Thorpe that ended Dorais' playing days. He recounted the incident decades later to Walter "Tillie" Voss, a former pro player and an All-American tackle from the University of Detroit:

> For some reason they had me playing half instead of safety on defense. It's early in the game and Thorpe gets near me and is high-tailing downfield as an eligible pass receiver. I fall in just behind him and execute a neat trip. He hit the frozen ground on his face, cut his lip, bloodied his nose and got a black eye. He looked like a gored bull when he got up—and just as angry.
>
> "Kid, I'm going to kill you," he said. I tried to pacify him, calling him Jim and telling him it was an accident.
>
> "Don't give me any of that Jim business," he shouted, "you just watch out."
>
> All through that game I kept "watching out" for Thorpe because he was glowering and his eye was getting bigger and blacker. He just missed getting me a couple of times. I'm plenty worried and very watchful and careful. The game had only about two minutes to go when I took the ball on one of those kind of sneaks along the line where you look for daylight and then try to leap through for a couple of yards.
>
> I saw my hole and jumped at it. I'm stopped after about a half a yard. I think the play is over, and for the first time I've taken my mind off Thorpe. But he hasn't forgotten me. He comes charging up and lands with both his knees in my back and kidneys.
>
> I'm sick all over, hardly conscious but I hear one of our guys say to Thorpe: "Why'd you do that to a little 150-pounder?" and I hear Jim say: "Because the brat is too little to be playing pro ball."[22]

In extreme pain, Dorais played the following week against the Dayton Triangles. When rain turned to snow, leaving the field a quagmire, the starters were pulled at halftime to save them for the remaining games. The contest ended a 0–0 tie, and the Tigers split the last two games of the season: a 7–0 win over the Cleveland Indians and 3–0 loss in a rematch with Canton. The Bulldogs won the last Ohio League Championship with a 9–0–1 record. Dorais didn't play another down professionally after being substituted for in the Dayton game, and his back was put in a tape cast for months. Subsequent diagnosis revealed a damaged kidney, removing any hope of taking the field again as a player. Despite the vicious play, Dorais always held Thorpe in high regard and bore no animosity toward him.

Notre Dame blew out Mount Union (Alliance, Ohio), 60–7, on October 11. Another classic Gipp tale took place:

> The sole aim and ambition of the Mt. Union boys was to score a touchdown against Notre Dame. That would make their season a success. So getting the ball up around mid-field, here came a pass play. An end came racing down through Gipp's territory wild-eyed with hope. Gipp stood there slouching and never made

a move as the long pass sailed over his head down to the goal line. Down there in the clear, the Mt. Union boy made a beautiful leaping catch, and it was a touch-down!

Over on the Notre Dame bench, Rockne woke up with his staccato barking to his assistant Gus Dorais: "What's the matter with the Gipper? Better get him out of there."

So Dorais wigwagged Gipp off the field. As he strolled nonchalantly up to the bench, not the least perturbed, "Rock" began on him: "George, George. What's the matter? What's the matter?"

Gipp looked up at him and sort of grinned sheepishly. "You know, Coach," he said, "I'd a bet ten bucks that guy would not have caught that ball!"

The Gipper was merely playing his idea of the percentages, and saving himself a lot of useless running down the field, as he figured it![23]

Other than the Mount Union dismantling, Notre Dame slogged their way to a 9–0 record in 1919, the first of five undefeated campaigns for a Rockne-led team. It was the ninth team in Notre Dame history to go through a season without a defeat. Big wins came away from Cartier Field, over Nebraska, Army and Purdue. The victory over the Boilermakers gave the Irish an outright Indiana State championship. A Western championship was also tallied. Notre Dame had a chance to further bolster their reputation, but a Christmas Day game against the Oregon Agricultural Aggies (now Oregon State University) in Portland, Oregon, was canceled. Under the tutelage of Dorais, the dynamic Gipp-to-Kirk passing combination gained the most attention.

On December 14, the annual Notre Dame football banquet was held at the Oliver Hotel. For the first time, the freshman team was present. Gipp, who received numerous post-season accolades, was named Captain for the 1920 season. Shortly thereafter, a few weeks into the basketball season, Dorais fell ill. He spent time at St. Mary's Hospital in South Bend with the flu in early January. He was one of over 1,800 people in the area who were hit by the ailment. Rockne had to put aside his disdain for basketball and run the team until Dorais recovered.

A year in, and Dorais and Rockne's relationship was paying dividends for Notre Dame's athletic department. Dorais made a daily habit of stopping by Rockne's office in the morning to talk about activities in the department. Of late, many of the conversations were dominated by the pair's trepidation about not having George Gipp in their backfield in 1920. On March 8, Father James Burns had expelled Gipp from Notre Dame. Since then, Rockne and Dorais heard that Gipp was considering several schools, including Michigan, Pittsburgh and West Point. Rockne and Notre Dame alumni pressed the school's administration to readmit Gipp. They did, but now Rockne had to track down the star, who was just as elusive off the field as on.

One spring morning, Dorais, who had just come down from the woods following spring break, was met at the door by a concerned Rockne. He received word that Gipp, along with Kirk—both Michigan boys—were at the University of Detroit, going through spring football drills. The pair was intrigued by the wide-open style of play that head coach James Duffy, a former quarterback at Colgate, had instituted. More importantly to Gipp, he could play football, basketball and baseball there.

"Gus, don't even take off your coat. Don't unpack. Get on a train and go to Detroit. Get Gipp back here," demanded Rockne.[24]

Rockne told Dorais not to bother coming back if Gipp wasn't with him, because neither of them would have a job if that was the case.

Dorais arrived in Detroit, and was directed to Belle Isle, a nearly 1,000-acre island park on the Detroit River. Three different squads were practicing under the tutelage of University of Detroit assistant coach Bingo Brown. Dorais kept his distance, but when practice ended, he moved closer. When Gipp saw Dorais, he coolly went over to speak with his backfield coach from the previous year. Dorais questioned why Gipp was there, to which the student replied that his ineligibility at Notre Dame led him there. Gipp was guaranteed that he could play multiple sports here without concerns for eligibility.

"Listen, George," replied Dorais. "They held a board meeting last week

Canton Bulldogs vs. Massillon Tigers game, November 16, 1919. The great Jim Thorpe, Rockne and Dorais can be seen in the action. During the game, Thorpe ended Dorais' playing career with a vicious knee to the kidney (Associated Press/ Pro Football Hall of Fame).

and they ruled you would be eligible for everything at Notre Dame, You've got to go back with me. It's my job if you don't. Rock says it's his job, too."[25]

Gipp returned to Notre Dame, but Kirk did not. He opted to enroll at the University of Michigan to play for Fielding Yost, who was recruiting Michigan-born players (Gipp considered, but declined the offer). Ineligible to play for the varsity, Kirk was a standout on the freshman team in 1920, before gaining several All-American honors as an end in 1921 and 1922. He helped the Wolverines to an 11–1–2 record over those seasons and a Big Ten co-championship in 1922. Like his former teammate, Gipp, Kirk died young. Less than a month after the 1922 season, Kirk and four friends were returning to Ann Arbor after a late night in Detroit. The vehicle they were traveling in slid off an icy road and crashed into a telephone pole. The other occupants received minor injuries, but Kirk fractured his skull and suffered internal injuries. Initially, it looked like Kirk was going to recover, but he contracted meningitis and passed away the morning of December 23, 1922.

While Dorais coached a winning baseball team during the spring of 1920, he looked elsewhere for work. He and Vi had been married for two years, living in three states (Iowa, Texas and Indiana), not to mention Gus' pro football career, which had him traveling all over the Midwest. They had also resided in a few different spots in their short time in South Bend. With Vi newly pregnant, Gus was looking to settle into a long-term, well-paying job. Without the added income from playing professionally (his last season with Massillon he made around $1,000, perhaps more), Dorais needed to find a position with responsibilities similar to those he held at Dubuque College, equating to a larger salary. It just so happened that a Catholic University in Spokane, Washington—Gonzaga University—was looking to hire a big-name coach.

Gonzaga's interest in Dorais was certainly based on his reputation as both a player and coach. As a player he had enjoyed success, and by now, his much-publicized career as an All-American and the Notre Dame quarterback of the storied 1913 team that beat Army. He also was legendary in the fledgling pro leagues of the Midwest. He found success as a coach at Dubuque and now with Rockne he helped lead Notre Dame to the Western Football Championship and National Champion by some critics. The stature gained from these successes only enhanced Gonzaga's view of Dorais.

There was also a strong link between Notre Dame and Gonzaga. The Pacific Northwest as a whole had been a beacon for Notre Dame alumni for years, and relations between the two universities dated back to the late 1800s. Both were Catholic schools, so there were certainly connections on an administrative level, as most Catholic institutions were a tight-knit group in those days. In football, the universities were indelibly linked. Gonzaga's first football coach was Dr. Henry Luhn, a Notre Dame graduate and captain of the school's first football team in 1887. Whatever conduit existed between the schools in 1920 would be used to bring Dorais west.

From Dorais' perspective, there were certainly many appealing features regarding the Gonzaga vacancy. He was a devout Catholic, and this position, like his previous ones at Dubuque and Notre Dame, was at a Catholic institution. He would be the full-time Athletic Director in charge of all sports and physical training and would be the head coach for all of the major sports, most notably for his passion—football. And not least of all, the salary was twice what he was making at Notre Dame. Another attraction to the job was the region itself. For an avid outdoorsman, the Pacific Northwest offered a multitude of those activities. Even after Dorais left Gonzaga, he returned west every other year during the summer to conduct coaching schools and camp in the wilderness, forever holding a fondness for the region. When Gonzaga offered him a starting salary of $3,500, Dorais accepted. "It would have been nice to stay on at old Notre Dame as Rock's assistant," he said, "but every football coach who is worth his salt wants to be a head coach."[26]

CHAPTER 6

Invading the Inland Empire, 1920–1925

In the 1921 edition of *Spalding's Official Foot Ball Guide*, Walter Camp wrote that "schools, colleges, universities—all recognize that foot ball is practically the central power plant of their athletic system."[1] It was a trend, particularly amongst Catholic colleges, that reached Gonzaga University in the post–World War I years. Under the leadership of new University President Father John McHugh, athletics became a focal point. In early 1920, Father McHugh established an Athletic Board of Control, made up of himself, a faculty moderator, three alumni, the graduate manager (a precursor to an Athletic Director), and the president of a student body of roughly 200. One of the board's first duties was to find a reputable football coach to bring the school to prominence and help in the Greater Gonzaga Campaign, a major fundraising effort.

Gus Dorais wasn't the first person that the Gonzaga Athletic Board offered the head football coaching job to. That person was the biggest football name in the country—Jim Thorpe, who turned the offer down. He was under contract not only to play for the Canton Bulldogs of the newly formed American Professional Football Association, but also served as the first president of the league that would morph into the National Football League a few years later. The coaching job was then offered to Dorais by the board. On May 29, 1920, Dorais signed a one-year, $3,500 contact to coach the football team and head physical training for the university students, regardless of whether they participated in athletics. He was the college's tenth coach, seventh in the last seven years, and ninth in the last decade. Over the next five seasons, Dorais would bring Gonzaga's Athletic Department to a higher standing.

On October 1, 1881, civic leaders of the newly incorporated Spokane Falls wrote to the Society of Jesus, an order of Roman Catholic priests and brothers. The men requested that a college for boys be started. Less than two weeks later, Father Joseph Cataldo, SJ, a Jesuit priest and missionary, purchased 320 acres along the Spokane River from Northern Pacific Railroad for $832. Cataldo's vision for the college was as an educational center for Upper Spokane Indian men, whom he had been teaching in a school house 12 miles outside of Spokane for over a year. City officials were adamant that it only be open to white students.

The Jesuits moved forward, starting construction in 1883. Cataldo persisted with his goal, too. He lobbied for the college to be an all-Indian school, before changing to an integrated institution. The first building was completed on a small budget and volunteer work. Gonzaga College, named for the patron saint of youth, Saint Aloysius Gonzaga, opened in September 1887. Cataldo's concession was not recognized, when two Indian boys were denied entrance in the first few days of classes. That first fall seven students—all white males—were registered, and by the end of the year that number grew to 18.

A fire destroyed much of Spokane Falls' downtown commercial district in 1889. It was rebuilt, and in 1891 the city was reincorporated as "Spokane." A year later, the Great Northern Railway built a railroad terminal. A revitalization began over the next few decades as the population went from nearly 20,000 in 1890 to over 100,000 in 1910. The same year that the Great Northern arrived, Gonzaga expanded with a new hall, dormitory and church—all wired with electricity. By the turn of the century, Gonzaga was the largest Catholic college in the Northwest. The student body swelled to 483 in 1906, and in 1912—Gonzaga College's 25th Jubilee year—the institution became Gonzaga University.

The first organized football game at Gonzaga was played on Thanksgiving Day, 1892. A group of students was led by Dr. Henry Luhn, a recent transplant to Spokane, having moved in October to open his first medical practice. Luhn knew the game of football rather well, having captained Notre Dame's first football team in 1887 (record of 0–3). The students did not, many of them having never played the game. Just two days before the contest, Luhn got the makeshift team together to teach them the basics. Gonzaga's first opponent was the Spokane Amateur Athletic Club, made up of young professionals from the East. Many had played football collegiately, including Luhn's brother, William. Gonzaga appeared overmatched when the teams took the field on the college campus in front of some 500 spectators. The Athletic Club was adorned in the proper football equipment and uniforms of the time, while the student squad wore painters' coveralls. With Luhn at fullback for Gonzaga, the college boys held their own over two 25-minute halves, tying the Athletic Club, 4–4.

Luhn remained head football coach until 1898. That year, a player from Spokane's Blair Business College was seriously injured, leading Gonzaga school officials to drop the sport as a university-sponsored program. The game was limited to intramurals until 1901, when the school banned the sport due to the high number of injuries being sustained. Once the forward pass was made legal, a movement was made to reinstitute football, which happened in 1907. In 1908, George Varnell, a former player for Alonzo Stagg at the University of Chicago and now sports writer for the *Spokane Daily Chronicle* in Spokane, coached Gonzaga to a scoreless tie with Blair Business College. Later that winter, Varnell, also a former Olympic hurdler, became Gonzaga's first basketball coach. He went on to become a respected sporting official on the Pacific Coast as well as the sports editor for the *Chronicle* and later the *Seattle Times.*

It wasn't until 1913 that Gonzaga made a serious bid to field an intercollegiate team by hiring its first full-time coach, Robert E. Harmon. The following year, the university applied for membership in the Pacific Northwest Intercollegiate Conference—Northwest Conference for short—but was rejected for not meeting various requirements. The program floundered for several years. The school abandoned the professional coaching system due to financial losses, relying on a series of student managers. Finally, a shift in priorities came in 1919, a year before Dorais' arrival. That team was led on a part-time basis by Gonzaga alum Dr. William Higgins, a local dentist. He was a football player a decade earlier, before finishing his education at St. Louis University, where he captained the football team. He returned to Spokane after graduating, coaching Gonzaga's basketball team to a 2–7 record during the 1915–1916 academic year. Higgins didn't have the time to dedicate to the university team on a full-time basis. However, Dorais persuaded him to become Gonzaga's first high school football coach in 1920 and then his assistant a few years later.

A new football field was in the works as an enticement for a new coach. The old Athletic Field, which had a gravel playing surface, was replaced in 1913 when Gonzaga moved to intercollegiate play. Tons of dirt were hauled in for the facility that could seat 2,000 and accommodate 50 vehicles lined up to watch. The new field quickly became dated and was all but abandoned as bigger games were played at the Spokane Interstate Fairgrounds. The only seating there was the racetrack grandstand across the track, a distance from the field. The athletic board was simply following the trend. A major benchmark for collegiate football during that time was the building of stadiums—some of them massive—to cater to the growing fan base. Now that Gonzaga had a big-name coach, they needed a new football field. The athletic board called for a new sports complex, the centerpiece being a new football stadium. A hastily formed building committee's first plans called for a horseshoe stadium with concrete stands that seated 23,000. Due to steep post-war construction costs and the recently completed Greater Gonzaga Campaign that raised $300,000, the estimated $100,000 stadium cost was deemed too much. The new stadium plan was put off a few years, with a goal of opening in the fall of 1922. In the interim, funds would be raised in part through a plaque-selling campaign. One hundred dollars earned a donor full stadium privileges for five years. Two hundred, ten years.

A stadium was ambitious, and the financial losses that led to the lapse in coaches a few years earlier brought hesitation about dedicating university resources to support an athletic board with a full-time Athletic Director. As a result, Dorais was only offered a one-year contract. Fears of a financial drain on the university by the football program pushed an enlistment of the alumni association to raise funds. The goal was to sell 1,000 sets of season tickets at $15 apiece in hopes of raising $15,000 to offset costs. Although the exact amount raised was never disclosed, the program survived the first year with its new athletic board and Athletic Director.

Not everyone was thrilled with the gradual takeover of football as a focal point of a college that had a student body of a few hundred during Dorais' first year. Yet the Athletic Board of Control had their eyes on the new stadium. There lay the problem of the football boom that Gonzaga historian and archivist Father Wilfred Schoenberg called "the era of big stadiums and small libraries." He pushed some of the blame on an earlier generation of educators that "produced the alumni who were now demanding coaches of Dorais' caliber."[2]

Dorais and Vi arrived in Spokane on the morning of August 28, 1920. A large group, many of them Gonzaga alumni, met the new coach downtown at the Davenport Hotel. Dorais deflected questions about assessing the talent of his new team and the upcoming season, but he did say that he had come to his new job "with a wholesome respect for the brand of football played in this section of the country," and that he "thoroughly realizes that it will be necessary to develop a speedy team if Gonzaga is to hold a place in football among the institutions of the northwest."[3]

The naming of Dorais as coach brought an invitation of admission to the Northwest Conference of Colleges. The athletic board turned down the offer, wanting to get the athletic department's policies in place before accepting. It was an error on the part of the board, as the school's petition to join over the next few years would be rejected. The move caused much consternation for Dorais and the athletic board during that time.

Gonzaga was yet to be known as the "Bulldogs." Instead, when Dorais came they were most commonly referred to as the "Blue and White," "Fighting Irishmen," "Fighting Irish" and "Catholics." One of the first appearances of the "Bulldogs" name in the local papers was in the *Spokane Daily Chronicle* on January 11, 1921, in an article announcing an upcoming basketball game. The origin of the "Bulldogs" moniker can be traced to an innocent reference from the school publication, *The Gonzaga*. The student writer is unknown, but they were certainly the unwitting originator of the school's nickname.

In the October 1920 issue, the following passage appeared in a preview of the football team: "Such, then, are the prospects for Gonzaga's 1920 football season. As each and every one of us realize, Coach Dorais has his hands full of work, the Notre Dame style must be taught to his cohorts, gaps left by the leaving of last year's letter men must be filled. All in all means bull dog tenacity and persistence on the part of both coach and team."[4]

Fall went by quickly as Dorais got acclimated to Spokane and the university climate. He and Vi settled into an apartment a few miles south of campus. Dorais continued his alumni-led tour of town, being introduced to various civic organizations, many of them Gonzaga backers. In the coming years, he took part in numerous community activities, frequently speaking on the local banquet circuit, occasionally refereeing high school and college football games, and once serving as president of the Spokane Amateur Athletic Club's indoor baseball league. In those early days, football was never far from his mind. He instituted the "G" Club, an honorary society for those competing in an intercollegiate sport. He knew that backing from the student body was a necessity, so he approached the athletic board about awarding an athletic "G" monogram to the "rooter king" who was elected by the student body to lead them in cheers during home games.

Dorais saw firsthand that there was potential for the Blue and White. With a small squad—never more than 18—Dorais regularly scrimmaged with the team. It was then that his players were privy to his abilities on the field, which Raymond Lower, a right halfback on Dorais' first team at the university, described three decades later. "I remember he had a wonderful 'soft' pass. You could pluck it out of the air on a dead run if he threw the ball anywhere near your fingertips. It was that throwing method that he taught us players. The ball was fatter then—and Dorais coached us to throw it nose-high to make it easier to catch."[5]

A difficult task lay ahead for Dorais. He was hired to build a reputable collegiate program, but three of his seven games were against non-college teams. He was also putting into action the offense he and Rockne had run at Notre Dame the year before. It was a struggle. Dorais' backfield had strong runners—especially freshman Jim McIsaacs—but passing didn't come easy. On the line were team captain Frank Benolken and 24-year-old underclassman Nick Busch at the tackles. The latter showed a talent at grasping the system, would be voted captain in 1922, and played professionally for the short-lived Los Angeles Buccaneers in 1926.

The most recognizable name from the 1920 team never played a down. Harry Lillis "Bing" Crosby was a freshman studying pre-law. Sources say he was a student manager, others an assistant yell leader, and a few fourth-string quarterback. A local boy who attended Gonzaga High School, Crosby was a decent prep athlete, excelling at swimming in his early teen years. At Gonzaga University the only organized sport he played was baseball in spring 1921. In later years, after Crosby gained fame, Dorais liked to recount the time Crosby stowed away on the train to Idaho for a game in 1921, players smuggling him food.

Tom Dorais recalled his father's tale:

Bing Crosby (right rear, number 17) played baseball and served in a few non-playing roles for the football team under Dorais (far right, dark uniform) (Gonzaga University Library, Gp_sp0110_01).

Bing Crosby was on his [Gus'] team but not a very good player—too small. While Crosby could never make the traveling squad for out of town games, the other players had a pullman berth key fashioned and would put Crosby in the upper berth when the conductor came through counting heads and punching tickets. From the time he was at school—he never missed a road game. Of course he always brought his guitar and entertained all.[6]

Gonzaga opened with a game against Washington State College (Pullman, WA), now Washington State University. In what may have been the first fly-over of a football game, a decorated football was dropped on the field from an airplane as part of the pre-game ceremonies. It was the fifth meeting between the two schools, dating back to 1911, and the first since 1916. The Cougars had won all four contests, outscoring the Blue and White, 150–0. The 1920 game was no different, Washington State dominating Gonzaga, 35–0. The Cougars were led by second-year coach Gus Welch, a man who held several parallels to Dorais—beyond name. The two men knew each other—at least on the field. Both came from Northern Wisconsin: Dorais, Chippewa Falls and Welch, Spooner. They played quarterback at top-rate programs: Dorais, Notre Dame and Welch, Carlisle Indian School and then top professional teams: Dorais, Massillon and Welch, Canton Bulldogs (albeit briefly). Finally, each was overshadowed by a more successful good friend and roommate: Dorais, Rockne and Welch, Thorpe. Like Thorpe, Welch was also a member of the 1912 Olympic track team, but was ill and could not compete.

It was feast or famine for Gonzaga in the 4–3, 1920 season. In the three losses—all against college teams—the Blue and White were shut out twice and outscored, 48–7. In the four wins, they recorded three shutouts and outscored opponents, 157–7. After being dominated by Washington State, Gonzaga won four of five. The loss was a 3–0 heartbreaker against Montana State in a Bozeman blizzard. Played in a mess of snow and mud, a late field goal was the difference. Dorais was confident, but realistic when he spoke to *The Gonzaga* in early November. "Gonzaga's future looks bright," he said. "We are building from the bottom and hope is a year or two to be a worthy rival for the representative teams in this territory."[7]

By mid-season, Dorais had began plotting Gonzaga's path to a larger stage. Plans were made for him and Graduate Manager, Eugene H. Russell to travel to Palo Alto, California, to attend the annual Northwest Conference meeting. Though Gonzaga didn't meet the requirements to apply for membership in the conference—made up of: University of California Berkeley, Stanford University, University of Oregon, Oregon State College, University of Washington and Washington State College—Dorais intended to schedule as many football, basketball and baseball games with those schools as he could. There was optimism in his actions. An overall new level of enthusiasm swelled around campus, especially for football. Newspaper coverage for the program expanded locally, thanks to former Gonzaga coach George Varnell's presence at the *Spokane Daily Chronicle*. Eventually, lead-up to games consisted of heavily attended pep rallies with loud cheers and students marching around in snake formations, all around roaring bonfires. Crowds even began congregating to watch practice, which Dorais occasionally made private in fear of opposing teams finding their way in to scout the Blue and White game plan.

Gonzaga ended the 1920 football season on a high note, despite it being a loss. The Blue and White brought a three-game winning streak into the finale against the University of Idaho at the Fairgrounds. Gonzaga jumped out to a 7–0 lead, but the Vandals rallied, winning 10–7 on a field goal in the last few minutes, despite the Blue and White having the total yard advantage. In the eight games that the schools had played since 1911, Gonzaga had won just once. It hadn't been close in recent years. Optimism was high at the team banquet on December 7, with 16 men earning a letter "G." A tentative 1921 schedule was announced, the highlight being Washington State playing in Spokane. Numerous season reviews commented on the surprising success of Gonzaga, crediting Dorais. Over the next few months he was sought after by a half-dozen colleges to come kick-start their football program when his contract was set to expire in June 1921. Knowing the type of person that the university had in Dorais, he was offered a three-year contract at $4,000 per year to remain in his current position through June 1924.

Stability is exactly what Dorais was seeking. On January 25, 1921, Gus and Vi welcomed their first of five children—Charles Emile Dorais, Jr., or Tommy as they called him. In later years, Charles Jr., legally changed his name to Thomas Charles. Soon after the contract was signed, Gus and Vi purchased their first home for $4,250, moving from their small apartment to a modest five-bedroom house on W. Buckeye Ave, several blocks northwest of campus. This is where they intended to stay and raise a family.

Dorais began his basketball coaching duties in December and was unable to return east to pay his respects when George Gipp passed away on December 14. Though Gonzaga would one day become known for its basketball program, that notoriety didn't begin under Dorais' tutelage. He brought his game plan from Notre Dame and over his five years on campus added stability to a program that had seen ten coaches since it began in 1907–

1908, when there was no coach listed. Several of Dorais' football players were on his squads during those years, but success was seldom met. He had one winning season, 10–8 in 1922 and an overall record of 34–53.

In spring 1920, Dorais was on the baseball diamond and put together a track and field schedule for the school, despite it not being an official university-sanctioned sport (he also added boxing). He and Gonzaga University officials were continuing efforts to find their way into the Pacific Coast Conference. After Dorais' rejection in the fall, University officials applied for membership in the Conference. They too were rejected, but were given some hope when they were advised to spend another year adhering to Conference rules and regulations as a probationary measure. In their first full summer in the Pacific Northwest, Gus and Vi fell in love with the Rocky Mountains, particularly trout fishing. Two decades later, the memories were still vivid for Viola: "It's such marvelous fishing out there that even when you back-cast, you get them," she recalled to the *Detroit Free Press*.[8]

Dorais sent letters to prospective players in August. He expected a modest returnee count, but also several new faces, including some transfers from University of Santa Clara, a Catholic College in Los Angeles, California, rumored to be dropping its intercollegiate athletic program. One of the transfers was Mike Pecarovich, who served as a utilityman for Dorais over the next few years. Pecarovich would one day return as both the head football and baseball coach, as well as get uncredited roles in a few Bing Crosby films.

For early drills, Dorais took two dozen players, a cook who boasted of once being the personal chef of an Army General, and a tiny bull terrier mascot named Teddy Gonzaga, across the border into Idaho. They traveled to a resort on Robertson's Island, in the middle of Spirit Lake, usually reserved as a summer rest camp for Gonzaga faculty. Dorais called on his military days to put together a strict daily itinerary. For two weeks, the prospects underwent strength-building exercises such as running, hiking, swimming, volleyball and rowing. Dorais planned to fully implement the Notre Dame system, so there was a heavy dose of football lectures, chalk talks and signal drills. He also added an assistant coach, R.C. Barlow, a former Purdue star and lineman, who was put in charge of the line.

After a 36–0 shutout of the College of Idaho in Caldwell, Idaho, to start the 1921 season, Dorais was hopeful Gonzaga could make some sort of statement on October 15 against Washington State at the Interstate Fairgrounds. The pep rally the night before reflected the fever pitch of Spokane and the University. A huge turnout of 1,400 was highlighted by a naked man in a barrel who held up a sign saying: "I've bet my clothes on Gonzaga," a cheerleader who passed out from yelling too loud, and, finally, an insurgent who disrupted the proceedings by trying to give a speech lauding the Cougars. He was booed, hissed, pulled from the platform, and escorted out.

The next day, less than two minutes into the game, Gonzaga captain Jim McIsaacs brought the crowd of over 4,000—many of them alumni—to their feet with a 70-yard touchdown run. The Cougars scored 54 unanswered points for an easy 54–7 victory over the Blue and White. Dorais took most losses in stride, always looking for something to build off of, but defeats at the hands of Washington State were particularly difficult to stomach. He was hired to compete against teams like Washington State, against whom the Bulldogs were now winless in seven games.

Plagued by fumbles, Dorais continued to have trouble with his offensive scheme. He tried a handful of players at quarterback, none of whom stood out. Gonzaga went 2–2 following the loss to Washington State, bringing a 3–3 record into the annual match against Idaho at the Fairgrounds. Trying to gain a foothold with alumni, a bevy of Homecoming festivities were planned. The night before the game, a large pep assembly was organized, with cheers and speeches from students, alumni and faculty. It culminated with a bonfire where a dummy football player was to be burned in effigy. An alumni-faculty dinner at the university dining hall followed. Game day entertainment consisted of a student-organized serpentine formations for the sideline and a halftime burlesque football game between the "leans" and "fats."

The afternoon before the game, Dorais and a group of students scraped ice from the field. On game day, temperatures were in single digits, and the Fairgrounds playing surface was covered in snow and ice, negating their hard work. Idaho's feature back, Gus Irving, was injured early and it turned into a punting duel. Gonzaga outgained the Vandals in total yardage, but fumbles were once again the Bulldogs' downfall. The only score came on a 50-yard fumble recovery for a touchdown by Idaho's Dale Vohs. A late drive by Gonzaga was halted on the 20-yard line with a Vandals interception. The frigid affair ended 6–0, in favor of Idaho. In the Thanksgiving Day season finale against the University of Montana, the Bulldogs squandered over 400 yards of offense, repeatedly faltering at the Bruins' goal line, ending in a disappointing 0–0 tie. The 3–4–1 record was a regression. So was the 70–93 point differential, but brighter days were ahead for the program.

As an aside, Dorais almost got his wish to play a game against Rockne and Notre Dame. The Irish were scheduled to play Centre College (Danville, Kentucky) in San Diego on December 26 in the inaugural East-West Christmas Classic bowl game. Rockne made tentative plans for Notre Dame to meet Gonzaga the following week. Those plans were snuffed out when the Notre Dame faculty board put an end to the West Coast trip. Centre College went on to defeat the University of Arizona (Tucson, Arizona), 38–0.

In March 1922, Dorais deflected an offer from Marquette University to become the athletic director and head coach of multiple sports. He reminded the institution that he still had two years left on his contract. He did the same when the University of Idaho offered a larger contract than his current earnings at Gonzaga to take over the position Tom Kelley vacated to take the head coaching job at the University of Missouri. It was enticing, though, as Idaho had just entered the Pacific Coast Conference. Dorais declined, suggesting that the Moscow, Idaho institution hire his former teammate at Notre Dame, Robert Mathews. Currently a freshman coach at the University of Washington, Mathews had spent the previous decade as a head coach at three different colleges, most recently Williamette University in Salem, Oregon (1915–1920). The University of Idaho took Dorais' advice. Relying heavily on the pass, Mathews proved to be a success. When Dorais casually asked his former teammate what kind of team he was going to have, Mathews replied: "Watch me and find out."[9] In three of his four seasons, Idaho beat nearby rival Washington State. Mathews, who also served as Athletic Director, remains the only coach in school history to have multiple wins against Washington State. He served as athletic director and head football and basketball coach at Gonzaga for one year, 1929. He led the Bulldogs' gridiron team to a 4–3 record.

Dorais had reason to stick around Spokane. At the football banquet in December, it was announced that the university would be breaking ground on a new sports complex in the spring. Five months later, on May 16, 1922, George Varnell broke ground for a $250,000 stadium on the east side of campus. Between May and October of 1922, a new $100,000 facility was built over seven-and-a-half acres. In addition to the football field, the grounds included a baseball field and an eight-lane, cinder quarter-mile track. The press boxes were equipped for telephone, telegraph and radio communication. There were clubhouses and restrooms. Seating would eventually accommodate nearly 10,500, and lights were added in 1931. Parking for 1,000 automobiles was within 600 feet of the crowned football field. The turf consisted of a mixture of ash, sand, loam and clay, and underwent testing over the next several months to make sure that the blend could absorb and handle rain adequately. The stadium was built with the pledge that "it shall at all times be available for public events, pageants and athletic affairs of all sorts," with maintenance, improvements and use of the stadium dictated by a five-member Board of Supervision. The agreement left the University hamstrung, leaving them financially responsible for any repairs or improvements.

In late August 1922, Dorais returned to the Midwest for visits with his mother and sister in Milwaukee and Vi's family in Iowa. After a stop in Chicago, Dorais was on to Notre Dame for a visit with Knute Rockne. While still out of town, Dorais had the athletic department issue a call for football candidates to report to Mission Field. Anticipating a large turnout, Dorais recruited Dr. William Higgins to return to the university as an assistant, which also called for him suiting up for practices, like Dorais. Forty

hopefuls reported in the opening days of tryouts. Returnees included Nick Busch, a lineman and team captain, and ends Dick Flaherty and Frank Needles. The final roster chosen by Dorais included several players who formed a nucleus for the program's rise over the next few years. Four were linemen: Marlon Ashmore, Ivan "Tiny" Cahoon, Hec Cyre, and Art Dussault. The backs were Matt Bross, John "Puggy" Hunton, Gil Skeate, and John Houston Stockton.

No player had a bigger impact than Stockton, known as "Hust." Born in Parma, Idaho, he was a record-setting back at Columbia Prep in Portland, Oregon. He scored 104 points—14 touchdowns and 20-for-28 on extra point attempts his senior year—nearly doubling the previous record of 58. He spent one year at St. Mary's College in Oakland, California (under former Notre Dame center Edward "Slip" Madigan), before transferring to Gon-

John Houston Stockton transferred to Gonzaga from St. Mary's College (Oakland, CA) in 1922. He became Dorais' first triple-threat back (Gonzaga University Library, Gp_sp0706_01).

zaga for the start of the 1922 academic year. On offense, he was a vaunted triple-threat back, terrorizing opponents with his physical running style, big throwing arm and accurate kicking. Defensively—some thought his strong suit—Stockton could break up a run at the line and seamlessly drop back into pass coverage.

The University of California's great coach, Andy Smith, who was in the midst of his "Wonder Teams" that went undefeated over a 50-game stretch from 1920 into the 1925 season (46–0–4) knew what Stockton was capable of. After a strong midseason performance by Stockton, Smith said that the Gonzaga back "will make the greatest halfback in the Northwest this year."[10]

Gonzaga opened with a 34–0 thrashing of the University of Puget Sound in Tacoma. The following week was the much-anticipated home opener against Washington State. It was to be the christening of the new stadium. Running north to south, much of the structure was completed between August 6 and September 12, but tweaks were still being made in the days leading up to the game. The once-planned concrete stands to fit 10,000 were substituted for with framed wooden units to hold 2,500, constructed to build upon for future expansion. The grandstands were filled and beyond on game day, as 5,600 watched the Bulldogs use an open style of play opposed to the Cougars' traditional gameplan. Washington State scored in the first quarter, Gonzaga in the second; both teams converted the point after. Thereafter, it was a game of punting and field position. The contest was decided on a field goal by Vernon Hickey in the last few minutes, giving the Cougars a 10–7 victory.

After a 35–20 loss at the hands of Multnomah in Stockton's return to Portland on October 21, the 1–2 Bulldogs ripped off a four-game winning streak at home that included a 77–0 dismantling of Wyoming and a modest 14–7 upset of Idaho on Homecoming Day. The victories raised Gonzaga's profile a bit on the West Coast and were a full unveiling of Stockton's talents. There were glimpses in the first few games as he became more comfortable in Dorais' offensive scheme. In the Bulldogs' 37–6 win against the University of Montana, Stockton totaled 378 yards of offense. He carried the ball 30 times for 310 yards and completed a pair of passes for 68 yards, showing a vertical passing game that had been missing in the previous two seasons under Dorais. In the Wyoming blowout, Stockton didn't enter the game until the second quarter. He proceeded to score six touchdowns and kick 10 conversions, tallying 46 points in Gonzaga's 77–0 defeat. The Bulldogs ran 92 plays from scrimmage. Stockton ran and passed for over 350 yards. Through seven games, he scored 99 points and passed for 786 yards, for an average of 112 yards per game.

An *Associated Press* article broke down the three traits that made Stockton a dangerous passer: "An ability to pass the ball like a baseball is hurled; a trick of leaping straight into the air when pressed and passing in the opposite direction that that faced when he left his feet, and a steely calm under fire."[11]

Ahead for the Bulldogs was a game with Stockton's former school, St. Mary's College (Oakland) at Ewing Field in San Francisco on December 9. That quickly became an afterthought following an invitation from the San Diego civic athletic authorities to play Notre Dame in the city's second annual East-West Christmas Classic bowl game (which the Irish were to have played in the year before). The allure would be the first game between Dorais and Rockne. A few days later, Dorais was given the okay to accept the offer, but the excitement was short-lived. After being upset 14–6 by the University Nebraska in Lincoln on November 30, Rockne decline the game with Gonzaga. Georgetown University offered to take Notre Dame's place, but in the end Gonzaga ended up being matched against 9–0–1 West Virginia University, regarded by some as one of the top teams in the entire country. In his second year, Clarence "Doc" Spears' Mountaineers had six shutouts and were going for their first 10-win season. The only blemish on their independent conference schedule was a 12–12 tie against Washington & Lee (Lexington, Virginia) on October 21. West Virginia hadn't allowed a point since. It would be the first bowl game for both schools—and Gonzaga's last.

The circumstances were bittersweet for Dorais. Since he arrived in Spokane, Dorais had lobbied Rockne for a game, touting the mountains, fishing and allure of Canadian beer. Rockne likely never intended to play Gonzaga. As Notre Dame rose to prominence and popularity in the early 1920s, Rockne scheduled games against Big Ten teams, Army and other powerhouses. He seldom made arrangements with Catholic institutions. Since he took over in 1918, three of the Irish's 55 opponents were Catholic universities. Not that it was a common practice before, but now that Notre Dame was the standard, Rockne was inundated with requests from other Catholic colleges.

As Dorais prepared his team for Gonzaga's first and only bowl game, he was petitioning to get the program into the Northwest conference. At a meeting in Seattle, conference officials denied the application, citing Gonzaga's use of ineligible players during the 1922 season, namely Stockton and Cahoon for transfer status, and Jim McDonald for academic eligibility. The Gonzaga Athletic Board erred, considering the pair as freshman rather than transfers, which made them eligible. Gonzaga was assured by the conference officials that admission would be granted at the 1923 meeting if no further violations arose over the next year.

Dorais was also being pursued heavily by the University of Detroit, which wanted him to not only coach the football team, but also become the school's first athletic director. Dorais considered the offer, but put the rumors to rest before departing for San Diego. "I decided that there was a greater field of endeavor for me at Gonzaga than at Detroit University," said Dorais, who described the offer by Detroit a "compliment." He furthered his explanation, obviously proud of what he had built over the past three seasons. "Personally I believe Gonzaga is started right and is on the way to recognition that fosters good clean athletics. I believe the hard pull at Gonzaga is finished and that with Northwest conference membership in sight for next year we can expect the institution to stride ahead in athletics."[12]

A young family in Spokane: Vi, Gus and Tom (Dorais family photo collection).

Severe weather kept the Bulldogs in the gymnasium much of the week leading up to their departure. Dorais let the group out for a brisk run through newly fallen snow. On the morning of Monday, December 18, 200 Gonzaga fans cheered on the team as they boarded the Spokane, Portland and Seattle Railway for the 1,300-mile trip south. They almost left team Captain Nick Busch, who had to fight through the crowd and make a last-minute sprint as the train was leaving the station. Noticeably absent from the sendoff was Dorais, who was reportedly staying behind in Spokane to be with his wife,

Vi, who was due any day with the couple's second child. She gave birth to William on December 24, but Gus had already left Spokane. He departed shortly after the team, traveling with a member of the Gonzaga Athletic Board, Leon Boyle. They met Idaho coach R.L. Mathews in Eugene, Oregon and traveled to San Diego in time to hold a few practices. Dr. Higgins was named chaperone of the team until Dorais' planned arrival.

In secret, Dorais traveled with the team to Sacramento, where he parted ways. From there, he journeyed over 400 miles southeast to San Bernardino. Wearing a disguise of wide-rimmed glasses and posing as a sportswriter, he boarded the Santa Fe train carrying the West Virginia team towards Los Angeles, where an announced practice was scheduled at Bovard Field on the campus of the University of Southern California. The Mountaineers' Coach Spears, suspecting that some sort of attempt at viewing practice, veered course at the last minute and held a practice in Pasadena. Unbeknownst to him, Dorais was able to watch the whole thing.

Gonzaga arrived in Los Angeles on the morning of December 20. The Bulldogs practiced at the Loyola College campus and were the guests of a luncheon at the Los Angeles Athletic Club. Afterwards they traveled south to their accommodations. Dorais soon joined them. For nearly a week the team stayed at the Hotel del Coronado, in Coronado, across San Diego Bay from San Diego, holding practices on the beach in their bathing suits. There was some initial skepticism from the hotel manager about a football team staying for an extended period, but his fears were quickly put to rest, and when the team departed he said the Gonzaga team was "the best bunch we ever had at the hotel," adding, "They can come back any time."[13]

On Christmas Day, fans in Spokane gathered at the American Theater on Post Street to hear the play-by-play report via Western Union. In San Diego, Balboa Stadium, with a capacity of 25,000, was half-full. The field had no sod and was extremely dusty. Heavyweight boxing champion Jack Dempsey was in attendance and decided to sit on the Gonzaga bench. Both teams featured a heavy passing game throughout, but West Virginia controlled the first three quarters. The Bulldogs' offense wilted, fumbling multiple times after long, sustained drives. The Mountaineers scored in the first quarter on a 12-yard run by right halfback Nick Nardacci, who set up the scamper with a 30-yard pass to end Jack Simmons. In the second quarter, both teams aired out the ball, passing on nearly every other play. Gonzaga advanced deep into West Virginia territory only to have Mountaineers captain Russ Meredith intercept a pass and go 80 yards unencumbered for a touchdown. A 16-yard touchdown pass from Nardacci to Simmons in the third quarter put West Virginia up 21–0, seemingly wrapping up the game.

Gonzaga's fortune began to change in the fourth quarter, when their passing game finally clicked. During the season, the Bulldogs gained a reputation as a second half team, and it once again rang true as cheers of "Come on, Gonzaga! Come on Gonzaga!" echoed throughout the stadium. Stockton led the comeback, throwing for 110 of his 225 yards in the final period, utilizing the short game with reserve halfback Matt Bross making several big plays.

An 18-year-old freshman, Bross, known as "Mal," began getting substantial playing time by midseason, and was an immediate receiving threat out of the backfield. He set up a one-yard touchdown run by Stockton with a 55-yard run on a dump off pass from Stockton, who missed the extra point. A few minutes later, Bross ran over from two yards out, and a successful point after by Stockton made the game 21–13. West Virginia fumbled the ensuing kickoff at their own 20, recovered by Gonzaga's Andy Murray. A Bross to Stockton pass brought the ball down to the Mountaineers' 7-yard line. On the next play Stockton threw a pass to a wide-open Pecarovich, who dropped a certain touchdown on the two-yard line. Three more passes went incomplete, and West Virginia took over on downs and ran out the clock. The final score was 21–13, Mountaineers.

Despite the loss, Dorais and Gonzaga were deluged with telegrams of congratulations. When word spread that the new football field was $7,500 in debt, civic organizations stepped up with a plaque-selling campaign, raising over $10,000. In the subsequent weeks, the team was honored with a public luncheon of over 600 at the Davenport Hotel, where they were gifted gold footballs. Days later at the team banquet, varsity letters were disbursed and the 1923 captain chosen. Marlon Ashmore, regarded as the best defensive player on the 1922 team, beat out fellow lineman Andy Murray. Individual post-season awards eluded the Bulldogs, but Stockton gained notoriety for his 1,000-yard passing season. His 126 yard per game average was being called a record by some, eclipsing a standards of 105 set in 1921 by Notre Dame's All-American halfback, John Mohardt.[14]

In March, Dorais was gifted an automobile by the Alumni Association and made an honorary member of the organization. By the end of the school year, the 1923 football schedule was nearly completed, highlighted by a trip east. On Thanksgiving Day (November 29), Gonzaga would play the University of Detroit in Detroit. Dorais also tentatively schedule a

December 1 game in Iowa against either Drake (Des Moines) or his old school, Dubuque College—now Columbia College. Open dates were discussed into June with possible games against either Notre Dame or Penn State. Neither materialized, and eventually the Iowa date was dropped, leaving Dorais scrambling to fill one of the three open dates with a game against an alumni squad on the October 6 opener at home.

Dorais had to replace the presence of Ashmore, Flaherty, lineman Al Grant, and Pecarovich, who joined Higgins as an assistant coach.[15] There was still a Flaherty on the roster, though, Dick's younger brother, Ray. A member of the first football team at Gonzaga High, Ray decided to attend Washington State his freshman year before returning to Spokane and Gonzaga University for the 1923 season. He served as a backup in 1923, emerged as a starter in 1924, and was an All-West Coast player by the time he graduated. Opting for professional football over baseball, Flaherty was an end for the New York Giants between 1928 and 1935. He stepped back to pursue baseball in 1930, playing second base for the Providence Grays of the Eastern League. That fall he returned to Spokane and coached the Bulldogs to a 1–7–1 record. He re-signed with the Giants the following fall as a player and coach, was named to his third and final All-Pro team, and won an NFL Championship two years later in 1934. His professional coaching career proved much more successful than his collegiate, leading to his induction into the Pro Football Hall of Fame in 1976. Over seven seasons, first with the Boston and then the Washington Redskins, he won four divisional titles and two NFL championships (1937 and 1942). Flaherty was credited with inventing the screen pass in 1937 when rookie Sammy Baugh was his quarterback. After serving in the military during World War II, Flaherty spent four seasons coaching in the All-America Football Conference for the New York Yankees (1946–1948) and then the Chicago Hornets (1949), where he hired Dorais as a scout.

Flaherty's affinity for Dorais was evident. When Dorais passed away four decades later in 1954, Flaherty had fond recollections of his college coach, ones that were shared by many who played under Dorais: "He had so much consideration for his players that they always gave their best for him. He was kind—always could see your side of things. On a road trip he was more like a father than a coach. Gus Dorais could afford to be considerate to his teams. He was a brilliant coach—and we all knew it."[16]

The highly anticipated 1923 Bulldogs season began with an early-morning game between the varsity and a contingent of alumni. A modest crowd showed up to watch Dorais quarterback the alumni in baseball pants and without headgear. The University eleven won, in a guarded 7–

6 contest, counting the win towards their season total. The margin was a missed extra point by Dorais. The alumni squandered multiple scoring opportunities, including several dropped passes from Dorais. The narrow margin left many wondering what kind of team the Bulldogs would have, especially with the upcoming game against Washington State. Dorais and members of the team traveled to Pullman following the alumni game to watch the Cougars defeat Pacific University, 19–0.

Washington State was ripe for an upset, as they found their way under first-year head coach Albert Exendine. Like his predecessor, Gus Welch, Exendine was a former Walter Camp All-American from Carlisle (1906, 3rd team end). For the past nine years, Exendine coached Georgetown to a 55–21–3 record and three South Atlantic Intercollegiate Athletic Association conference titles. In front of a record crowd of 9,000, Gonzaga picked up where they left off in San Diego. Shedding the second-half team reputation, the Bulldogs were on point from the start, beginning with a trick play on the kickoff that Dorais had literally dreamt up a few weeks earlier. From his halfback spot, Stockton acted essentially as a quarterback, calling plays and directing the offense. He completed his first eight passes, and 191 of his 226 passing yards came in the first half. He played the whole game and scored a late touchdown, despite suffering a fractured rib early in the second half. On that score, Matt Bross sustained a serious leg injury and had to be carried off the field. Gonzaga won the game, 27–14. Near the end of his life, Gus recounted the victory as one of his favorites: "Of a day as a coach at Gonzaga U., when we, always the chopping block in the opener against Washington State, rose up and beat them for the first time…. And of getting a ride back to the locker room on the shoulders of my players."[17]

The win resurrected discussions of a game against Notre Dame later in the season. Though 2–0, Gonzaga had three straight difficult road games ahead of them. Even with a large group following them to their destination each weekend, the Bulldogs managed one win—a 25–2 victory in Missoula over the University of Montana. Gonzaga was shut out in their two losses: Multnomah, 10–0 and Idaho, 13–0.

The Bulldogs returned to Spokane to renew their intrastate rivalry against Whitman College of Walla Walla. Much of the week leading up to the game brought talk of Gonzaga's off-field behavior that was affecting their on-field play. Stories about players enjoying the Spokane nightlife with alumni surfaced. Actions like these had the possibility of compromising the University's conference status, so Dorais stepped in and suspended several regulars for the upcoming game. It had little effect on the outcome. After three Bulldog drives stalled to start the game, Dorais substituted in Stockton, and three plays later he ran one in from 30 yards out. With the University of Detroit head coach, Adolph Schulz, in attendance to scout Gonzaga, the Bulldogs' second-string played much of the game, a 53–6 Gonzaga victory.

The Bulldogs had over two weeks to prepare for the Thanksgiving Day tilt in Detroit against the University of Detroit Tigers. Gonzaga would be only the second team from the west to cross the Mississippi for a game. The first was the Oregon Agricultural College team (now Oregon State), who defeated the Michigan Aggies 20–0 in East Lansing, Michigan, in 1915. During the training period, the Bulldogs lost their top end, Frank Needles, first to an ankle injury and then a bad burn. It was a difficult situation for Needles, a senior, who had been through the thin early years with Dorais. Needles originally had a ligament damage in his ankle, but continued to practice with heavy bandaging, determined to play his final college game. After a light workout, Dorais was removing tape from Needles ankle with the aid of ether. The wrap ignited and though quickly extinguished, Needles suffered a severe burn from ankle to knee.

Dorais prepped the team for the trip ahead—both the game and long journey. There were the occasional stops planned along the way as they crossed the plains. The itinerary included taking in a NFL game in Chicago and a three-day stopover in South Bend for a visit to the Notre Dame campus and a few practices in front of Rockne and his team. Stockton was tabbed to write a series of articles about the trip for the *Spokane Daily Chronicle*. More than a thousand well wishers saw Dorais and 20 players off at the Northern Pacific Railroad Depot. The usually stoic coach gave an emotional speech to the crowd. "I'm more than proud to be able to take this team back to Notre Dame, my alma mater, and show teammates a team that has the fight to meet Detroit, with its student body of several thousands."[18]

The throng responded, "Hooray, hooray, Gus Dorais!"[19]

On the trip east to Detroit, excitement abounded. It seemed victory was encouraged everywhere, as the Gonzaga team passed through the western states. At Livingston, Montana, Blackfoot Indians were interested spectators as the players went through their "grass drill" at the depot park. When told about the big game at Detroit, the chiefs, to show support of the westerners, adopted the entire squad into their tribe, naming Coach Dorais Chief Pohaska, meaning "Little Chief of Victory." Captain Ashmore was called Chief Oacohaskoma, which meant "Big Mother of the Braves," and Houston Stockton, the star of the team, Chief Onawhaonha, "Heap

Scrapper of the Foe." This ceremony left a big impression on Dorais. In later years, whenever he would vacation out west, he would take time to stop and visit with the Blackfeet.

Activities on the train included a vaudeville show in the observation car. The Bulldogs stopped in Chicago to watch a professional football game and then headed to South Bend, where they were greeted by a large number of students who accompanied them to Notre Dame. While on campus, the team practiced in front of Rockne and his squad, who had just moved to 8–1 with a win over Carnegie Tech a few days earlier and were preparing for a November 29 game in St. Louis against St. Louis University. During the run-through, Dorais was informed that Detroit planned on wearing the same color jersey as Gonzaga. Rockne offered the Bulldogs Notre Dame's green jerseys that the Irish wore in a 25–2 road win over Princeton (Princeton, New Jersey) in October.

Nearly 10,000 onlookers were in attendance at Dinan Field for the Thanksgiving Day game. Weather conditions were favorable, leaving a dry playing surface—a rarity at this time of year. That did little to help the much-anticipated Gonzaga passing attack that squandered a first quarter scoring opportunity. A 40-yard pass from Stockton to Bross brought the Bulldogs into Detroit territory. Thanks to a Tigers penalty, Gonzaga made their way down to the 10-yard line. Stockton attempted another pass to Bross, but the ball was just out of his reach in the end zone, giving Detroit the ball on downs. A pair of second quarter field goals by Tigers captain Larry Welsh gave Detroit a 6–0 halftime advantage. The field goals were aided under suspect circumstances. At the time, rules permitted that a mound of dirt on the field could be built to assist in extra points and field goals. The Tigers kept a lump of dirt they claimed came from the field to set the ball on for kicks. Dorais protested, but referee Walter Eckersall permitted its use.

Detroit's lead extended to 13–0 after a 30-yard touchdown run by halfback William Brett and a successful extra point by Thomas Thornton. Stockton threw a pair of interceptions, but in another fourth quarter gasp he almost brought the Bulldogs back singlehandedly. He intercepted a pass by Tigers quarterback Dan Curran, running it back 52 yards for a touchdown. Stockton's extra point made it 13–7, Tigers. Gonzaga regained possession of the ball and had a chance to score again, but a pass to Jack Garrity fell incomplete in the end zone, giving Detroit the 13–7 win.

There was some talk that the long road trip had hindered the Bulldogs' performance, but Dorais felt the opposite about road games—even ones as long as this. "Traveling doesn't take anything away from you," he said a decade later. "Instead, it helps you. You pile up energy and thus are in better shape."[20]

Many thought that Gonzaga had underperformed with a 4–3 record, but the football program and athletic department as a whole received validation on December 10. University dean Father Charles Carroll presented before the Pacific Northwest Intercollegiate Conference delegates in Portland. His findings were well received and Gonzaga was admitted to the Conference without a vote. Later in the month, Stockton was named honorable mention on Walter Camp's All-American team in *Colliers*, one of four players from the Northwest to be so recognized. At the team banquet, deemed "Gonzaga Night," Stockton was voted captain for the 1924 season.

The game in Detroit was undoubtedly a recruiting tool for the University of Detroit to lure Dorais to the city and show him what he could have as athletic director and head coach. Following the trip, telegrams between Dorais and John Scallen, a member of the University of Detroit's Athletic Association, escalated. The two continued to communicate, even after it was announced in January at the annual football banquet that Dorais had spurned Detroit's offer of $6,500 to stay at Gonzaga through June 1925. Scallen wouldn't back down and was willing to accept an oral agreement from Dorais to come to Detroit in fall 1925. Scallen offered a position similar to Rockne's, backing from the faculty, and a solid group of recruits.

Dorais' influence on Gonzaga's campus was felt both on and off the field, a sentiment expressed in the *Spokesman Review* when the Detroit pursuit intensified: "He has been more than a brother to the boys. He has taught them how to win gracefully and how to lose like sportsmen. The spirit has been reflected in the student body."[21]

By March, it seemed that Dorais was secretly crafting an exit to Detroit in 1925. He proposed that Mike Pecarovich go to the University of Detroit in the spring and begin implementing Dorais' offense. Scallen and other members could assess Pecarovich's ability to coach the team for the 1924 season, with the understanding that Dorais would come in 1925. If accepted, Dorais would come to Detroit in the middle of August as an advisor to Pecarovich until Gonzaga's season started in mid–September. He promised to expand upon the offense and begin implementing a special defense to combat Army's wedge attack.

None of Dorais' proposals came to fruition, and communications suddenly ceased. Dorais turned his attention to Gonzaga's 1924 football season, the Bulldogs' first in the Northwest Conference, or any conference for the matter. With anticipation of conference play, Dorais was able to institute spring football drills, which had previously failed due to conflicts with spring sports. Prospective players were able to participate, one of them being Mel Ingram. A prep star from Aberdeen, Washington, Ingram had spent early practices with Gonzaga in 1923, but quit the team and withdrew from school due to an illness. He went onto earn 15 letters, four each in football, baseball, and track and field. A back injury his senior year left him with only three in basketball.

The 1924 team would come to be considered the University's best squad ever. Undefeated at 5–0–2, the Bulldogs outscored their opponents, 138–26, and tied the University of Idaho as Northwest Conference champions. From the start, there was no mistaking that Gonzaga's game plan revolved around Stockton, who would ultimately earn second-team All-American honors on Walter Eckersall's squad. In a 27–0 shoutout at home over the State Normal College at Cheney (now Eastern Washington) to open the season, he completed all six of his passes for 108 yards, including a touchdown to Flaherty. Even in a 0–0 tie with Idaho the following week, Stockton's punting took center stage. With his younger brother, Chester, looking on as a member of the Vandals, Stockton punted 18 times for 732 yards, an average of 40.6 yards per punt. When Idaho coach R.L. Mathews was asked his thoughts on Stockton later in the season, he gave an endorsement like no other:

> Houston Stockton, as a forward passer is the best man in the world, and I bar none. On defense he is a whole football team. On the offensive he ranks with the best ground gainers in the country—he can buck or run the ends or dash through a broken field with equal facility and he is an awful man to tackle. He punts from 50 to 60 yards consistently and any kicker who does that has few superiors. He comes nearer being a whole team himself than any player I have ever seen.[22]

Dorais was doing much of the coaching on his own now, after Higgins stepped down to focus on his medical practice. He was getting some help on the line from Spokane native Charles Adams, a former standout at the University of Pennsylvania. For the first time under Dorais' leadership, Gonzaga won all three of their road games. On October 11, they edged Washington State in Pullman, 14–12. Stockton completed nine straight passes, two of them for touchdowns (including a 50-yard toss to Flaherty), and kicked the crucial extra points. A 14–0 shutout of Multnomah came next, thanks to another standout performance by Stockton. He completed seven passes for 168 yards, tossed a touchdown, caught another, rushed for 67 yards, and averaged 40 yards on six punts.

Stockton followed those performances with perhaps his best all-

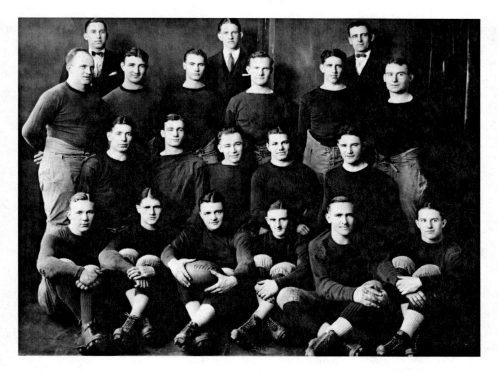

The 1924 Gonzaga University team went undefeated (5-0-2) and tied the University of Idaho as Northwest Conference champions. Captain Houston Stockton (front row, holding ball). Years later, Ray Flaherty (third row, far right), a future Pro Football Hall of Famer, would hire Gus as a scout in the All-America Football Conference (Gonzaga University Library, Gp_ov0105_02a).

round output in an epic 20–14 win in a muddy, rain-soaked game at Dornblaser Field in Missoula against the University of Montana. An injury-riddled Gonzaga team went into halftime trailing, 14–0. Dorais uncharacteristically chastised the team in the locker room with a single snarky statement: "What a fine bunch of football players!"[23] The Bulldogs responded, scoring 20 unanswered second half points. Stockton was the stalwart, amassing 310 rushing yards on 30 carries. He passed for 65 more and ran back five kicks, one for 35 yards, another for 25. Later in the season, the *Oregonian* in Stockton's hometown, Portland, used the game as a promotional tool to show that he was not only on par with the likes of Red Grange, but combined with Stockton's defense exceeded the back for the undefeated University of Illinois.

A two-week layoff left Gonzaga well-rested and gave Dorais enough time to implement some new wrinkles. He again went out of character and gave, as halfback Arthur Dussault recalled, "the only emotional pep talk I ever heard him give, and that was a very short one."[24] The result was a 63–0 pummeling of Whitman College. The Bulldogs set what was believed to be a record, when they returned successive kickoffs for touchdowns in the first two minutes. Ingram returned the first for 100 yards. Stockton followed with a 90-yarder. Stockton had 453 of Gonzaga's 875 yards from scrimmage. He completed seven of 11 passes for 147 yards. He ran for 306, including a 95-yard jaunt.

The season finale, a rematch with Washington State, was a week and a half later on November 27, Thanksgiving. Bleachers were added to Gonzaga Stadium to accommodate 1,500 more people. Stockton was a one-man wrecking crew on defense from the start, batting away a certain Cougars touchdown in the first quarter. Late in the fourth quarter, Washington State had four cracks at a touchdown from the one-yard line and were stopped each time. The game ended in a 0–0 tie. Stockton made two of the key tackles from his linebacker position. The *Spokane Daily Chronicle* called the game "Stockton's greatest exhibition of defensive play......time after time broke up forward passes, nailed runners at the line and was waiting for a man to pierce the Bulldog forward wall."[25]

There was little that Stockton could accomplish on offense. The *Spokesman Review* reported: "When Stockton dropped back to pass he was pursued by a flock of Cougars. When he stepped around end he again was pursued by the pack.....They tore his socks off, and most of his jersey, but Stockton ripped off the remains of his stockings and played the rest of the game bare-legged, his jersey flying in tatters.[26]

Stockton received his second team All-American honors from Eckersall. Stockton went on to play four seasons in the NFL. He won a championship with the Frankfort Yellow Jackets in 1926, beating the Chicago Bears, 7–6, at Philadelphia's Shibe Park. In the waning moments, Stockton threw a touchdown pass to Henry Homan. That year the Yellowjackets, located in Frankfort, the northeastern part of Philadelphia, had a regular season record of 14–1–2. That mark wasn't broken until the San Francisco 49ers went 15–1 in 1984. Stockton served as an assistant coach to Clipper Smith at Gonzaga in 1927.

Shortly after the conclusion of 1924 season, Gonzaga offered Dorais an extension at a yearly salary of $5,000, but Detroit continued its pursuit. The Athletic Committee of the Spokane Chamber of Commerce stepped in and started a campaign to raise another $3,000 to bring the total within $1,000 of Detroit's offer of $9,000. That wasn't enough for Frank McKevitt, a former standout athlete at Gonzaga and now a local businessman.

He felt the University was already saving on having one person serve as athletic director and coach of three major sports. "In the majority of instances fat salaries are being paid coaches for tutoring football alone, the remainder of their time being spent on other matters," he explained.[27]

On January 1, 1925, Dorais was at Rose Bowl Stadium in Pasadena, California. He had been invited by Rockne to join him on the sideline for Notre Dame's game against Glen "Pop" Warner's Stanford University. It was the Irish's first bowl game and the team's first trip to the West Coast. It was the last game for "The Four Horsemen" of Notre Dame: Harry Stuhldreher, quarterback; Jim Crowley, left halfback; Don Miller, right halfback; and Elmer Layden, fullback. The quartet had been together for three years, losing a game in 1922 and 1923, both to the University of Nebraska in Lincoln, Nebraska. The Irish capitalized on eight Stanford turnovers, scoring on three on their way to a 27–10 win.

Dorais took part in Notre Dame's celebratory festivities, first at the Hotel Maryland and then a dinner-dance put on by the Notre Dame Club of Los Angeles at the Hotel Biltmore. It was likely during this time that Dorais and Rockne discussed the University of Detroit negotiations that had now been ongoing for over two years, and, as telegrams show, grown contentious over the last month. Dorais accepted Detroit's offer by telegram, but then rescinded, causing a firestorm at both universities.

Much of the hesitation to move was on the part of Vi, who loved living in Spokane, but she, too, began softening her stance in the new year. In early February, it was announced that Dorais would not only succeed James Duffy as the University of Detroit's new football coach, but would also be the school's first athletic director. His duties would be on par with two of the higher profile athletic directors: Rockne of Notre Dame and the University of Michigan's venerable Fielding H. Yost. According to L.H. Northard of the *Detroit Free Press*, Dorais was given "complete control of all athletics, including the coaching of various teams, police of conducting all sports and training of all schedules."[28]

Dr. William Keane, Detroit's chairman of the Board of Control of Athletics was confident that Dorais' reputation and connections were a perfect fit for the newly created position. "It has been proven that this is the one satisfactory and successful way to handle collegiate affairs when the right man is placed in charge and we are certain we have selected the best man for our needs."[29]

Publicly, there was no animosity displayed towards Dorais by Gonzaga. In fact, it seemed the university felt it was inevitable that he would be moving on at some point. There were some assertions around campus that heavy involvement by local alumni had been looked down upon by other institutions and had begun to tax Dorais, leading to his exit. He made no mention of such and remained in Spokane longer than planned, helping with the transition of new coach Maurice "Clipper" Smith, a former Notre Dame guard. Dorais originally planned for Smith to be a member of his coaching staff in Detroit, but that invitation led to Gonzaga filling their head coach vacancy with Smith, continuing the Notre Dame and Gonzaga connection. Dorais still put out the call for a spring practice in early March, and a few weeks later was celebrated with a farewell dinner. The event was put on by the Spokane Athletic Round Table, an organization promoting athletics, particularly Gonzaga football. Gus Dorais was a founder of the club, formed in October 1920. Like many collegiate programs, football was shut down after the 1941 season, never to be revived. The field was razed in 1949 to make room for expansion.

There was no denying that Dorais had set a tone for the Gonzaga athletic department. The football team in particular found immediate success under Smith, a reflection on the program Dorais built in his five years there. "We never, for one moment, ever regretted hiring Gus. He was a gentleman and a great coach," said Leon Boyle, chairman of the Gonzaga Athletic Board that hired Dorais.[30]

CHAPTER 7

Motor City Man, 1925–1930

Detroit College was established in 1877, after the Roman Catholic Bishop of Detroit, Casper Henry Borgess, gifted his cathedral church and residence near downtown to the Jesuits. Classes began that fall under the guidance of the institution's first president, Reverend John Miege. The first commencement was held the following spring, and Detroit College was incorporated under Michigan law in 1881. Athletics were a part of campus life from the beginning. Football had been played sporadically at the school for years.

In 1896, faculty member William S. Robison ventured from the occasional scheduling of games against Detroit area teams. That year, on Thanksgiving, St. Ignatius of Chicago traveled to Detroit to play Detroit College at the Michigan Athletic Association grounds. Detroit lost, 20–0, but sparked interest for a set schedule. Robison took on this task and over the next three years found moderate success, including a 5–0 record in 1898. After he stepped down in 1899, there was a revolving door of coaches and a few years of no teams at all when there was a backlash from faculty about the violent nature of the game.

Detroit College incorporated as Detroit University in 1911. Increased enrollment brought a larger turnout for football, garnering recognition for the sport as a major part of university activities. The program continued to grow until Dorais' predecessor, Jimmy Duffy, helped advance the program into the modern game. Duffy began coaching at the University of Detroit in 1917. He took over for Gil Dobie, who grew frustrated just a month into his tenure due to poor practice field conditions. Duffy, a former freshman coach at his alma mater, Colgate, took over and helped Detroit get the first dedicated practice field and adequate equipment. That season, the then–Tigers, adorned in the school colors of cardinal and white, set an untouchable record for points in a season with 394. A good portion of that came in a 147–0 obliteration of Toledo University. The only loss

Detroit suffered that year was a 14–3 defeat in Ann Arbor at the hands of the University of Michigan—the last time Detroit played a Big Ten team until Dorais came along.

During his time at Detroit, Duffy, whose day job was as an attorney, groomed the school's first All-American—lineman Tillie Voss, who in 1920 was awarded a spot on the first team by Walter Eckersall (*Chicago Tribune*) and a third team slot by Walter Camp (*Colliers*). Other standouts included: Walter Ellis, tackle; Harold Lauer, back; Joe Gillis, guard; and Gus Sonnenberg, tackle, all of whom garnered some sort of post-season recognition. The best year under Duffy was in 1921. The Tigers went undefeated in the regular season (9–0), with eight shutouts, outscoring opponents, 250–10.

In 1924 the Tigers changed their nickname to the more unique "Titans." Stanley Brink of the *Detroit Free Press* noticed that teams seldom ventured from standard nicknames—and "Tigers" was one of the most common. When fall came around, it was easy to mix up headlines for the Detroit Tigers baseball club and the University of Detroit Tigers. In the spring, Brink wrote to graduate manager of athletics Charles Bruce, suggesting a name change to "Titans." Bruce passed along the suggestion to Father Foley, faculty moderator of the Board of Control of Athletics. The board liked the suggestion, and the University of Detroit Titans took the field in fall 1924.

The Dorais family traveled east, visiting relatives in Milwaukee and the Rockne family in South Bend, Indiana. There were undoubtedly hopes in Detroit that the Dorais-Rockne friendship would spawn a rivalry between the Catholic institutions—University of Detroit and Notre Dame.

On Tuesday, March 24, Dorais arrived in Detroit. On his first day on campus, Dorais announced plans for a hearty spring football schedule that would start the following Monday. He invited those interested to meet in a few days. He also touched on intramural sports, specifically baseball and track and field, thought to be the next intercollegiate sports for the university. Finally, he talked about plans for the physical fitness of all students, another of his duties. He ran this campus-wide campaign under the slogan of "Athletics for All."

The initial meeting was attended by 36 hopefuls. Dorais was disappointed in the turnout and put out word that the team was not handpicked, but rather anyone could try out. "Football men will not be a class apart, but will be drawn from the student body as a whole—from the Arts department, as well as the Engineering, Law and Commerce."[1] Later that week Dorais was a guest at a smoker held in the gymnasium by the student-alumni association. Outgoing coach Duffy wished him well and offered any help he could give. Dorais reiterated a point he had been stating since he stepped on school grounds—anyone interested should show up. His words seemed to work, and by the time the first spring practice was held on the following Monday at Grand Trunk Field, the number of candidates had increased significantly to nearly 60.

The Titans played their home games at Dinan Field, located on Six Mile Road and Livernois Avenue, west of Fairfield Street. When the university began moving to its current 40-acre location from downtown, in 1921, the football stadium was one of the first structures built. The facility opened in 1922 and was known by several names: University of Detroit Stadium, U of D Stadium, Titan Stadium, and most commonly, Dinan Field, in a nod to the Dinan brothers, Michael and John, the latter an alumnus. The Dinan brothers made their fortunes in grocery and real estate around Detroit. They were generous benefactors to the university, including helping to purchase the land that the stadium was built on and the plot that the university campus eventually moved to. Though the alumni association was the sole financier of the stadium, the Dinan brothers' philanthropic efforts to the university led the facility to be known as Dinan Field. Over the years the Titans would share the field with a few of Detroit's NFL teams: Panthers (1925–1926), Wolverines (1928), and, finally, for the first several years of the Lions' existence.

Dinan Field was part of an impressive sporting complex that would only grow. The school's student-run newspaper, the *Varsity News*, gave a full description of the facilities in the May 1925 issue:

> The University has one of the finest stadiums in the country. At present, it will seat 18,500 spectators; its capacity will be increased to 31,500, and it has been so constructed that, if necessary, its height can be increased and room made for 50,000 persons. It is of horse-shoe shape, and its greatest width between the forks is 261 feet.
>
> Around the field is a 30-foot, quarter-mile track, one of the widest in the country. A quarter-mile straightaway is being constructed also. This will enable track men to make better records than are possible on a curved track. No other college in the country has a quarter-mile straightaway.
>
> Adjoining the stadium is a practice field. This is being fenced in to prevent spying on secret practice. The baseball grounds are adjacent. They are being put into condition and will be used as a freshman practice field. The stands will be built next year.
>
> The equipment is on the new University campus. As soon as the new University buildings are completed, a large and complete gymnasium and tennis court will be added.[2]

Dorais settled into his office on the second floor of Reilly Hall. This location allowed him access to the football players who lived on the same floor. He worked closely with the graduate manager of University Athletics, Charles Bruce, who retired in late April once it became apparent that Dorais was able to manage the department on his own. Dorais showed his clout when Rockne spoke at a dinner in Dorais' honor. Before University classes dismissed for the summer, Dorais put together a coaching staff. He hired Ed Degree, a former guard for Notre Dame, to coach the line. A lawyer in Detroit, Degree had coached at Purdue University under fellow Irish alum Jim Phelan. Dorais' other assistant was faculty member Father John Markoe, an All-American on the Army team that Dorais opposed in 1913. The freshman were to be coached by former Titans star John "Bunny" Barrett.

Once again, Dorais had a large task ahead of him, one that he relished. Under the motto of "Plan carefully, work efficiently, and fight spiritedly," he set out implementing his modified version of the Notre Dame system. He would be coaching a team with a nine-game schedule for the first time in his coaching career. In a series of articles chronicling the history of football at the University, Tom Burke wrote, "It must be remembered that Dorais was faced with a dual problem because, besides building a team, he was required to teach the players the intricate shift plays."[3]

At the urging of the University's sixth president, Father John P. McNichols, Dorais looked to lay the same groundwork off the field that he had at Gonzaga: engage alumni, grow the fanbase and build upon tradition and rivalries. In June 1925 he started the "D" Club to include anyone who earned a varsity letter at the university. A student band was formed and debuted in the fall. Pep assemblies, bonfires and cheering squads were an essential, as was the organization of a publicity office for the Athletic Department. Annual banquets for each team were started. Dorais thought it was important to gain interest from the student body of nearly 1,700. He said, "The greatest thing a university can bestow upon its undergraduates is that traditional something we call college spirit, undergraduate spirit."[4] Game programs provided spectators with as much information about the opposition as Dorais could gather. He based them on observation, media contacts and a questionnaire he sent out to each of the schools. He instituted an "All-Opponent" team from the teams played the previous year, and in the late 1930s started an annual spring game against an alumni team.

Another aspect of life in Spokane that Dorais tried to emulate in Detroit was community and civic engagement. He became a sought-after speaker, and there were plenty of opportunities. The city, located in Wayne County, was in the middle of a population boom. Since 1900, the number of citizens had quadrupled, surpassing the 1,000,000 mark by the mid-1920s. For several decades, Detroit was the fourth-most populous metropolitan area in the country. Much of the decade leading up to the Great Depression was a prosperous one for the city. In 1922, the world's largest municipal streetcar system, the Detroit Street Railways, was created. An already booming auto industry was bolstered when the Chrylser Corporation was opened by Walter Chrysler in 1925. At the time, there were 37 automobile manufacturing plants, 250 auto accessory manufacturing plants, and over 3,000 major manufacturing plants.

In the summer, Dorais received a correspondence from A.G. Findlay, his old high school coach back in Chippewa Falls, Wisconsin. Findlay, now working as an insurance agent, asked Dorais for assistance in helping one of the Chippewa Falls High School's recent graduates get a job in South Bend, Indiana, in hopes of eventually attending Notre Dame and playing football. The student was Tom Connell, a star athlete who grew up just a few blocks from Dorais' childhood home on the city's east hill. Connell was an all-state basketball player, despite being academically ineligible for several games (the Chippewa Falls High Yearbook, the *Monocle*, said of Connell: "Poor in words, but in deeds, most rich.").[5] It was on the football field, as a running back who frequently passed, where his athletic talents were best suited. Had it not been for an ankle injury, Connell would have likely been recruited by big-name schools for football.

After hearing about Connell's athletic feats, Dorais reached out to the recent graduate several times. He finally convincing him that the University of Detroit was a better fit for him. The sales pitch worked and Connell enrolled. He went on to be the school's only two-time captain (1927 and 1928) and helped lead the team to a 19-game win streak that stretched over three seasons. Connell would be the number two scorer in the country in 1928 with 18 touchdowns (126 points) and set the school record for the longest kick return, 98 yards. He also lettered in basketball.

On September 3, 1925, 45 Titan hopefuls assembled at Camp Ozanam in Lexington, Michigan, for training camp. It was a tradition started by Duffy, and one that would last until after the 1928 season, when Dorais moved all spring and pre-season practices to the field adjoining Dinan Field. For the next two and a half weeks, Dorais and his staff put the players through an intensive regimen. They practiced three times a day—twice on the field (morning and afternoon), followed by an evening classroom session or "skull" practice. Early in the season, famed sportswriter E.A. Batchelor, who was freelancing for the *Detroit Saturday Night*, commended Dorais on being able to work with the team he inherited:

> Mr. Dorais took hold of a squad that was perhaps weaker than the casual critic realizes. It included a small percentage of men that could be classified as good football players, a small percentage of men that needed only experience to become good football players, and a large percentage of men whose value even under the best coaching and with all the experience permitted by an intercollegiate career never could be anything better than fair performers.[6]

By the time Dorais arrived in Detroit, Batchelor was an institution, and his opinion carried significant weight. For nearly two decades, he had written for the *Detroit Free Press*, and then was hired on as a war correspondent for the *Detroit News*. For years he covered the Detroit Tigers and served as a charter member of the Baseball Writers Association of America (BBWAA). He covered the University of Michigan football team and is credited by some as making the first mention of Notre Dame as the "Fighting Irish." He left the *Detroit News* after World War I, becoming involved in advertising and the occasional freelance writing job, plus a monthly column for the *Detroit Athletic Club News* to keep his membership in the BBWAA. He and Dorais struck up a friendship, and within a few years Batchelor became the first Director of University of Detroit Sports Publicity.

Dorais held steadfast to his vision, and all things considered, the 1925 season turned out to be a success. In the opener, an intrastate game against Alma College, it took Detroit just three plays to get into the end zone. Later in the first quarter, team captain William "Binker" Brett threw the game's first pass, a 25-yard touchdown to Bob Maniere. Detroit's defense allowed just one first down on the way to a 26–0 shutout. The *Red and White* (soon to be the *Tower*), the university yearbook, described Dorais' game plan as the "fastest and smoothest ever seen."[7]

Reality set in the next week when the Titans traveled to West Point to play Army. The result was a sound 31–6 victory by the Cadets. Detroit rebounded with a 6–0 win over Dorais' old school, Dubuque College, now known as Columbia College. They were coached by former Notre Dame running back Elmer Layden, a member of the "Four Horsemen," who had taken over for another Irish alum, Eddie Anderson, now coaching DePaul. A shutout loss to Georgetown (24–0) was followed by three consecutive victories, guaranteeing a winning season. It was needed as Detroit dropped their last two contests to finish with a 5–4 record.

Dorais found himself in a controversy in November when he suggested that the presence of females on campus was a distraction for football players. He told E.B. McLaughlin of the *Detroit News*, "We have no coeds here and that is the reason that this team is going to develop as it should."[8] The only problem was that the University of Detroit was a co-ed campus, with over 200 females enrolled. He was chided by a co-ed in the *Varsity News*, which turned to Vi Dorais for her take on the subject. She, too, found fault in her husband's statement. "Coeds are essential to a football team," she said. "Their cheers, their support and, sometimes, their love, help carry the team to the heights. 'Gus' knows this, but he is too stubborn to admit it."[9] He exacerbated the situation with further comments, and the flub followed him for a few years, but never reached beyond the occasional jab at him in the *Varsity News*.

Basketball was next, but it was evident where Dorais' priorities lay. He missed the first week of practice while attending the Football Coaches Association meeting in Chicago. There, he made contacts for games two or three years in advance. He was heavily sought after to join a conference of other independent schools from the Midwest, which he ultimately declined. Once he returned to Detroit, Dorais enjoyed the best season of his four years as the Titans' basketball coach. The 13–6 win total tied a school record for a single season set in 1918. Overall, he amassed a 36–30 record before handing the team over to Louis Conroy for the 1929–1930 season.

Even with athletic director duties, football was still Dorais' central focus. During the struggles of those first few years, he was developing talent on the freshman team. Though he had little chance of convincing players to come to Detroit over the University of Michigan, he knew what kind of players to seek out. Years later, Batchelor noted that Dorais found great success in recruiting "players on the small parochial school teams who didn't get enough publicity to warrant other coaches going after them," and those who "gravitated to the U. of D. because they could live at home and get a college education at minimum expense."[10]

Tom Connell took over as the right halfback (wingback). He came to be known as "Five Yard Connell," for his positive outcome every time he touched the ball. He was more popularly known around campus as "Cowboy," thanks to his love of Western movies and books, with a particular affinity for Zane Grey novels. Jerry Donovan of the *Varsity News* wrote that when Connell wasn't on the football field or studying, he could "be found in some theater, drinking in a drama of the 'wide open spaces.'"[11] Early in trials at Camp Ozanam, Dorais was instructing Connell on his throwing. The sophomore fit into Dorais' longstanding practice of making the halfback the main backfield threat, both running and throwing. The tutorial drew a crowd. John M. Carlisle of the *Varsity News* described the scene:

"Why not do it like this, Tom?"
    With that, he began to pass. Soon, every man in the squad of 50, who should
have been hard at work, at fundamentals, stopped to watch him. They watched
with an intentness that rendered them oblivious of everything but his movements,
for they were envisioning, not merely their athletic director passing to his ends,
but the reenactment of a performance by the "frail youth of 145 pounds" which
had astounded the whole football world.[12]

Also at camp was a freshman who would change the direction of the
program, but not until 1927, when he was eligible to play varsity ball. Lloyd
Brazil was Dorais' first great in-state recruit. A standout from Flint Central
High School, Brazil was twice an All-State halfback, was a standout in
basketball, and turned down offers to play baseball professionally. "He
didn't look like an athlete," Dorais said of his early impressions of the
young, loose-jointed Brazil. "He was a skinny, sallow kid—but put him
into a football uniform and he was a whirlwind. He was as good as they
come, as good as any player I've ever coached."[13] Brazil would excel in
every aspect of the game.

In addition to building tradition in those early years in Detroit, Dorais
fostered a positive attitude that went through the team, into the student
body and onto the fan base. "Sportsmanship! That's the big thing," Dorais
told W.F. Dorn of the *Varsity News*. "I am trying to impress the boys with
the fact that victory in sportsmanship is as desirable and more far-reaching
than victory in the game itself. One of the most cherished traditions of
the University of Detroit is the sportsmanlike way that our team and student body always treat visiting teams and their guests."[14]

The Titans took a brief step back in 1926. Detroit was shut out five
times during a 3–6–1 campaign, thanks in part to injuries and what Dorais
deemed as distractions. On any given day, dozens of fans showed up to
watch practice. That number grew to hundreds as the season progressed,
before Dorais finally made practices private. There was also the constant
tinkering of rules, which Dorais became a vocal opponent of. In 1926 a
five-yard penalty was assessed to a second incomplete pass of any series.
"Too many rules threaten to deprive football of the color of which it
belongs," he told the *Varsity News*, "and the penalty on forward passes
merely puts on football a burden of more officiating where there is already
too much officiating."[15]

After winning two of their first three—the loss, a 21–0 defeat at West
Point to Army—Detroit went into a free-fall, even with their last six contests at Dinan Field. The Titans lost five of their last seven games and tied
one of the other two. During the stretch, Dorais took the team to New
Orleans to play Loyola (lost 38–0), the longest trip since 1920, when

Detroit beat Tulane, 7–0, in New Orleans. The Titans battled the tough Carnegie Tech Tartans in a 7–0 loss on a mud-caked Dinan Field. In a month, the Tartans would hand Notre Dame their sole loss of the season, in shutout fashion, 19–0.

The only Detroit win in the second half of the season was against St. Louis University, now coached by R.L. Mathews, Dorais' old Notre Dame teammate and coaching rival on the West Coast. The Titans were shut out in four of those games and outscored, 105–42. It was the programs first losing season since a 1–4 mark in 1915. Dorais wouldn't have a losing campaign for the last 16 years as head coach at the University.

Dorais scoffed at the recent talk of cutting back or even abolishing football in collegiate athletics. While speaking at an athletic banquet at St. John's High School in Jackson, Michigan, Dorais' thoughts were quite the contrary. He was adamant that the game was "bound to keep on growing and expanding in a healthy manner merely because of its character-building qualities for the students who take part in it whether on the first team or only on the squad." Dorais saw many men "who enter college for the athletics and learn a great deal which makes them better citizens before they graduate."[16]

As the Athletic Director at the University of Detroit, Dorais eloquently expanded upon these thoughts in *The Red and White of 1926.*

> On the other hand, when it is apparent that the habit of self-reliance, initiative, discipline self-control, and courage are acquired and fostered, it will be simultaneously agreed that there is also a mental and moral advantage to be gained in the proper conduct of competitive sports. The practical application of the Golden Rule is nowhere stressed more than in the playing of our college games. Living up to its principles is one of the most helpful aids in character building at the formative period when the so called "sinking in" does the most good.[17]

In January 1927, Dorais was chosen by George Trevor, esteemed sportswriter for the *New York Sun*, as quarterback on "Notre Dame's All-Time Eleven." Trevor's said of Dorais: "Charles Dorais wins the quarterback assignment from Harry Stuhldreher by a gnat's whisker. Dorais was the perfect field general. He could punt, drop kick, run the ends and forward pass. He was a good interferer, blocker and true tackler. What a treat to watch him catch punts, and run 'em back often for touchdowns."[18] When Dorais brought his basketball squad to South Bend a few days later, he was given a large ovation and described as "a former Notre Dame man, and perhaps the most famous in the early years of the institution."[19]

The following month, the Titans' 1927 football schedule was released. The obvious highlights were games on consecutive weekends in October.

First the team were to travel to West Point, New York to play Army, followed by Rockne bringing Notre Dame to Detroit. The situation was ripe for reminiscence. "Rockne and I had considerable success with our strategy when he was making touchdowns back in 1911, '12 and '13. Somehow, it seems like it was only last year that we amazed Army," said Dorais when asked what the two-week stretch meant to him. "Just how the strategy will work when it comes from rival benches is another matter and a question that only the game will decide. At any rate, I am looking forward to a new thrill in matching wits with my former team mate."[20]

Dorais was finally getting his wish to play Rockne, something he had been vying for since taking over the Gonzaga job in 1920. It was a long time coming for Detroit University, too. The same year Dorais took over the reins in Spokane, Father M. Matties, a missionary priest, approached Rockne about a game between Detroit and Notre Dame, with all game proceeds going towards a mission fund. Rockne showed great interest in the proposal, but never followed through. The Irish hadn't played another Catholic institution since 1923 (University of St. Louis), so it took much persistence from Dorais, including a meeting with Notre Dame's Athletic Board, for the game to happen. They decided on a two-year, home-and-home arrangement.

There was no denying the impact that Rockne and Notre Dame football had over football programs throughout the country. At the start of the 1927 football season, 68 former Irish players—50 of them under Rockne—were coaching as either a head or assistant in exactly 50 institutions at the college or preparatory level. Of those schools, roughly half were considered major schools by measure of their size or past record of success. This gave a wide audience to the Notre Dame system. Yet, Rockne was reluctant to play other Catholic institutions, claiming they seldom abided by the strict athletic policies that were in place at Notre Dame. This couldn't be used as an excuse for not playing the Titans. Numerous schools were adopting the by-laws of their Athletic Association. College football historian Raymond Schmidt thought Rockne's motivation was more of a self-serving nature. "Considering Notre Dame immense popularity by the mid–20s, as reflected in the media publicity for its football program, the attendance figures attracted to its games, and the substantial recruiting advantage Rockne already held among Catholic high school athletes, the refusal to share any part of the wealth by playing other Catholic schools is an indication of the Notre Dame coach's exploitation of the Catholic 'network' for his own gain," said Schmidt in *Shaping College Football: The Transformation of an American Sport, 1919–1930.*[21]

In the early summer, Dorais hired Art "Bud" Boeringer, an All-American lineman for and soon-to-be graduate of Notre Dame. Boeringer, a St. Paul, Minnesota, native, came highly recommended by Rockne, replacing line coach Ed Degree, who left to focus on the growing demands of his law practice. The intense Boeringer became Dorais' line coach and first dedicated defensive coordinator. Over the next 16 years, Boeringer's defenses recorded 65 shutouts. He also ran the university's newly formed outdoor intramural sports program and coached the new hockey team, another sport that he excelled in at Notre Dame.

Boeringer proved to be just what Dorais needed, as explained by Gus' son, Tom, who played under both for the Titans:

> He was the antithesis of my father, in that my father was very quiet, never got angry, never lost his cool. I guess you could say from the standpoint of getting a team emotionally up, he didn't do that. Bud was a rough, tough, tobacco chewing line coach who the players loved and respected. He was just a perfect match with Gus. He [Boeringer] would get these guys so they would run through a wall. I can remember before and when I played with the team, before we went on the field, Bud whipping up the team with all the profanities known to man—then turning to Father Shipel and quietly saying: "Alright Father, now lead us in prayer." Father Shipel led us in a Hail Mary. The second after the word "amen" was spoken, Bud would yell, "Alright god dammit! Get out there and kick their ass!" And then the team would go out screaming.[22]

A few weeks later, Dorais was in South Bend for Commencement. He had extra incentive in that the 1913 team was having a reunion. Earlier in the year, Dorais had sent a tongue-in-cheek message to the Notre Dame Alumni Board about the possibility:

> Bout time that team of '13 (which I captained) got together as a mutual admira-tion society again. We were good and we should get together and admit it among ourselves where we would be assured of a good hearing. They probably have out-grown the respect they have for me, but I will add my efforts to yours in rounding up that crew. If you would assure them of another barrel of water like we had in Texas I'm sure there would be a stampede.... I'll be there.[23]

In July 1927, Dorais announced the addition of Michael Hebert Butler to the athletic department staff. When Dorais began planning the imple-mentation of a track team, Butler, better known as "Dad," was the first person he thought of to lead it. He would also work as athletic trainer, a post he would hold for 17 years. A native of the Catskills, he was regarded as the first runner in the county to run the half-mile in under two minutes at 1:59. He moved to Chicago, beginning his career in 1896 as trainer for George "Kid" Lavigne, world's lightweight champion. Butler spent years working at a gym in Chicago, having the distinction of serving as Knute

Rockne's first track mentor. Dorais first came into contact with Butler during his time at Gonzaga. During a game, Dorais' Bulldogs suffered several injuries. Butler, who was serving as a trainer at Oregon State, was in the stands. He came over to Gonzaga's bench and offered his assistance. Years later, Dorais called Butler "the most successful man I've ever known."[24]

At Camp Ozanam, Dorais could hardly contain his excitement. In the backfield he had the reigning team MVP and captain, Connell at right halfback. Joining him were Brazil, left halfback, and Ed Maloney, fullback. The line was anchored by the big center, sophomore Merrill "Ring" Lardner, a 330-pound All-State player from Bay City, Michigan. The much-anticipated 1927 season began with a blowout of Adrian College, 44–0.

A bit of nostalgia lay ahead for Dorais: Army and Notre Dame. Both ended in losses for Detroit, but the manner in which the Titans performed had people taking notice. Dorais was confident in the 23 men he brought east to the United States Military Academy. On October 1, Detroit played spectacularly in a 6–0 loss at West Point. A long touchdown pass by Army—the Cadets' only completion of the game—was the difference. At the insistence of the Military Academy, the Titans played without one of their main offensive weapons—the shift—yet they held their own against a team that would go 9–1, including an 18–0 win over Notre Dame.

The following Saturday, Dorais and Detroit hosted Rockne and Notre Dame. The Irish brought a huge student following with them, over 1,000 making the 220-mile journey to Detroit as part of the official student trip. The students were met by buses, that gave them a tour of the city and various landmarks, including a luncheon at the General Motors Building and a viewing of the new campus. The weekend coincided with the University's Golden Jubilee. Notre Dame was included in the celebration. Dorais' old mentor in South Bend, Father John Cavanaugh, gave the Golden Jubilee sermon.

Dorais and Rockne never saw eye-to-eye on how to defend the pass. For years, Dorais looked forward to the challenge of proving Rockne wrong that man-to-man defense could handle all passing attacks. Detroit was pass-heavy and Dorais had concocted several new plays he thought were impossible to cover in man coverage. Deviating from his usual game plan, and on the heels of having to play without the shift, Dorais was confident he would succeed. "Now is my opportunity to really show Rock that he doesn't know anything about pass defense," Dorais recalled thinking. "I am going to show the Old Master this time."[25]

Neither team performed particularly well passing the ball, but Rockne and Notre Dame got the upper hand. Each squad attempted 13 passes, with the Fighting Irish completing eight, for 74 yards and a touchdown. The pass played a major part in Notre Dame's other two scores. Detroit had six completions for 41 yards and an interception. It was only towards the end of the game, when the outcome was already determined, that the Titans' offense was able to string together a few passes, albeit for short gain. The 20–0 loss was a learning experience for Dorais, who was focusing too much on the pass trickery and not enough on a balanced attack. It brought him back to the fundamentals and began a 19-game winning streak that spanned parts of three seasons.

Nearly a year after Rockne's death in 1931, Dorais reflected on what he was reminded of in that game:

Rockne and Dorais together before the kickoff of the 1927 game between Notre Dame and Detroit—the only time the two met head-to-head as coaches (Digital/print image from the University of Detroit Mercy Archive and Special Collections, University of Detroit Mercy).

We all know that the backbone of football is the running game. The pass attack is dependent for its success on the success of the running game, which will always be the fundamental basis of attack in football and which will be the most important. There must be a balance maintained, however, and it is unwise, I think, to put all our eggs into one basket. I learned that by sad experience.[26]

This would be the only game played between Dorais and Rockne. When Dorais reminded Rockne the following spring about the two-year arrangement, the latter never returned the inquiry. It was unfortunate, as Dorais would have one of the top teams he ever coached in 1928, and Rockne, record-wise, the worst at 5–4. The Irish scored only 99 points the entire season and suffered the first home loss since 1905, a 27–7 setback to Carnegie Tech.

A scary incident took place at the Dorais home following the game when the Rockne's paid a visit. At some point, Rockne's 11-year-old son, Bill—with the middle name "Dorais"—nearly strangled Dorais' oldest, Tom, just six at the time. "Billy Rockne took me behind the garage and ended up on top of me, choking me to death," recalled Tom, nearly half a century later. "Someone heard the commotion. When they hauled him off of me my face was blue. I didn't remember anything except being told what a terrible thing it was and how lucky I was to be alive."[27]

Following the two setbacks, the Titans whitewashed Columbia College, 58–0, and began a 19-game winning streak that stretched into the 1929 season. After an open date, Detroit played Michigan State for the first time in four years and the just sixth time since 1902. State held a 4–1 advantage. The Titans got the scoring started early. On the eighth play of the game, Connell went around left end for a 59-yard touchdown run. Later, Brazil tossed a 52-yard touchdown pass to Maloney—the longest in school history to that point. The Titans won, 24–7. Detroit won handily over the Haskell Indians, 38–7, and shut out St. Louis, 21–0, thanks to a pair of touchdown runs by Brazil, one for 81 yards. Tom Connell bested him, tearing off a school record 86-yard jaunt, eclipsing Hans Loving's 1919 mark of 85.

The week leading up to the Carnegie game was a personal matter for Bud Boeringer. The year before, the Notre Dame team he captained went into Pittsburgh undefeated, having outscored opponents, 197–7. A victory for Notre Dame was so certain that Rockne opted to travel to his hometown, Chicago, to watch the dedication game for Soldier Field between Army and Navy. In a contest regarded as one of the great upsets in college football history, Carnegie shut out the Irish, 19–0. Even more infuriating for Boeringer was that Carnegie coach Walter Steffen stalked the sidelines yelling insults at the Notre Dame players.

Boeringer got some revenge. As time ran out, and a 12–7 Titans victory was imminent, he jumped to his feet and ran up and down the sideline, yelling his own set of cheers to antagonize Carnegie. When Dorais reminded Boeringer that the sportsmanship he expected of the players was the same for coaches, Boeringer only yelled louder. Dorais walked away without further discussion. Years later he would say that he was afraid that he had "signed a wild man."[28]

Detroit finished the 1927 season with a 38–7 win over South Dakota State. The six straight wins gave the Titans a 7–2 record. The win total was the most for a Dorais-led team since he won seven in back-to-back years at Dubuque College in 1915 and 1916. A few weeks after the season ended, Connell was named a repeat as captain at the football banquet—

a first for the university's football program. Knute Rockne was among several people who feted the players at the celebration. The Notre Dame coach commended Dorais and his young Detroit team for their clean style of play and perseverance, particularly in the recent come-from-behind win against Carnegie Tech.

Dorais began to feel the struggles of having a successful program. He would no longer be able to schedule the likes of Notre Dame or Army. Major L.M. Jones, then coach of West Point, summed up the situation to Dorais. "You are just too good, Gus," Jones said. "Sooner or later your team is going to whip West Point and I can't afford a whipping from anybody but Navy, Yale or Notre Dame or perennial rivals. If we beat you, our rooters don't get excited, but if you beat us, they will get my scalp."[29]

E.A. Batchelor surmised that Dorais was a victim of his own talents and his team's success:

> Gus was perhaps too good a coach for his own peace of mind. His teams were so uniformly strong that every opposing coach feared them. They were hard to scout because their attack was so varied and their repertoire so extensive. Scouts complained that they took back a voluminous report of the Titans' offense and a defense was planned to meet it. Then, the very next week, the Detroit team would play a game with their team and show an entirely different offense.[30]

If Rockne couldn't fit Detroit into Notre Dame's schedule, at least he could help Dorais with finding opponents. Four of the Titans' first seven games were against teams coached by former players of Rockne: Eddie Anderson, DePaul University; Tom King, University of Louisville; Harry Baujan, University of Dayton, and Hunk Anderson, St. Louis University. Since Detroit's loss to the Irish the previous October, Dorais had been scheming how to handle the Notre Dame Box, and each of Detroit's opponents—faithful to Rockne—ran it. W.W. Edgar of the *Detroit Free Press* noted that these "disciples of Rockne" often "clung to the old defense until they encountered Dorais' teams. And when they saw Gus riddle the box with passes right down the middle, they were forced to shift their defenses."[31] The Titans won all of these contests in shutout fashion, outscoring the opposition, 169–0. But for a close 7–0 game in sloppy conditions against Baujan's University of Dayton Flyers—the first score against Dayton since 1926—Detroit never scored less than 38 points. This total came in a win over St. Louis University Billikens on November 3, in a game that left both team's coaches with hard feelings.

St. Louis traveled to Detroit with high expectations. The schools had played four times since 1920—all Titans victories. Due to Detroit's inconsistent schedule, the series, albeit brief, was the closest the Titans had to a tradition. There were a few subplots, notably Detroit's winning streak and the Notre Dame alums going head-to-head. Due to injuries, Dorais started his "shock squad." As the end of a scoreless first quarter neared, he put in his first team, including Connell and Brazil, the latter of whom had been struggling with a finger injury for a few weeks. He showed no signs of being hindered in the Titans' victory, setting a school record for total yards in a single game: 396 (187 rushing and 209 passing). Connell scored 20 points on three touchdowns and two extra points. For the season he had 71 of the Titans' 182 points.

Both of their accomplishments were overshadowed by a rift between the coaches: Dorais and fellow Notre Dame alumnus Heartly "Hunk" Anderson. Each coach insisted that the other's team was playing dirty. By halftime, Anderson was openly calling Dorais crass names, which was quickly relayed to the Detroit coach. Dorais claimed that he only put his first stringers in because of the rough style of play that the Billikens were exhibiting. In the subsequent days, Anderson took to the press, calling the Titans out for intentionally hurting his players. Anderson was also upset with former Notre Dame lineman and captain (1923), Harvey Brown, who was interning as a doctor at a hospital in Detroit. Anderson took exception that Brown, who served as an assistant for St. Louis for a few seasons prior, scouted the Billikns for Dorais the week before and spent significant time in the St. Louis locker room after the fact, visiting with players and coaches.

Anderson was already making plans to drop Detroit from the 1929 schedule. Dorais responded, but in a more reserved manner, saying that he too thought the series should end, while defending his team's sportsmanship. Both coaches turned for advice to Rockne, who was cordial to each of them. In Dorais' letter he said: "Hunk is a friend of yours and was a friend of mine" and that Anderson's Billikens were "eleven pop-eyed maniacs."[32] In his correspondence with Dorais, Rockne voiced his regret for setting up games between Notre Dame alums: "There has been more bad blood between Notre Dame coaches than is good for the game and personally there is no one more sorry than I am that these things happen."[33]

The biggest early-season challenge—and what was ultimately the closest game of the season for Detroit—came against the University of Tulsa Hurricanes on October 6. After traveling 1,000 miles, the Titans had to withstand 98-degree heat and an odd playing field that sloped to one side and measured just 90 yards. When the ball reached the goal line, play was halted, and the ball was returned to the 10-yard line. The circumstance made Dorais furious, and his team seemed rattled by the ground rules. The Hurricanes jumped out to a 14–6 lead in the first quarter and held a 14–13 lead into the fourth quarter, when Connell connected with Brazil on a 45-yard touchdown pass. Connell dragged three defenders over the goal line for a final score. The game lasted 3½ hours. Detroit held on for the 19–14 victory. Brazil rushed for 150 yards.

On November 16, the Titans put on a 39–0 trouncing of Michigan State. The Spartans were under first-year coach Harry Kipke, in his one year at the school before moving on to his alma mater, the University of Michigan. Brazil set a school record with 209 rushing yards on 22 carries. Each of the backs had long scoring runs: Connell, 75 yards, Brazil 62, and Maloney, 45.

The Titans traveled to the Polo Grounds in Upper Manhattan to take on the Fordham University Rams. There was a sparse crowd in the stands, but back in Detroit the alumni association had to turn away more than 3,000 fans and alumni from a gridgraph showing party at the Statler Hotel. The Rams' game plan revolved around stopping Brazil. It worked. On Detroit's first four offensive plays, the Titans lost 40 yards. Brazil football intellect was on full display. With the Titans back on their 5-yard line, he called a daring triple pass. Starting the trick play, he was on the final receiving end for a 67-yard gain to kickstart the offense. Brazil's knowledge of defense showed. When Eddie Barbour came in the huddle and called for Detroit's big ground gainer off tackle, Brazil checked the play twice. When Barbour called it a third time, Brazil relented. "On it, I was supposed to block the right end so Braz could cut inside me," recalled Barbour. "I belted my guy real good and figured Braz was in the clear. But when I looked up, he had been thrown for a three-yard loss."[34]

"We didn't call that play again all day. Braz had seen things nobody else could see. Not even Dorais. That's the kind of player he was," added Barbour. "He was born with football intuition. Nobody knew it more than Dorais. Braz was his alter ego out on the field. He'd change plays on Dorais and Gus let him do it. But Lloyd was the only one."[35]

Except for one brilliant pass, the Rams shut down Brazil. They didn't account for Connell, who scored all of Detroit's 19 points in a shutout—the Titans' sixth straight.

Detroit went nearly two weeks before playing Georgetown University in the season finale. In the interim, six Titans were named to the All-State first team by Detroit sportswriters, including all three backs: Connell (named team captain), Brazil and Maloney. On the brink of an undefeated season, celebrations were held each night on Detroit's campus—pep rallies, bonfires and speeches. It wouldn't be an easy victory, as the 8–1 Hill-toppers, coached by Lou Little, a two-time All-American tackle from Penn, was one of the top scoring teams in the country, outscoring opponents by a margin of 293–29.

On the opening kickoff, Connell turned a near disaster into a touch-down. Georgetown kicked towards a waiting Connell and Brazil. Each back thought the other was going to field it, watching it land between them on the 10-yard line. Connell picked the ball up right as a Hilltoppers end arrived. The back eluded the defender and followed Brazil downfield for 20 yards, before cutting all the way across the field and up the sideline for a touchdown. What could have broken the game wide open, instead had the opposite effect. "Instead of loosening us up, that early score seemed to tie a rope around our necks," recalled Lloyd Brazil. "We couldn't do a thing afterward. Georgetown pushed over two touchdowns and should have made a few more."[36]

Down 13–7 at halftime, Detroit entered the locker room expecting a tongue lashing from Dorais. One of the coaches was already instructing them on adjustments for the second half. Dorais stopped him. Instead, the team sat around doing nothing in particular until the referees told them the half was to begin in three minutes. Dorais addressed the team:

> The happiest days of my life were spent playing football at Notre Dame. They are the fondest memories I have. Why? Because I got a lot of fun out of playing foot-ball.
>
> You fellows are taking it too seriously. You have made work out of a game. The stadium will still be here tomorrow if you lose and the field house and all the other buildings will stand. Let's see somebody smiling out there. Now go out and have some fun. Even if you must get beaten, have some fun while it's happening."[37]

Detroit went out and scored 26 unanswered point in the second half. They won, 33–13, and completing an undefeated 9–0 season and pushing the win streak to 14 games. For the year, the Titans outscored their oppo-nents, 267–27, and recorded six straight shutouts and seven overall. The points allowed total was the lowest for a Dorais-led team (Gonzaga Uni-versity gave up 26 in seven games in 1924, compared to the 1928 total accomplished in nine). Edmund J. Barbour, a member of the undefeated team, said of his coach: "Gus Dorais was a man of profound football knowl-edge, with infinite patience, and a sound teacher. He ... came up with star-tling answers [to football problems] a number of times."[38]

An undefeated season didn't lead to many individual national post-season accolades. Overlooked was the two-time captain, Connell. He scored 125 points (18 touchdowns and 17 PATs) in 1928, ranking second in the nation to future NFL Hall of Famer Ken Strong, New York University's featured halfback who scored 162 points and amassed over 3,000 total yards. In Connell's three years, he scored 218 points (32 touchdowns and 26 PATs)—both school records. He approached nearly 1,000 rushing yards his senior season, even though he shared the backfield with Brazil and played limited minutes in certain games when Dorais started his second-stringers or the Titans were ahead by a large margin. Connell did win the Titans' Loyalty Award for the second time.

It was hard to look past the season that Brazil had. Besides the school's individual game records he set during the season, Brazil also established the single season total yards mark, 2,159 (1,393 rushing and 766 passing). The rushing yards was also a school record, accomplished on 164 carries (8.5 yards per carry). Some sources have him at 2,330. Collegiate football statistics weren't kept consistently until 1937, but that number wasn't eclipsed again on a major college level until Drake Uni-

The 1928 University of Detroit undefeated (9-0) football team, part of an unbeaten streak that lasted 22 games over three seasons (Dorais family photo collection).

versity's Johnny Bright had a 2,400-yard output in 1950. Brazil became the first University of Detroit All–American since Tillie Voss in 1920. Brazil was selected as a utility player on Grantland Rice's *Collier's Weekly* squad and third team on Frank Getty's *United Press* team. That made Brazil an easy choice as captain for the 1929 season. He was the only player in school history to be captain on both the football and basketball teams.

The Titans' undefeated season garnered minimal attention, other than the vague "Midwestern Champion" title. There was some consolation a few years later, when football historian Parke Davis named a national champion every year dating back to 1869 for the 1933 edition of *Spalding's Football Guide*. Davis split the 1928 title between Detroit and Georgia Tech.

Dorais spent an exasperating 1928–1929 offseason trying to schedule major schools to help bolster the program's reputation. Over a two-month period, he wrote an endless number of letters and took trip after trip, but for the most part his efforts were for naught. In early February, a banquet was held to award sweaters to members of the football team. Dorais was gifted a La Salle sedan by the school's Alumni Association. It was painted in school colors: red and white with black fenders. A week later he signed a five-year contract extension. In the spring, Dorais decided to cease the decade-old tradition of training at Camp Ozanam. His reasoning was that Big Ten teams could automatically decline his overtures because Detroit held practice at a camp, which was against Big Ten Conference rules.

While trying to schedule opponents, one of Dorais' selling points was that Dinan Field would have a lighting system for the 1929 season. There had been few modifications since Dinan Field opened in 1922. In July 1926, a committee decided to sod the field with creeping bent grass, and it was soon considered one of the best playing surfaces around. Shortly thereafter, Dorais pushed for lights as his team became an attraction and began competing with the University of Michigan for fans on Saturday afternoons. This allowed for Dorais' plan of Friday night games, a practice that other private schools followed in the coming years. The $25,000, 56,000-watt, six-tower lighting system was hyped by the University as "The World's Greatest Lighting System." Designed by University of Detroit alum Edwin Labadie, it flooded the field with 50-foot-candles of light, compared to the highly regarded Pasadena Rose Bowl's eight. Eventually, Dorais came to feel that the arrangement left his team at a disadvantage due to there being one less day of practice.

Dinan Field was now illuminated for night games, and the first three contests of the 1929 season showcased the new set-up. Detroit opened the season against Eddie Anderson's De Paul Blue Demons. After a scoreless first half, the Titans scored 14 points in the third quarter on their way to a 27–7 win, running their winning streak to 16. The game was almost an afterthought, as 22,000 fans packed into Dinan Field for the first night game. The highlight of the game was a 76-yard touchdown pass from Brazil to Herman Young, the longest passing play in the nation for 1929. Brazil ran for another, and Connell's replacement, Charles Ross, a two-time All-State football player and sprinting champion from Detroit Northwestern, ran for two. Known as "Snitz," he complemented Brazil nicely, ripping off several long touchdown runs throughout the 1929 season.

Wins over Dayton (18–0), Tulsa (21–6) and Loyola (20–6) followed for the Titans. They were without big center Ring Lardner, out with a serious leg injury. In the Tulsa game, Brazil matched his school record rushing mark of 209 yards (on 19 carries), achieved the year before against Michigan State. He also started a triple pass that went for a touchdown. With Detroit's winning streak now at 19 games, the Titans were re-engaging with Marquette University for the first time since 1923. On November 2, 1929, they met the previously unbeaten Golden Avalanche (also known as the Hilltoppers), who would go undefeated in 1930. Dorais played an uncharacteristically conservative offensive scheme through the first three quarters. In the final period, Brazil opened up the game plan with passes, but was unsuccessful. The contest finished in a 6–6 tie, ending not only an overall winning streak at 19 games, but also a 14-game run at home.

The tie did little to shake Detroit's fan base. A large group followed the Titans to Morgantown to watch them overwhelm the West Virginia University Mountaineers, 36–0. In a showcase to Easterners, Brazil played so well that an ovation got so loud when he was substituted for at the end of the game that the referees halted play. Ross scored three touchdowns, including a 65-yard scamper. When the final whistle blew, the Titans revelers swarmed the field and dismantled the goal posts. The crossbar was brought back to Detroit and briefly stored in the Field House. Engineering students raised funds to construct a trophy to commemorate the yearly games between the two schools—the aptly named University of Detroit–West Virginia Trophy. The crossbar was painted with the colors of each school and had two hands clasped together. A bronze plaque was also placed on it to engrave the score of each contest.

A 25–0 win in East Lansing over Michigan State was next. The victory was marred by a drunken riot by fans after the game. "If it is allowed to get a start, it will ruin the game," Dorais said of drinking at games.[39] The Titans returned to Dinan Field on November 23 to play 4–4 Oregon State, losers of their last two. Detroit jumped out to a 7–0 lead in the first quarter, thanks to a sustained, 62-yard drive and a touchdown by sophomore Louie Berg. Once it was apparent that Brazil was going to be a non-factor, the Aggies were able to handle the Titans' sputtering offense. Detroit attempted a school record 41 passes, including a triple pass that was intercepted deep in their own territory. Oregon State used a lateral pass of their own to score the decisive touchdown. After 21 games, the Titans finally lost a game, falling to the Aggies, 14–7. A few years later, Oregon State coach Paul Schissler admitted he had been inadvertently tipped off about Detroit's use of the triple pass at the hotel the night before the game by an overzealous Titans fan.

After much consternation, it was decided that Brazil would sit out the season finale, and what would have been the final game of his career at Detroit, due to the lingering leg injury. As he watched from the sideline, the Titans won a hard-fought, 14–13 battle at home over Georgetown in single-digit temperatures. Detroit finished with a record of 7–1–1.

Brazil held numerous single-game and season records, as well as career marks, including total yards of offense—5,790–3,833 rushing and 1,957 passing. Both the rushing and passing numbers were records, too. Over the three years he was in the backfield, the Titans amassed a 23–3–1 record. According to longtime *Detroit Free Press* sportswriter George Puscas, "Only once in the 26 games was Brazil, a powerful runner, held to fewer than 100 yards, and 19 times he carried the ball for more than 200 a game."[40] The sub-100 game came in 1928 against the University of Dayton on a rain-soaked field, while playing with a badly sprained thumb. Dorais held Brazil in the highest regards: "As far as I'm concerned there were only three great collegiate backs in my lifetime—Jim Thorpe, George Gipp and Lloyd Brazil."[41]

Brazil was once again showered with post-season accolades. He was on three different outlets, at a variety of positions: second team, quarterback, Davis Walsh's International News Service Team; third team, Newspaper Enterprise Association; and third team, fullback, International News Service. He was also named to the East-West All-Star Game, playing despite his injured leg.

In the Titans' spring drills, Dorais saw that the program was in for a down year in 1930. Of the 130 candidates, there were just two regulars returning—team captain William Storen, fullback, and John Hackett, end. There were players who emerged in standout roles, most notably lineman, Art Masucci, who would gain All-American and All-Catholic honors and was selected to the North-South All-Star Game in in January 1931. Noticeably absent was Snitz Ross, who left the team for unspecified reason a few days into fall practice. For the most part, it was a struggle for the Titans in 1930, particularly on offense.

There was no replacing a player of Lloyd Brazil's caliber, and Dorais knew it. He told W.W. Edgar of the *Detroit Free Press*, "Football moves in cycles and we are about due for an off year."[42] Brazil was still around and joined the coaching staff. He spent the next four decades within the athletic department as athletic director, business administrator, and chairman of the athletic board, as well as coaching the basketball and baseball teams. He also worked as an NFL official and was the highest-ranking football and basketball official in the Michigan High School Athletic Association. Though numerous alumni would help Dorais in one capacity or another over the years, Brazil joined the core group of Boeringer and Butler for the duration of Dorais' tenure at the university.

Nothing was taken for granted during the 1930 season. Dorais' teams had always been deficient when it came to kicking extra points, a fact for which he himself took blame. "I always thought kicking points was so easy, it didn't require any coaching and I just didn't bother with it," he said the week leading up to the opener against Adrian. "But it will be different from now on."[43] Dissatisfied with his scout team, Dorais occasionally played quarterback to prepare his defense for that week's opponent.

A high point on Detroit's now 10-game schedule was the November 1 game against Iowa. It was the Titans' first Big Ten opponent since 1917, a 14–3 loss to the University of Michigan in Ann Arbor. The Titans came into the game with the Hawkeyes undefeated, 4–0. Detroit had outscored their opponents, 177–6, in three easy wins over Adrian, Albion and Grinnell, and a hard-fought shutout of West Virginia, 20–0. After a scoreless first half, the Titans got on the board first with a third quarter field goal. Iowa responded in the fourth quarter on a 53-yard touchdown run by reserve back John Warrington, the game-winner. The 7–3 loss was just Detroit's second setback in the last 28 games.

Dorais seldom had disagreements with the referees, at least publicly. After all, it wasn't uncommon to see an ex-teammate or opponent officiating the game. If there was, it often resulted in a civil discussion—except when it was with the explosive Larry MacPhail. He became a Hall of Fame front office executive for the Brooklyn Dodgers and spent several years refereeing Big Ten football games. Dorais and MacPhail were friendly, frequently fishing together, but that friendship didn't stop a terse post-game interaction.

Following the loss to Iowa, Dorais walked into the officials' room and quietly remarked to MacPhail, "Larry, I thought you missed a couple out there this afternoon."

MacPhail jumped to his feet. "I missed them?" he shouted. "Don't tell me I missed anything. Before you go criticizing referees you had better teach your quarterback the rules. He asked three different times this afternoon what he should do when he had a choice."

Dorais remained quiet as MacPhail continued his diatribe. "Looks like you better stick to finishing your job of coaching, Gus, before you start telling officials they're missing anything,"[44]

Detroit won just one more game the remainder of the season, but their 5–3–2 record was deceiving. A strong Fordham team won their 16th straight with a touchdown in the final seconds, defeating the Titans, 13–7, at Dinan Field. Detroit played a pair of 0–0 ties on the road; first to a previously unbeaten Marquette team in Milwaukee—the Golden Avalanches' only blemish on their record—then in East Lansing against Michigan State. The Titans recorded their first win in over a month, a 12–0 shutout of Georgetown, before losing the finale in New Orleans against Loyola, 9–6. Detroit's defense was one of the best that Dorais and Boeringer put on the field. The Titans allowed a paltry 32 points in ten games, just five more than the legendary 1928 squad did in nine contests. The season included four shutouts, six if the two 0–0 ties counted.

In the winter, Dorais worked on launching an ambitious intra-mural program at Detroit. In late December he was among the athletic directors at the Coaches Football Association meetings in New York City. He openly defied any team in the country to play the Titans. Dorais also critiqued the meeting, feeling that just because coaches were convening, changes didn't need to be made. In recent years, he saw the constant alterations to the game was being lost on fans. He said as much to his contemporaries: "Each year we are attempting some changes in the rules and the changes have come so often that the vast portion of the populace that crams its way into the stadia throughout the country cannot keep up with the game."[45]He suggested a cessation to the yearly manipulations for a five-year span, which the congregation agreed to. In a few months, the handling of rules became trivial when tragedy befell the football world and changed Dorais' life.

CHAPTER 8

Changing Landscape, 1931–1936

Dorais loved driving his red and white LaSalle around Detroit. It was one of the few respites from the demands of his job at the University of Detroit. The daily rides gave Dorais time to clear his head and contemplate issues of the day. Of late he was pushing for a field house and gymnasium to expand the Department of Physical Education. He wanted to broaden the intramural program, add a boxing team led by Dad Butler, and begin a handball tournament for both student and faculty (he had recently picked the game up and was taken with it). March 31, 1931, was no different. Dorais was likely thinking about spring practice. For the first time he had split his candidates up into three teams led by himself, Boeringer and Brazil: the Reds, Whites and Blacks. The team was just days into drills after several weeks of twice-daily lectures on the fundamentals. Returning to his office, Dorais was flagged down by Harold Kahl of the *Detroit Times*. The reporter was wondering if Dorais had heard the news—Knute Rockne was dead. Dorais had not. He was blindsided.

Earlier that day, Rockne had been onboard a TWA Flight 599 airplane when it crashed into a wheat field near Bazaar, Kansas. En route to Los Angeles to help with the filming of *The Spirit of Notre Dame*, Rockne had stopped over in Kansas City to visit his two sons, Knute Jr. and Bill, who were attending the Pembroke-Country Day School.

Kahl asked Dorais if he could speak with him about Rockne's passing. Dorais agreed to, but first he excused himself and got back into his automobile. He drove around without a destination, contemplating the horrible news of his friend. Dorais was one of the first people worldwide to reach out to Rockne's wife with a sympathy-filled telegram. "Please call on me if I can be of the slightest help. God bless you and the children in your terrible loss."[1]

Dorais returned to campus, where he corralled a few members of his coaching staff who were associated with Rockne. Team trainer Dad Butler was Rockne's first track coach at the Chicago Athletic Club when he was still a teen. Defensive coordinator Bud Boeringer was an All-American lineman for Rockne at Notre Dame. The threesome sat down with Kahl to reminisce about Rockne. Though each gave their feelings, no one spoke more at length or as eloquently as Dorais. In between, he chewed nervously on a cigar and occasionally took long pauses to stare blankly out the window.

Over the next several hours, Dorais fielded calls and in-person interviews from multiple publications within the city and beyond. All the while, he was beginning to craft a lengthy public eulogy of Rockne that appeared in newspapers all over the country. This was a position that Dorais would hold the rest of his life—primary spokesman for the legacy of Knute Rockne. In the immediate future, Dorais helped organize tributes in Detroit, including a memorial radio program put on by the Notre Dame club of Detroit. Gus and Vi prepared a spiritual bouquet for the Rockne family that included 1,000 low Masses, 14 high Masses and 200 Communions.

The plane crash wasn't far from Rockne's and Dorais' coach Jesse Harper's Clark County, Kansas ranch. Harper rode with Rockne's body on the train back to South Bend and remained in town for the funeral. Dorais was a member of the honor guard, as were several teammates of the storied 1913 team at the funeral mass on campus at Basilica of the Sacred Heart. Harper eventually took over Rockne's Athletic Director position as a favor to former school president Reverend Matthew Walsh. Before Harper resumed his duties, it was decided that former Rockne assistants Hunk Anderson and Jack Chevigny would serve as co-coaches, with Anderson having the title of "senior coach." It was a disaster, as the two fought throughout the 1931 season, with Chevigny departing to coach the Chicago Cardinals in the NFL. Anderson, hamstrung by the budget mandated by the Great Depression and Harper's strict academic requirements to play, was fired after a 3–5–1 record in 1933. Only 33 points were scored in the first losing season in school history.

If there was ever a conversation about Dorais being considered for the Notre Dame job, it was never made public. That didn't mean it wasn't a topic of conversation. "I don't for the life of me know why Notre Dame itself was muddling around several years ago with all those suggested successors to Rockne, the old master, when a natural and seemingly logical choice was not many miles away," wrote David Walsh in a national column.[2]

Dorais thought back to the last time he saw Rockne. The two had gotten together when Rockne was in Detroit to speak at an automobile convention. He confided in Dorais that his physician had advised him to slow down his pace or he'd be dead within a few years. Rockne had a health scare a year earlier when he fell ill during the summer of 1929. He was diagnosed with a thrombosis, a circulatory disease, causing him to coach that fall from a wheelchair. He would have none of the doctor's most recent diagnosis. "I'm not going to slow down," he told Dorais. "I don't like to take things easy, and I want to make all the money I can for my family. So I'm going right ahead!"[3]

Rockne's death brought Dorais closer to his alma mater. He was now the oldest Notre Dame man coaching in the college ranks. He had already been an active participant in Notre Dame's large Detroit alumni chapter and frequently returned to South Bend for commencement. He would soon be manning the Michigan chapter of the Rockne Memorial, join on the Board of Directors of the Monogram Association, and help with a George Gipp Memorial. Dorais had a permanent seat at the head table at Irish Football Banquets, was often tabbed to be the toastmaster of Rockne Memorial Dinners all over the Midwest, and never missed a Rockne Memorial Program at Notre Dame or any other tribute to his friend on campus. Dorais was a go-to for reporters for a Rockne story, and in 1938 he penned a three-part story, "Rock and I," for *Smith's Sport Story Magazine*.

In June 1931, Dorais had a lengthy written correspondence with Father Cavanaugh about Rockne that lifted some of the mystique off his former roommate. Dorais' reputation as one of the preeminent minds in college football swelled by the day. At the same time, he became more giving with strategic advice. In the spring, he appeared in a "talkie" series, *One of a Series of talks by Famous Coaches*, giving a brief explanation and demonstration of the forward pass. Dorais also appeared in a series of sketches that were shown before *The Spirit of Notre Dame*, where he and former Notre Dame teammates paid tribute to Rockne.

Dorais' public persona expanded in the fall. He became a staple on Friday night radio, talking all things college football with Sam Greene of the *Detroit News*, and began selecting a post-season All-Midwest Team that was distributed throughout the country. Dorais decided to make some of his knowledge public with his October book release, *The Forward Pass and Its Defense*, dedicating it to Rockne, "my old pal and the receiver of many a winning pass." Though just 59 pages, Dorais was forthcoming in his strategies and, according to E.A. Batchelor, the book soon became "the bible" on the subject."[4]

With all the outside distractions, there was still a football season to be played. Dorais managed a few new opponents on the 1931 schedule, highlighted by the first meeting with Villanova University. A spirited rivalry between the Titans and Wildcats took place over the next few years, thanks in part to Villanova being coached by former Notre Dame quarterback Harry Stuhldreher. He often rivaled Dorais for the title of greatest Irish quarterback of all time. There was also talk of a post-season game with Notre Dame to be held in Ann Arbor at the University of Michigan Stadium. Leading up to the season, improvements were made to Dinan Field, including ventilated and heated locker rooms.The stadium improvements were curious to some. In the midst of the Great Depression, the University was struggling, and the fall of 1931 was the beginning of true financial hardships for the school.

By 1935, gifts dwindled to less than a third of what they were in 1929 ($66,959.66 to $20,436). For an institution that relied heavily on tuition, a decreasing enrollment—down 1,200 between 1930 and 1935—proved detrimental. Dorais tried to establish a student loan fund in 1935, but it did little to help. In March 1933, the University defaulted on its debt of $3.5 million. Threatened with foreclosure in February 1935, the institution filed for bankruptcy and begin a reorganization in November 1936. For years, Dorais quietly took a reduced salary to help save money, with the understanding that it would be paid in full at a later date. When he left the University in 1942, he was still owed nearly $25,000.

In the 1931 opener, the Titans reengaged with Eddie Anderson's DePaul Blue Demons after not playing each other in 1930. DePaul, thought to be a warm-up for the season, had 17 returnees. They completely stifled a flat Detroit offense that seemed to have no direction. In sultry conditions, the Blue Demons scored two touchdowns in the fourth quarter for a 12–0 victory. The loss was the first time since 1909 that the Titans met defeat in an opener. It was a particularly embarrassing game for Dorais, as it was played in front of a large crowd from the Legionnaires convention in town—several of them former football stars at the university. Detroit rebounded, shutting out four of their next five opponents before being steamrolled, 39–9, by Fordham in the Titans' first road game of the year, at the Polo Grounds in Manhattan. It was the first time in 40 games, win or lose, that Detroit surrendered more than 14 points in a game.

On November 14, the Titans returned to Dinan Field to play Villanova University for the first annual Dad's Day, which brought fathers to campus to get a feel of what their children were up to. An added sidelight to the game was that the Wildcats were coached by Stuhldreher. Dorais was home sick for much of the week leading up to the game, and an all-night rain the night before made the field conditions poor as both teams combined for just four scoring opportunities. The outcome was an anticlimactic, 0–0 tie—the Wildcats' second tie in three weeks. Detroit won the final two games, coming away with the Smead Trophy against Michigan State (21–13) and a victory towards the Georgetown Trophy against Georgetown (6–0) to finish with a record of 7–2.[5,6]

Another off-season was thick with rumors of Dorais fleeing Detroit. This year it was two Big Ten teams: Wisconsin and Iowa. In the spring, Detroit president Father McNichols, who had been on medical leave since early October, expressed the college's intentions to re-sign their veteran coach. It would be one of the last public endorsements of Dorais by Father McNichols, who passed away on April 26, 1932, of a heart attack. Dorais served as a pallbearer at the funeral. "The boys will miss his inspiration," said Dorais of the man had who helped shape the University over the past decade. "He appealed to them for what he was—a forceful man, a

Dorais had the same coaching staff nearly every year at the University of Detroit: (left to right) Lloyd Brazil, Arthur "Bud" Boringer, Michael "Dad" Butler, Gus Dorais (Digital/print image from the University of Detroit Mercy Archive and Special Collections, University of Detroit Mercy).

man's man."[7] Father Albert Poetker was installed as president a few months later.

In late June, the Dorais family traveled to the West Coast for a month-long schedule of coaching clinics led by Gus. The highlight was a return to Spokane, Washington, where Dorais took part in the six-day Gonzaga coaching school, along with Hunk Anderson of Notre Dame and Dad Butler, the Titans' trainer. Anderson took the first three days, lecturing in the morning about line work, followed by an afternoon of on-field demonstrations. Dorais took the last three days, discussing mainly backfield play. Butler talked about training and taping players.

Dorais had been on the lookout for his next game-changing back, and in 1932 he found one in left halfback Douglas Nott. Detroit's 1932, 1933 and 1934 seasons revolved around the play of Nott—the good and the bad. He came to the Titans as a stout blocking back from Ann Arbor High School (Ann Arbor, Michigan), where he lettered in football, basketball, baseball and swimming. As a triple threat back for the Titans, Nott twice led the nation in passing, and most of his school passing records stood for 30 years. He held several Detroit career passing records, including: attempts (346), completions (143) and yards (2,741). Over 261 punts, he averaged 35.4 yards per kick—both school marks. Detroit went 15–3 in the 1932 and 1933 seasons. In September 1932, Dorais said that Nott "is farther advanced right now than Brazil was in his first year on the varsity squad [and] that is no idle boast."[8]

The 1932 Titans finished 8–2, the second-highest win total of Dorais' tenure at Detroit, second to the undefeated 1928 team's 9–0 mark. The 1932 team won their first two games, but the offense sputtered, especially the passing attack. It was a trend that lasted throughout the season. Detroit set a school mark for fewest total yards in a season with 2,073. As a result, Nott set a high with 94 punts on the season. Dorais finally decided to alter his game plan after an embarrassing 9–7 loss at Holy Cross (Worcester, Massachusetts), when the Titans set school records for futility. Detroit threw just one pass (which was incomplete) for 0 yards. Moving forward, much of the offense filtered through Nott. A strong defense allowed a meager 59 points (5.9 per game) for the season, and Nott's punting ability fortified the Titans' success moving forward.

After three quality wins at home over West Virginia (26–13), Georgetown (13–0) and Marquette (7–0), Dorais and his Titans traveled to Philadelphia to play Villanova. Of late, there had been polls released that gave Wildcats coach Harry Stuhldreher the nod as the greatest Notre Dame quarterback. Dorais brushed off the question when asked, but it quietly gave him further motivation for the game. The night before, Dorais and Stuhldreher met for dinner. Dorais applauded Villanova's new hand-waving offensive formation that had been so successful. The Villanova coach confided that it was all distraction, and you can tell where a player is going by watching their feet. That was all Dorais needed to hear. Prior to the game the next day, he gave a rare pre-game speech. "There's one thing I want you to remember. You are the underdogs today," he said to his players huddled around him in the locker room. "They say you'll lose by two touchdowns. So, when the opening whistle blows I want you to feel that you are two touchdowns behind, and you can't win unless you score three. Go out there and get those two back just as soon as possible. Then you can make a game of it."[9] When the Detroit offense came to the line the next day, they used a hand-waving formation—distracting the Villanova defense. Nott completed seven of his first eight passes—two of them touchdowns—on the way to a 28–12 Titans victory.

Stuhldreher was in tears after the game. Dorais consoled him and passed along some advice that changed the young coach's game plan. "Harry, you'll find out the longer you stick in the coaching game that the traditional defense used against passes at Notre Dame is weak," said Dorais. "You'll have to get out of the box defense, spread your backs a little more. That's what went wrong this afternoon. We went right down the middle of the box."[10]

Since Rockne's death and the release of *The Forward Pass and Its Defense*, Dorais was increasing his transparency regarding his football methodologies. Rather than hoard information, he was more than happy to dispense it. He was not opposed to dissecting offenses that were growing dated—including Rockne's Box. Before heading back to Detroit, he was approached by Tom Conley, captain of the 1930 Notre Dame National Championship team, who was now coaching at LaSalle University in Philadelphia. Conley spoke to Dorais in the club car and expressed his frustration with trying to run the offense he did at Notre Dame.

"Tom," Dorais replied. "If you're going to stick in the coaching game, you'll have to change that. It's one of the weak points in our system and you'll find the other fellows making you look silly if you stick to it."[11]

Dorais' influence was showing. Former players were spreading what Jack Cummings of the *Varsity News* called the "Dorais System."[12] Dorais had distanced himself even further from the aging Notre Dame system, providing flexibility to suit the current team's talents. Detroit area high schools, particularly the Catholic High School League (13 of 37 schools), were littered with his blueprint, and in the 1930s, schools in Canada were, too. "Let's call it unorthodox," Dorais said of his system. "It's built on the surprise attack, the method of calling plays the opposition isn't expecting."[13] Defensively, he ran a six-man line and two-two-one secondary, opposed to Notre Dame's seven-man line and two-two defense.

The Titans stumbled in their next game in East Lansing against Michigan State. Detroit's starting quarterback Clifford Marsh was absent, called to the bedside of his sick mother. His replacement, Earl "Midget" McCracken, who usually played halfback, was injured in the first quarter. That left Nott to try to run the offense by himself. Hampered by numerous dropped passes, the Titans mustered a paltry 85 yards, completing just eight of 26 passes. A 35-yard scamper by State's Bernard McNutt in the first quarter held up, giving the Spartans a 7–0 win—the first in six tries against Dorais' team. Detroit finished strong with a pair of victories. The first was a 14–6 win over Oregon State at home, the difference being a 55-yard touchdown pass from Nott to Howard Young at the end of the first half. In the season finale, the Titans went on the road to New Orleans to play Loyola. Detroit trailed 12–7 in the fourth quarter, but Nott threw two of his three touchdowns to overtake the Wolfpack for the 21–12 win. The game was Clark Shaughnessy's last as head coach of Loyola, before moving on to the University of Chicago to replace Alonzo Stagg. It was also the last time the two schools played. Between 1928 and 1932, Dorais' Titans beat Shaughnessy's Wolfpack in four of the five games played.

When Dorais released the Titans' 1933 schedule in late January, the Alumni Association voiced their disappointment. Not only was the slate too moderate for their liking, but there were two fewer games, the shortest schedule since a seven-game docket in 1916. Alumni pressed Dorais to find top-notch competition, but he continued to have difficulty. To complicate matters, there were only two road games, which had been popular amongst alumni. There were also grumblings from other athletic programs at the University about his strong focus—as athletic director and head football coach—on the football team. Dorais moved a number of duties to Boeringer and then looked to add both an indoor and intramural baseball league, as well as boxing (all of which wouldn't come to fruition until the late 1930s and early 1940s). He hired Mike Peters, a former player Dorais' son Tom described as a "devoted, loyal secretary to my Dad," who did "all the grunt work in the office."[14]

Dorais knew that the only thing that attracted top-notch football programs was big crowds. After the schedule was complete, Dorais focused his attention on ticket sales for the coming year. He began an incentive-laden initiative—including four new automobiles as giveaways—that he hoped would increase student participation at games. For the first time, partial payments were also being taken. Dorais and the Athletic Department hoped to sell 100,000 tickets to make the people of Detroit "U. of D. conscious."[15]

Over the years, Dorais forged close relationships with several writers from Detroit newspapers. One of them was W.W. "Eddie" Edgar, who came from the *Allentown Record* (Allentown, PA) to the *Detroit Free Press* in 1924, the year before Dorais arrived in Detroit. The coach was a frequent subject in Edgar's column, "The Second Guess." These pieces often came from the time Dorais spent surrounded by sportswriters in his office with a view of the football field. By now, Dorais received frequent overtures from different schools, but Edgar recalled one unnamed school that had Dorais agonizing during this off-season (likely Michigan State).

"Why don't you take it, Gus," Edgar and the others implored. "You've had a hard time here, what with a shortage of material and inability to obtain a schedule to your liking. You've been hiding your light under a basket and it's about time you were stepping out to take your place with the leading coaches of the country."

Dorais listened quietly, before turning his back to the group and reaching for the phone. He called the telegraph company. His dictation was curt: "Not at all interested. Have decided to stay here."

Dorais swiveled back around to face the surprised group, with a small smile on his face. "Now, I suppose you wonder why I've done that," he asked rhetorically.

"I'll tell you why I did that," he continued without response. "I could go to that school and possibly build up a winning team. It surely is a great spot for a coach. But it's not for me. I still have a job to do here.

"When I came here it was with the understanding that I would build up University of Detroit's athletic department. That hasn't been accomplished yet and I intend to stay until I have finished the job."[16]

Not everyone was happy that Dorais was sticking around. Some University of Detroit faculty were tired of Dorais and what they viewed as press-hungry behavior. Exasperating the situation was that Dorais' salary ($10,000 a year) dwarfed professors of equal rank in other departments. Compounding the disdain for Dorais was that many of the lay faculty members had waived a portion of their 1933 salary. A vitriolic letter from several professors to Dorais ended with: "Why the hell didn't you move to other schools offering a higher salary than U. of D.?"[17]

This contempt for coaches wasn't isolated to Dorais and Detroit. A few years prior, Westbrook Pegler of the *Chicago Daily Tribune* wrote about the ongoing scorn for football coaches and the sport in general, by professors who, beyond salary discrepancies, thought "the physical side of education in the United States has been exaggerated at the expense of the intellectual."[18]

Dorais' salary was one of four points highlighted in April when the North Central Association of Colleges dropped and then reinstated the University of Detroit's athletic department as a warning that changes needed to be made. The other violations were: lack of a gymnasium, failing to have physical examinations, and athletes not paying the same tuition as non-athletes. Dorais released a statement addressing each accusation, including his salary, to which he said he "had opportunities to move to several other schools at a higher salary, and these institutions are not accused of 'bad athletic conditions.'"[19]

Dorais was always upbeat, but the stress of his job was visible. He had noticeably aged since moving to Detroit. He drank Four Roses Whiskey, chain-smoked Camels and snacked on black licorice throughout the day. When he came home, Dorais often went downstairs and cooked a steak on an iron grill without butter or lard. The smoke wafted upstairs, much to the annoyance of Vi. Still, Dorais remained active. He was almost a scratch golfer and was in a poker club. He and Vi often found time to take to the dance floor. In recent years, Dorais implemented and became involved in the campus-wide handball craze, winning a University Championship when he was in his early 50s. Few students or faculty could keep up with him. He was also an expert fly fisherman. Golfing became a summer pursuit, and he won several tournaments around Michigan. He continued to write, and in 1933 contributed a weekly column to *The Varsity News*, analyzing the previous game and the Titans' upcoming opponent. He also made predictions for notable games around the country. On Sundays, the Dorais' opened their home for Gus' famous pancake breakfast.

Dorais had many stories of his back-country adventures. His son, Tom, recalled one of his father's favorites:

> Once when Gus was out west camping, he went fishing by himself. He had caught several fish and was on a trail heading back to camp. As he rounded a corner he came face to face with a bear. In a panic he dropped the fish and ran back the way he had come. He found a tree to climb up and stayed there for a good half hour. After he came down from the tree he carefully went back up the trail to find his fish still sitting where he had dropped them. Apparently the bear was as startled as Gus and fled the scene as well.[20]

After nearly two decades of coaching, it was a given that football was a priority within the Dorais family. Vi rarely missed a game and was one

The Dorais family owned a home on Tecon Lake in Michigan. Gus was an avid fly fisherman. Gus and Vi always spent summers away from football (Dorais family photo collection).

of her husband's biggest supporters. The boys were often on the bench for home games and the occasional road contest. Gus considered their presence a good luck charm. Dorais' duties as athletic director caused his family to make numerous sacrifices. Gus missed two of his children's births: Bill in 1922, when he took Gonzaga to San Diego to play West Virginia, and Joan in October 1928, when the Titans were playing in Tulsa. Sam Greene of the *Detroit News* encapsulated the demands laid on Dorais: "In the fall he stays on the field almost every afternoon until dusk after which he retires to a private room to sketch new plays. He takes trips with the team that keep him on the road for three or four days at a stretch and when he returns there are alumni gatherings, athletic board meetings and accumulated correspondence to demand his attention. It is a great job for a man capable of working a 24-hour shift."[21]

Spring practice began on March 17, St. Patrick's Day. Shortly thereafter, Dorais began implementing a new scheme, which came to be known as the "muddle huddle." He worked on it all spring and invited his coach at Notre Dame, Jesse Harper, to provide feedback. It went as follows:

> The right tackle stands immediately to the left of the center, the right guard stands to his left and next to the left end. The left tackle stands to the right of the center and the left guard to his right. Then when the backfield shifts, the tackle and guard on the left of the center walk to their proper positions on the right side of the line and the tackle and guard on the right of the center go to their regular positions on the left.
>
> The shift works as a screen for the backfield and tends to confuse the opponents as to the time and direction of the play.[22]

A week before the first game of the 1933 season, Dorais invited fans to a public football clinic—likely the first of its kind. "I have come to the conclusion that we coaches take too much for granted," Dorais said of the clinic's creation, "and judging from the many queries I am asked to answer it is time to help the public understand just what is going on during a game."[23] For over three hours, Dorais, explained to a packed Dinan Field the basics of football, via a spotty public address system. With the help of Boeringer, Dorais ran his players through different formation and plays as visual aids.

For the second year in a row, the Titans' offense set records for futility: fewest team rushing yards, 1,073, and first downs, 66. That didn't seem to hinder the pass-heavy offense, employing the single wing attack guided by senior quarterback and captain, Clifford Marsh. He called the signals, but true to the single wing, either the tailback or fullback—in this case, often Nott from his fullback position—received the snap in a shotgun style and either passed or ran. A daring passing game made the Titans' offense go in 1933, as Nott led the nation and set a school standard with 1,092 yards. He completed 51 of 116 passes at an average of 21 yards per completion, with eight touchdown passes.

Detroit opened with a pair of shutout wins against in-state schools: Michigan State Normal, 31–0, and Western State Teachers College, 26–

0. A 14–0 win over Washington and Jefferson followed. In the game, end Norb Reisterer emerged as a favorite target for Nott with a school record 103 receiving yards, 67 of them coming on a touchdown reception. Reisterer, a Kalamazoo native, would set school highs for a season with 29 catches for 367 yards. For years, he held the career receptions and yardage record.

On October 20, the Titans suffered their only loss of the season in Pittsburgh at a poorly lit Forbes Field against Elmer Layden-coached Duquesne University. The Dukes held Nott's passing game in check for much of the evening, and Duquesne halfback, Arthur Strutt scored on runs of 51 and 1 yards in the 14–0 shutout. The Dukes went on to win the Festival of Palms Bowl, a precursor to the Orange Bowl, finishing the season 10–1. Detroit returned to Dinan Field, defeating Marquette, 22–6, before entertaining the undefeated Holy Cross Crusaders for Homecoming and Dad's Day.

Coached by Notre Dame alum, Eddie Anderson, the Crusaders were coming off wins against Harvard and Brown and boasted one of the top lines in the East. Confidence was high in the Holy Cross locker room, where telegrams of encouragement were pinned to the wall. Supposedly the week before, Crusaders scout (and future Holy Cross head coach) Joe Sheeketski came into the Titans' locker room following the Marquette win and predicted that the Crusaders would pound Detroit by at least four touchdowns. In the Titans' pregame locker room, tensions were high. Since the Duquesne loss, Detroit had been secretly practicing an old play— receive the kickoff and immediately kick it back, trying to pin the kicking team by their own goal line. Dorais calmed his team, telling them that he would take the blame if the plan didn't work out.

The Titans placed four punters back for the opening kickoff. Detroit's Vincent Kadi received the kick on the 5-yard line, ran ten yards and then punted the ball nearly the entire length of the field, where it was downed on the Holy Cross 3-yard line. The play seemed to knock the Crusaders off of their game plan. When they tried to punt after three unsuccessful plays, the punter sliced the ball, leaving the Titans in easy scoring position. Detroit played inspired ball, with Nott throwing for a school record 283 yards, including a pair of touchdowns, and running for another on a wide reverse.[24] Kadi finished the scoring with an 80-yard run through nearly the entire Holy Cross defense. The Titans' 24–0 victory was one of Dorais' favorites.

Dorais and Detroit took the momentum of the Holy Cross win, shutting out Catholic University in Washington, D.C., 26–0, thanks to a pair of touchdown passes by Nott, who also returned an interception 55 yards for a touchdown. After the game, the Flying Cardinals' head coach, Dutch Bergman, was in awe of the halfback. "I thought possibly Detroit would beat us by two touchdowns at the most," said the former Notre Dame half-back, "but we never expected to see anything like Nott threw at us. He is a marvel and just spelled the difference between what should have been a close game and a complete rout."[25]

In the season finale, at home, the Titans shut out Michigan State, 14–0, finishing the season 7–1. The win marked another undefeated season at Dinan Field and 18 straight wins at home dating back to the second game of the 1931 season. The Titans allowed just 20 points for the eight-game 1933 season. Nott, who would be moved to fullback, and end Bill Storrie were named co-captains for the 1934 season at the annual football awards banquet. The end-of-year celebration was always bittersweet for Dorais. In reflecting on the the trials and tribulations of the season, he would often grow emotional when addressing the seniors, whom he would no longer be coaching.

During another successful season, Dorais worked behind the scenes to try to get Detroit into a conference. In late November, a proposal was made public to form the Great Lakes Conference, to include Carnegie Tech, Detroit, Marquette, Michigan State, Washington & Jefferson, and West Virginia. Despite the efforts, nothing materialized. Over the next few years, Dorais made it his mission to create a Catholic League, with such schools as Catholic University, Boston College, Villanova, Creighton, Xavier, Marquette, St. Louis, Fordham, Manhattan, Georgetown and Duquesne. "I don't think any conference would be able to show more strong football teams than a league of the dozen best Catholic schools of the country," said Dorais.[26] That idea, much to his disappointment, never came to fruition.

In early December, Dorais was named as the leading candidate to replace Hunk Anderson at Notre Dame. "Gus was called down to Notre Dame to discuss the coaching position, but I didn't want him to take it," recalled his wife, Vi, who was due any day with the couple's fifth child. "When the train stopped in Jackson, Michigan, Gus phoned me. I again pleaded with him not to take the position."[27]

The offer may have been just a public relations move by Notre Dame to appease one of the largest alumni populations in Detroit that lobbied for Dorais to take over as both head coach and athletic director. University President Charles O'Donnell and Vice President Father John O'Hara liked the dual role, but, according to author Murray Sperber, the pair felt that

Dorais was "too old and lacking the personality necessary for the N.D. job."[28]

Duquesne's Elmer Layden was hired to replace Anderson and Harper as athletic director. A few days later, on December 12, 1933, Gus and Vi welcomed their fifth child, the couple's third son, David. Contract talks went on for a few months as Dorais sent out telegrams to potential opponents. He attended the coaches conference in Chicago and made frequent appearances on WXYZ radio's "Sportslog," sponsored by the *Detroit Free Press.*

Despite continued jealousy and dissension for Dorais on Detroit's campus, other universities courted him for the 1934 season, including the University of Texas, Auburn, Northwestern, and Ohio State. The most aggressive was Harry Heneage, athletic director at Dartmouth, who came to Detroit and met with Dorais for several hours. Of 106 candidates, Dorais was a finalist. He was bypassed for Earl Blaik, an assistant from Army, whose Dartmouth team would achieve a 22-game win streak from 1934–1937.

In early February 1934, Dorais signed a three-year, $10,000 per year contract extension. He retained his varsity staff of Boeringer, Brazil, Maloney and Butler. Dorais also hired former quarterback Ed Barbour to serve as the main scout, traveling to upcoming opponents, while the Titans were playing their games. Barbour also served as an assistant on the freshman team under another former Titan, Bill Storen, before taking over the head caching duties in 1934. Between 1931 and 1942, the freshman team was undefeated.

Shortly thereafter, Dorais found himself at odds with his alma mater about Detroit using a black player when the two schools met in basketball. The player in question, sophomore Laurence Bleach, had already played several games without incident, and Dorais himself had told Bleach upon admittance to school that he would be eligible to play in all games. Irish coach George Keogan allowed Bleach to play, but loudly protested throughout Notre Dame's 36–17 victory. In correspondence following the game, Dorais was deliberate in his words as to not offend his alma mater, but regarding the "gentleman's agreement" that Notre Dame had referenced about not playing "colored" ball players, he wasn't in concurrence.

In the spring, the football program suffered a major blow when the University of Detroit was expelled from the North Central Association of Colleges and Secondary Schools due to "academic administration, academic standards, and athletic conditions."[29] This was not a warning like the year before. If the expulsion lasted beyond the 1934 season, Dorais would be even more hamstrung when it came to scheduling, as members of the Association were not supposed to play non-members. It also would toughen Dorais' chances of attracting top-notch competition.

Dorais didn't take the allegations against the school lightly, challenging Dr. George A. Works of the North Central Association. Dorais stated, "The athletic situation at the University of Detroit is absolutely clean and I challenge comparison in this regard with any school in the country."[30] He pointed to the recent expulsion of two members of the football team who didn't have honor points equal to the number of hours they had taken. Dorais claimed that "This is an internal rule of the university and not a standard required by either the North Central association of the Big Ten."[31] After fixing the issues, the University was reinstated in mid–April 1935.

Dorais had to contend with the re-entry of professional football into Detroit's sports landscape. George A. "Dick" Richards, owner of WJR radio, led a group of investors who purchased the Portsmouth Spartans (Portsmouth, Ohio) for $7,952.08, moved the franchise to Detroit, and named them "Lions." According to Arch Ward, Dorais "came close" to signing an offer to coach the Lions but declined, and the job was given to Potsy Clark.[32] Though the arrival added competition for a fan base, Dorais seemed unfazed. He saw a professional team as another way for his team to get better. An agreement was made with Clark to scrimmage during the week when both teams were scheduled to play at home. Together they shared Dinan Field from 1934–1937 and 1940, and that first fall saw the establishment of the Lions' annual home Thanksgiving Day game, won by the Chicago Bears, 19–16. Over the years, several Titans players were signed by Detroit, and Dorais would serve as one of the team's main scouts, before finally taking over head coaching duites in 1943.

The summer of 1934 marked the first College Football All-Star Game, devised by Dorais' good friend, Arch Ward, now at the *Chicago Tribune*. Ward had found success with the Major League Baseball All-Star Game in Chicago in 1933 as part of city's centennial celebration and the 1933 Chicago World's Fair. All proceeds went to disabled and needy major league players. Ward looked to replicate the success with a football game. The 1934 Chicago Charities College All-Star Game was to be played on August 31 at Soldier Field between the Chicago Bears and a team comprised of college All-Stars. Proceeds from the game benefited Chicago-area charities. A poll was held in July and early August to see who would coach the All-Stars. Dorais finished 17th in the vote, with a total of 69,784 points, spread out over a first- (8,762), second- (14,557) or third-place (14,384) votes. Purdue's Noble Kizer was the winner with 261,485 points.

With the 1934 season approaching, Dorais took over syndicate writing duties for the *Associated Press* from Dr. C.W. Spears, head coach of Wisconsin. Spears stepped down from scribe duties after his Badgers struggled in 1933 (2–5–1, winless in the Big Ten, 0–5–1). Dorais continued to stress the importance of tradition. He looked to alumni, specifically former letter winners, to help boost attendance at games. Dorais formed a "D" club to have a more organized setting for these former letter winners to convene. The group was given several perks, including a lifetime pass for games played at Dinan Field. He also put on his second annual Grid clinic, explaining the intricacies of the game to over 17,000 attendees. With a heightened alumni presences, Dorais knew that he had to win or the blame would fall squarely on him. "If the coaching staff does its part, this could be one of Detroit's best teams in history," he said in the preseason.[33]

Misfortune struck the Titans in late August. Days before camp was to begin, halfback Vincent Kadi was killed in a horse riding accident. The death of the popular player, who was the surprise star of the Holly Cross game in 1933, dampened the 1934 season. Still, Detroit got off to their usual fast start. In the opener, a 38–0 shutout of Central State, Dorais played his starters in the first and third quarters, but that still wasn't enough to keep his team healthy. In the third quarter, Nott, who had played in every game the last two seasons, tore tendons in his right foot. On crutches the following week, he suited up and played sparingly to keep his streak alive in a 25–7 win over Western State, and he did the same in a 12–0 victory over Washington & Jefferson College. When it came out later in the year that the private school in Washington, Pennsylvania had spent in excess of $40,000 in subsidization to football players, Dorais quipped: "They got cheated. We don't pay players at of U. of D. and we beat W&J this fall, 12–0."[34] Always the innovator, Dorais addressed his players' hydration with pineapple juice, rather than water. He felt that it "takes less of the pineapple juice than of water to position a player's mouth and appease his thirst."[35]

Detroit squandered numerous chances near the goal line in a disappointing 0–0 tie in Philadelphia against Villanova. The Titans then lost consecutive games at Dinan Field for the first time since 1930. The 20–6 loss to Duquesne snapped Detroit's home winning streak at 21. In the game, Nott, still nursing his sore foot, set a school record for pass attempts in a game with 32. The next weekend, the Titans fell, 19–6, to Oklahoma A&M. A 7–6 loss to Michigan State in Ann Arbor followed, handing Dorais his first three-game losing streak as a coach since his Dubuque

College team dropped four straight in 1917. Detroit rebounded and won the last two games of the season: a 13–6 victory over Marquette in single-digit temperatures in Milwaukee, and a 6–0 shutout of Dorais' former Gonzaga rival, Washington State, at Dinan Field. The Titans finished a disappointing 5–3–1.

Nott's injury was the biggest setback of the season. In a campaign that was supposed to be a record-setting season for the big back, the only school record he set was for punts with a 39.4 yard average on 40 kicks. His 35.4 yard average per kick over 261 punts are a school record. He was still thought highly enough of to play in the 1935 East-West Shrine Game in San Francisco and a pair of exhibition games in Honolulu.

It was those post-season games that caused a controversy and almost cost Nott his professional eligibility for the 1935 season. He missed classes and fell behind in his studies. Some faculty threatened to not pass him, which would keep him from graduating and, in turn, disallow NFL teams from pursuing him (there was a rule in place that stated that either a player or his class graduate before joining a team). Nott was barred from class, but the situation ended up not hurting him. In February, he signed a contract with the Lions, but his professional career was short-lived. He played one season, 1935, splitting time with the Lions for the first five games and the Boston Redskins for the final four. He rushed for a total of 101 yards and passed for 204.

Following the Titans' Marquette game on November 24, Dorais traveled back home to Chippewa Falls, Wisconsin, for a two-day celebration of the silver anniversary of the 1909 high school state championship. Along with former teammates, their wives and 50 others, Dorais reminisced for hours at the Elks Club atop downtown's Hotel Northern. The event was a much-needed reprieve from the recent trials of the Titans' season. He was the speaker of the evening, comparing the prep win to his collegiate victory over Army in 1913 and how the high school triumph was the bigger thrill. According to the *Chippewa Herald-Telegram*, Dorais stated, "He had made no friendships in his life since that he felt were as intimate and as genuine as those of 25 years ago."[36] He was so proud of the event that he made sure that the story of the banquet and reunion would be broadcast over WJR, Detroit.

Shortly after the season at the football testimonial dinner, John Sloan, president of the Alumni Association, stepped forward to try to mend the continually growing divide between Dorais and alumni, whom he had referred to as "apathetic," resulting in a slew of spiteful letters and telegrams to his office in the days leading up to the dinner.[37] Like staff members, the alumni had grown tired of perceived spotlight grabbing and name-dropping of Rockne. Sloan had a stern message for alumni: "Gus Dorais is the greatest football genius in the United States and deserves our undivided support."[38]

The Dorais-friendly Detroit press had been surprisingly harsh on him, too, particularly towards the end of the season. They referred to it as not only the worst year of his tenure, but of the whole program, including a 1897 team that lost to three high schools and a 1915 squad that beat only a forgiving alumni team. The situation worsened when Michigan State declined Dorais' request to play in 1935—the first time since 1926. A despondent Dorais called the situation "deeply regrettable.[39] It was a tough off-season for Dorais, but in a few years he was vindicated on a national stage.

During spring drills in 1935, it was evident that a new movement was emerging that could have major effects on the game. "We are headed for a new trend, a trend that will feature lateral passes and open the game up much further than it ever has been before." Though it would affect offensive game plans, Dorais felt the largest impact in other facets of the game, including "those thrown on punt returns, pass interceptions and kick-offs."[40]

Detroit was fortunate to have team captain Kinsey Jones at quarterback, who Dorais called "the best quarterback I ever had out here."[41] Jones would gain honorable mention on Grantland Rice's All-American team for his efforts in 1935. In the Titans' backfield, hard-running sophomore Andy Farkas filled the void left by Nott. Farkas took over as a starter in midseason and began a storied collegiate career. He was sometimes chided for being just an adequate passer and punter, but there were few who were tougher to bring down than the thick 190-pounder. On defense he was a standout from his safety position. As a prep player, he won all-state honors in two states: as a junior, he was an all-state halfback at Waite High School in Toldeo, Ohio. During his senior he was an all-state back for University of Detroit High School. He struggled with a lingering foot issue and then a knee injury during the 1935 season, but still took over starting duties. He led the Titans in scoring his junior (66) and senior (97) seasons, the latter good enough for third in the nation. He made a number of All-American teams after his senior season and played in the East-West Game in San Francisco. He played seven seasons for the Washington Redskins, where he was an All-Pro halfback in 1939. He missed the entire 1940 season due to a knee injury suffered in training camp and was never the same player thereafter. He finished his career with the Dorais-led Detroit Lions in 1945.

For the third year in a row, the Titans opened with three consecutive wins—all shutouts—at Dinan Field, now equipped with a scoreboard with a giant game clock that gave time down to the second (provided by the Chevrolet Motor Car Company at the direction of their Vice President of Sales, Hugh Dean, a Notre Dame alumnus and good friend of Dorais). Detroit suffered their first loss of the year on October 19, a 13–7 heart-breaker to a tough Catholic University team. With just a few minutes to play, the Flying Cardinals got the ball on their own 40-yard line, trailing 7–6. What transpired was called one of the "wildest finishes ever staged in the stadium on Six Mile Road," by W.W. Edgar of the *Detroit Free Press*.[42] In the waning seconds, Bill Adamaitis, Catholic's star halfback connected with George Mulligan, who hauled the ball in on the 12-yard line and headed for the end zone. The Titans' Dick Lutz was bringing the tall end to the ground when Mulligan lateraled the ball to the other end, Herman Schmarr, who crossed into the end zone for the winning touchdown. Dutch Bergman's Cardinals went on to a 7–1 record and a 20–19 win over Mississippi in the Orange Bowl.

Dorais' squad had little time to wallow in the loss. Up next was unde-feated and unscored upon Villanova. In the first occurrence of its kind, not only for the university, but for college football as a whole, the Titans and Wildcats played a home-and-home series. The teams split the games, with the home teams emerging victorious. The loss, another frustrating 13–7 setback, once again came in the final minutes on a long pass to a lanky receiver. In a moment of exasperation, Dorais confided in E.E. Edgar of the *Detroit Free Press* about the unpredictability of his job. "You work all year and then have to depend on luck after the opening whistle blows to learn whether you are a success or a failure," he said.[43]

Detroit erased the memory of the tough Villanova loss with a 53–0 Homecoming whitewashing of Bucknell University in the Titans' final con-test of the season at Dinan Field. In the game, Lutz—a shifty halfback and the team's leading scorer in 1934—caught a 98-yard TD pass from quar-terback Jack Wieczorek—the longest in school history. The play was a good chunk of the Titans' record for total yardage in one game—585. Detroit finished the season with two road games. Following a two-week layoff, Detroit suffered another tough loss in Pittsburgh, falling to Duquesne, 13–6, at Forbes Field. Once again, the Titans gave up a late fourth quarter touchdown pass. It was the third consecutive loss to the Dukes, the first time that Detroit had lost three straight to an opponent since falling to Army in 1925, 1926 and 1927.

The season finale took place in Lubbock, Texas, on November 28,

Thanksgiving Day. The Titans emerged victorious, 12–6, over Texas Tech to finish 6–3. Several years later, Dorais recalled the memorable defensive effort at the end of the game that culminated with Farkas intercepting a Red Raiders pass. "That was the greatest goal line stand I ever saw. They had the ball on our three-yard line. Because of penalties, they got seven plays for a touchdown but our boys held them," said Dorais.[44]

Dorais' decade of leading the University of Detroit football team to a consistent and at times dominant style of play was beginning to be lost in the success of the city of Detroit's athletic scene as a whole. Expectations intensified as other sports teams and athletes from Detroit reached the pinnacle of their respective sports in 1935. These successes gave Detroit the label "City of Champions." In September, Joe Louis defeated Max Baer at Yankee Stadium, knocking down the former heavyweight champion for the first time in his career. The Tigers won the World Series in six games over the Chicago Cubs, and the Detroit Red Wings took the Stanley Cup in April 1936. On December 15, 1935, Dorais was among the 15,000 onlookers at Dinan Field to see the Detroit Lions win the NFL Championship game over the New York Giants, 26–7.

At the end of December 1935, Dorais was at the National Collegiate Athletic Association meeting in New York. Now serving as the chairman of the public relations committee, he touched on a number of topics in his annual report. Last year, he had said that drinking at games and betting on games was becoming a serious problem. Though happy to say that the latter seemed to have decreased, Dorais felt there was still much work to be done. He then turned his focus to greater cooperation between coaches and the press. He called on his fellow coaches to be truthful about their players' weights and jersey numbers. Though he knew that much of it was to mislead scouts, he felt that any coach using this methodology was "only fooling himself."[45] A final point put forth by Dorais for contemplation was whether the growth of major college bowl games was a "healthy appendage" of the game or a "cancerous growth."[46] In 1930, the sole major bowl game was the Rose Bowl. In 1935 alone, the Sugar Bowl, Orange Bowl and Sun Bowl were added. The Cotton Bowl came along in 1937.

By the 1930s, college football moved from a game of regional to national appeal. Over the next few years, more concrete innovations were implemented for greater recognition of teams and players. In 1935, the Downtown Athletic Club in Manhattan awarded the Downtown Athletic Club Trophy to the country's top college football player, Jay Berwanger, a halfback for the University of Chicago. The following year it became the Heisman Trophy, after the Club's Athletic Director, John Heisman, died of pneumonia on October 3, 1936. Berwanger was the first player picked in the first-ever NFL draft on February 8, 1936, chosen by the host city's Philadelphia Eagles.

For years there was never a clear-cut way to rank college teams. In 1926, University of Illinois economics professor Frank G. Dickinson came up with Dickinson System to rank teams in the Big Nine. Impressed by the system, Jack Rissman, a Chicago clothing manufacturer and rabid football fan, convinced Dickinson to rank the entire nation's teams and award the Rissman Trophy. This system lasted from 1926 to 1940. In 1934, the *Associated Press* (AP) College Football Poll ran for the first time. The following year, Alan J. Gould, creator of the AP All-American team, decided on a controversial three-way tie for national champion between Minnesota, Princeton and Southern Methodist. His colleagues suggested that he create a poll of sports editors, and in 1936 the modern-day AP Poll was born, ranking the top 20 teams.

In April 1936, it seemed there were daily discussions about Dorais leaving for Villanova. The Pennsylvania university was seeking a head coach after Harry Stuhldreher left for the University of Wisconsin to take over as athletic director and head football coach. Of the hearsay, Dorais explained his stance: "Of course I'm interested in any job better than the one I have, but I'm a little doubtful that Villanova can offer me a better job. We'll know soon."[47] At that same time, Dorais saved the university money by directing a group of about 50 players in resodding the field. He also made plans to lead a 33-day tour to the Berlin Olympics, leaving July 23 on the *Britannic* and returning August 15 aboard the *Laconia*.[48] There are no records of the trip taking place.

Even with Farkas at the top of his game, the senior-heavy Titans started the 1936 season with mixed results. The situation got worse when the team's top passer, halfback Jimmy Piper, broke his wrist against Manhattan. Detroit, playing a 10-game schedule for the first time since 1932, held a 3–2 record and were set to host Duquesne on October 30. The Titans hadn't beaten the Dukes in their three meetings. The game had Dorais abnormally tense. "It seems the longer I'm in this coaching business the more nervous I am before a game—especially a game like this," he told W.W. Edgar. "You've taught the boys all you can and you begin to wonder if you've equipped them well enough to withstand the charge of a powerful rival."[49]

Duquesne was coached by first-year coach Clipper Smith, a Notre Dame alum and the man who succeeded Dorais at Gonzaga. The Dukes had been ranked 11th in the initial AP Poll on October 19, before being dropped from the poll following a tough 2–0 loss at home against West

Virginia Wesleyan. The Titans handed Duquesne their second straight—and final loss—of the 1936 season that ended in a 13–12 win over Mississippi State in the Orange Bowl (the Dukes were given the bid over Dorais' squad). Detroit scored on two passes from Ed Palumbo to a heavily bandaged Farkas from 50 and 28 yards. The final score was 14–7, Titans. Following the game, Dorais' players gave him what the *Detroit News* called "the most spontaneous outburst any college team ever gave a coach." When he entered the locker room spent from the stress of the game, "players jumped up on benches and yelled their lungs out for their coach." Embarrassed, Dorais responded, "Well, I'm nothing to cheer about—you oughta be cheering your selves, you did it."[50]

The Titans won three of their last four to finish 7–3. The loss, a 14–13 upset by North Dakota, kept Detroit from gaining a berth in the Bacardi Bowl in Havana, Cuba, on New Year's Day. The Sioux were led by sophomore running back Fritz Pollard, Jr., who had won a bronze medal in the 110 meter hurdles at the Olympics a few months earlier. Pollard, Jr., an African-American, was the son of Fritz Pollard, Sr., a highly regarded individual in football circles. A halfback at Brown, he was the first black player selected on Walter Camp's All-American Team and was one of the first players of color in the NFL and the league's first black coach (Akron Pros). Pollard, Jr., would gain some recognition over the next few years, including being named to Collier's Little All-American team in 1938, but couldn't help North Dakota come close to duplicating their success against the Titans, being defeated soundly in 1937 and 1938.

Late in 1936, Michigan coach Harry Kipke, new president of the Foot Ball Coaches Association, put together a committee to look into the gambling epidemic that was affecting the collegiate football game. Professional bookmakers infiltrated the college game in the 1930s with pool or parlay cards, which had been used in baseball for decades. For 25 cents, bettors picked at least five wins from the bookies' list of nine competitive national games. By 1941, parlay cards became a $5 million a year business.

The Kipke-appointed committee leaned heavily on the suggestions of a report from Dorais, serving as the head of the public relations committee for the National Collegiate Athletic Association. He recommended studying the "entire situation."[51] During his presentation, he said:

> We who are responsible for the integrity and the moral well-being of football are confronted with a serious menace. The increase in gambling on our games in the last year are unbelievable. Professional gamblers have interested themselves in a big way. I have been informed more money was wagered last season on football than on horse racing.

When professional big-time gamblers interest themselves in the results of our games, I do not need to tell men what might happen. Foot ball always has been played on the square and the responsibility rests on us to see that it continues to be played that way.

We know that gamblers now send these men around to various colleges to get inside information on team preparations, player injuries, etc., so that bets may be made or odds fixed with the latest facts in hand. This means we, as coaches, must guard against any possible attempt to "fix" games for the benefit of gambling elements.[52]

Dorais also took time to comment on the proposal to make jersey numbers mandatory: "We know that there is a distinct advantage in favor of the coach who does not use front numbers for the reason that the work of scouts is made less effective, also the players who have studied the opposing team's numbers are at a loss when no numbers are visible."[53]

The esteem in which Dorais was held by his colleagues was evident. That only grew in the coming months.

CHAPTER 9

A Sage Coach, 1937–1942

For all the bickering that took place between Dorais and University of Detroit alumni, the latter stepped forward with a plan to get bigger crowds and better opponents to Dinan Field. In the summer of 1937, they started a movement to get Dorais elected coach for the College Football All-Star Game against Curley Lambeau's NFL champion Green Bay Packers, September 1 at Chicago's Soldier Field. First, a group had to convince Dorais to put his name up for consideration. He relented, but messaged from the family's summer home on Otsego Lake that he would take no part in the campaign. An election committee was already in place and put out a statement of their purpose. "Ever since these All-Star games have been played," said co-campaign managers Paul Sanderson and Frank Potts in a press release, "we've sat back and watched some other coach chosen for the job and later hailed as the outstanding coach of the country. And even though we kept silent, we knew all the while that the outstanding coach in the country was right on our campus. This year we decided that Dorais should reap some of the honor and we've nominated him. What's more, we'll elect him."[1]

There were no formal ballots, instead voters could send in their support to either the *Detroit Free Press* Sports Department or the *Chicago Tribune*. Throughout the country, over 150 associated newspapers participated in advertising the poll. An unprecedented push for Dorais began. Letters were circulated to alumni touting Dorais, giving directives on how to vote, and asking to buy season tickets for the coming year, all with the tag line, "Better Crowds Mean Better Schedules." W.W. Edgar of the *Free Press* wrote several lengthy complimentary pieces on the Titans' coach. Coaches Charley Bachman of Michigan State and Harry Kipke of the University of Michigan took to the radio to stump on Dorais' behalf. Detroit Red Wings coach Jack Adams joined them in praising his friend. Governor Frank Murphy did the same. A resolution to get Dorais elected made it

Dorais was elected by popular vote as Head Coach of the 1937 All-Star team. Here he is with his coaching staff days before the game against the Green Bay Packers. The All-Stars won, 6-0. (left to right) Jimmy Phelan, University of Washington; Gus Dorais, University of Detroit; Lynn Waldorf, Northwestern University; Bernie Moore, Louisiana State University (Dorais family photo collection).

to Michigan's House of Representatives committee on rules and regulations.

University of Detroit co–eds descended upon Navin Field during Tigers games to garner support. Bing Crosby, Dorais' old student manager at Gonzaga, was sent a telegram urging him to endorse Dorais on upcoming radio appearances. Harry Wismer, radio broadcaster for the Lions, even went as far as digging up political petitions from a county building and replacing the office seeker's name with Dorais'. The results were resounding. By the end of July, he was leading by nearly a quarter million votes. The support didn't stop. Up through the last day of balloting, a steady stream of families stopped by the *Free Press* office to cast votes for Dorais. When final ballots were tabulated in the second week of August, he had a record 1,241,658 first-place votes and 5,269,179 total points from first-, second-, and third-place votes. Support came from all corners of the country, but the majority of votes were cast in Michigan, specifically Detroit. Congratulatory telegrams and phone calls flooded his office.

Dorais cut short a trout fishing trip on the Manistee River and returned to Detroit for a testimonial dinner and national radio broadcast in his honor, hosted by Wismer. The following day, Dorais was off to Northwestern University in Evanston, Illinois, to begin preparing for the game, just three short weeks away. He met with his 67 players, also chosen in a national poll, as well as his four-man coaching staff that included Notre Dame alums Jimmy Phelan (University of Washington) and Elmer Layden (Notre Dame), along with Northwestern coach Lynn Waldorf, who finished second to Dorais in voting, along with Bernie Moore (Louisiana State University). George Halas of the Bears gave the early advantage to the All-Stars, saying, "If those smart coaches can't plan an offense to pierce that sturdy Packer line, no one can."[2]

The next 17 days were exhausting for Dorais and his staff. They assessed talent, implemented the University of Detroit's game plan, and prepared for Green Bay's offense. The Packers were led by the record-setting passing combination of the NFL's leading passer, quarterback Arnie Herber, and his end, the great Don Hutson. In 1936, Herber set league records with 177 completions, 1,239 yards and 11 touchdowns. Hutson set marks with 34 catches, 526 yards and eight touchdowns. Emerging as Dorais' main passing threat was Sammy Baugh, a strong-armed quarterback from Texas Christian University, named All-Star team captain by his teammates. Dorais was excited to see what the two-time All-American and MVP of the first Cotton Bowl could do against the pros, calling Baugh "the quickest observer of an uncovered receiver I ever saw."[3]

As was the case in years past, the two coaching staffs had to decide on what rules to adopt. Dorais did not have an easy time coming to terms with the combative Lambeau, but finally, a hybrid of college and professional rules was agreed upon. Then there was the issue of George Sauer. The former Packers fullback retired after the 1936 season and was now coaching at the University of New Hampshire. Though technically not on the roster, Lambeau wanted him to play. When Dorais objected, Lambeau threatened to boycott the game because numerous members of the All-Star team were already under contract with NFL teams. Dorais pacified the Packers coach by dropping his protest. "Our coaches do not wish to handicap your champions," Dorais told Lambeau. "On the basis that Sauer was a member of the championship eleven last year, he is eligible this year although abandoning pro football for coaching."[4]

After two-a-days, secret practices, a scrimmage at Soldier Field, and numerous press inquiries and photo ops, game day finally arrived. Dorais' game plan was "to run from side line to side line, quick kick and throw long forward passes to tire Green Bay and back them up so we could use inside and flat passes which were to be used as our main offensive weapons in the later stages of the game."[5] He also planned an exhausting rotation of players that would wear down the Packers and completely rethink future coaches' game plans. The night before the game, Dorais told Arch Ward, "I don't know how many times they will score on us, but I know one thing—they can't hold us scoreless as long as we have Baugh firing passes."[6]

A crowd of 84,650 showed up, with proceeds being split up between United Charities, Catholic Charities and Jewish Charities of Chicago. WGN, Mutual, and NBC network provided radio coverage. The All-Stars won the toss and chose to kick off. The Packers were forced to punt, and the college men missed a field goal. After the teams traded punts, Dorais' squad retained the ball and Baugh and the offense went to work. After a few short runs got them into Packers territory, Baugh rifled a pass to his receiver, Gaynell Tinsley, 22 yards downfield. The two-time All-American receiver from LSU, who went on to set an NFL record for receiving yards the following year for the Chicago Cardinals, did the rest. He weaved his way through Green Bay's defense and up the left sideline, scoring a 47-yard touchdown. Sam Francis, the Nebraska fullback and 1936 Olympic shot-putter, missed the extra point.

Despite the Packers completely dominating the stat sheet for the rest of the game, the 6–0 lead held up and Dorais' squad became the first College All-Star team to defeat the NFL Champions. The All-Stars had two more chances to score but came away empty, including another field goal miss by Francis. They snuffed out a fourth-quarter threat by Green Bay on their own 3-yard line to secure the victory. The All-Stars defense was formidable, led by Johnny Drake of Purdue, who had 12 tackles in the game including the goal line stop. Baugh shined on defense, too, making two of the three All-Star interceptions. Dorais called the win "one of the grandest experiences in my long association with football."[7]

The victory added to Dorais' legacy. He became a frequent quote source for the game for the next couple of years, attended it and even provided coverage for a few Detroit papers. There was a clamoring for any football wisdom he could bestow on the masses, so in addition to his annual grid clinic in September he was talked into writing supplemental articles for the *Varsity News*. He also provided a weekly radio broadcast of a simulated football practice.

A few weeks after the game, Dorais was feted at the Detroit Athletic Club by prominent sportswriters such as Arch Ward, Billy Cunningham of the *Boston Post*, and E.A. Batchelor. A who's who of Michigan footballers were dispersed throughout the crowd. Dorais was given an honorary membership to the Athletic Club, just the fifth man to be bestowed the honor—the others being Charles Lindbergh, John Lodge, Fielding H. Yost and Eddie Rickenbacker. University of Detroit President Rev. Albert H. Poetker, S.J. gave the most rousing tribute, calling Dorais "a man loved for his sense of values; his courage; his balance; his high ideals; his unswerving loyalty to his players, to his principles and to his institution where he has become a tradition."[8]

In the coming months, Dorais became a spokesman for Chrysler's Airtemp, a home heating and air conditioning system, and was a salesman of plumbing fixtures and supplies. He was also approached by Harry Bennet, an executive at Ford, about opening a car dealership. "I want to give you a Ford dealership," Bennet told Dorais. "I think you ought to be a car dealer, so pick out a city you'd like to be in."

"Spokane," blurted out Dorais.

Bennet pointed at a large wall map of all the Ford dealerships on the wall.

"You already have a Ford dealer there," said Dorais when he looked closely.

"Well, we'll sell it to you," said Bennet.

"Suppose he doesn't want to sell it, Harry," Dorais questioned.

"Well, then we'll build one across the street," responded Bennet. "We'll force him out of business."

"I'm a football coach, not a car dealer," said Dorais, ending the meeting.[9]

Dorais carried the momentum of the All-Star win into the Detroit season. He had 13 letter-winners—eight of them seniors—headed by Farkas, a two-year starter. "Anvil Andy" would make several All-American lists, in part because of being third in the nation in scoring—16 touchdowns—despite playing limited minutes with a leg infection in the last few games. He gained much of his yardage running behind guard John Shada. In the first year of official scoring, the Titans set school records for pass attempts (200) and completions (94). Detroit led the nation with 253 points—the most for the Titans since the legendary 1928 team scored 267. Not to be outdone, the defense was equally as stingy, allowing just six touchdowns.

For years there were calls for a centralized way to track statistics throughout the country. Finally, in 1937, a 29-year-old sportswriter from Seattle named Homer F. Cooke convinced the NCAA to begin the process. The only catch was that he had to finance the project himself. Working under the company name, the American Football Statistical Bureau (AFSB), Cooke was determined to make the venture work. "It seemed to me that college football needed statistics," he once explained. "One could make a case for the value of college statistics to youth in placing emphasis on how they played the game, not who won or lost and by what point spread."[10] In 1941, the Official Scoring Rules were put in place for more accurate statistics. In 1946, the NCAA finally paid Cooke for his efforts.

Detroit was fierce in the 1937 opener, a 60–0 thrashing of Hillsdale College (Hillsdale, Michigan) in front of a large crowd at Dinan Field. Farkas lived up to the pre-season hype, scoring five touchdowns in the 20 minutes he and the starting lineup were in the game. The touchdowns and points scored, 30, were both school records. It was an all-around special day for Farkas. It was the first time that Andy's father, Dr. Geza Farkas, had seen his son play for the Titans. Just days before Andy left for college, his father was partially paralyzed in a car accident in Toledo, Ohio. Dr. Farkas kept up on his son's exploits via newspaper and shoddy radio reception, while Andy's mother and sister traveled to Detroit for home games.

As Farkas went, so did the Titans. They jumped out to a 5–0 record, including two impressive road wins. In the first, Detroit shut out Catholic University in Washington, D.C., at Griffith Stadium, 30–0. Farkas scored on runs of 50, 70 and 80 yards and piled up 231 yards from scrimmage. The next week, the Titans traveled to Boston and shut out Gilmour Dobie's undefeated Boston College squad, 14–0, despite a school record for fewest yards gained with 91. Swampy conditions at Alumni Field hindered both teams' offense. The Titans touchdowns came on an 88-yard interception by Albert Oliveto—also a school best—and Farkas crossing over from one yard out after a 42-yard scamper by halfback Ed Palumbo. The poor playing surface and being the focus of Boston College's defense kept Farkas—auditioning for All-American honors—in check for much of the day; an 11-yard run was his best gain. He also developed a leg infection from wounds caused by cleats, leading to admittance to Providence Hospital upon returning to Detroit.

With losses by Wisconsin and Northwestern, the win by the Titans made them the only undefeated major college team in the Midwest. Detroit found themselves ranked 18th in the AP rankings, tied with Holy Cross. The Titans were primed to climb even higher when they returned to Dinan Field for the annual Dad's Day game, hosting 16th-ranked and unbeaten Villanova. Farkas played, but with a high fever and feeling the effects of medication to combat the infection, he was mostly ineffective. The Wildcats' All-American tackle, Jon Mellus, blocked a punt in the first quarter, which was followed by a seven-yard touchdown pass from half-back Raymond Stoviak to fullback Arthur Raimo. That was the game's only score. Detroit fumbled at the goal line on their best scoring opportunity of the day. Villanova won, 7–0, knocking the Titans out of the AP poll. Following the loss, Dorais had one statement: "Villanova had a better team than Detroit."[11] He was correct. The Wildcats, who allowed just seven points all season, finished undefeated (8–0–1) and ranked sixth in the AP Poll in 1937 and undefeated (8–0–1) and ranked 18th in 1938.

Farkas returned to the hospital after the game and remained there when the Titans traveled to Brooklyn to take on Manhattan College at Ebbets Field. His health had worsened, and Dorais saw that it went beyond winning a game. "I don't want to take any chances with this youngster's health," said Dorais, perhaps thinking back to the blood poisoning that led to his former Notre Dame teammate had Ralph Dimmick's death in 1911. "Two Saturdays of that might be too much."[12] Farkas starred in the game between the two teams the year before, scoring all three Detroit touchdowns. Even without their featured back, the Titans could have won the 1937 contest had there not been a key penalty late in a scoreless fourth quarter, deep in Titans territory. Manhattan capitalized with a score, then ended a Detroit threat with an interception, winning 7–0.

After back-to-back devastating losses, Dorais was surprisingly upbeat at his luncheon with reporters on Monday. When they tried to prod him into self-pity, Dorais had none of it. "I'm just as proud, maybe a bit prouder of my kids today than I would have been had they won," he said. "I've been coaching football teams for 19 years, but my team this year is giving me a bigger thrill than any I've had before. They're a great gang of kids."[13] When asked to expand upon his thoughts, he did. "They're not equipped physically for a great team but they're making up for this shortcoming with fighting spirit."[14]

Detroit shut out North Dakota, 39–0, at home and then traveled to Omaha, where they pounded Creighton, 48–7. Four days later on November 25, Thanksgiving Day, the Titans were back on the road, this time in Pittsburgh to battle Duquesne. The game was broadcast on a radio connection from coast to coast. Farkas returned to play as a final All-American audition, but was still not healthy. On an icy and slushy Forbes Field, Detroit could muster only 11 rushing yards, a school record for futility. The Dukes won, 14–7. The Titans ended the season 7–3 for the second year in a row.

For the first time in recent memory, Dorais had the backing of alumni, and in the spring his biggest candidate pool turned out, causing him to split squads up into four teams. This coincided with one of the more aggressive recruitments for his services. Dorais was named as a candidate to succeed Harry Kipke, who stepped down at Michigan after a 10–22 record between 1934–1937. Even Kipke thought Dorais should get the job. "Gus Dorais would make a good man for Michigan" said the future College Football Hall of Famer. "I don't know where they could find a better football coach."[15]

In late December 1937, papers were even calling it a done deal, with Boeringer named as Dorais' replacement at Detroit. Ultimately, Dorais was bypassed for the position by Fritz Crisler. Again, Dorais' salary played a factor, as the Big Ten had a rule that a coach couldn't be paid more than a faculty member of equal experience. The decision didn't sit well with the Michigan Alumni Association or the student organizations that lobbied for the hiring of Dorais. With backing from four of the nine members of the Board of Regents, the Alumni Association proposed the immediate removal of Yost as Athletic Director and supplanting him with Dorais, but nothing ever materialized. "I hereby deny all reports of a similar nature up to and including Jan. 1, 1939," said an exasperated Dorais. "And all newspaper men are hereby empowered to write the denials without consulting me."[16]

The captain of Dorais' 1938 squad was end, Alex Chesney, but the leader was halfback Ed Palumbo of Cleveland, Ohio. The two-year letter winner, who added 10 pounds of muscle in the off-season, resumed his duties as the main passing threat out of the backfield. The best game of his career came during the 1938 season against Tulsa in his final game at Dinan Field. In the 39–14 Titans victory, he passed for three touchdowns and ran for two more. Palumbo was selected in the seventh round of the 1939 NFL draft by the Pittsburgh Pirates, soon to be renamed Steelers.

The Titans were finally playing a first-rate team to start the season. The opponent was Purdue University, coached by Dorais' end at Notre Dame, Mal Elward. It was Detroit's first game against a Big Ten team since the 1930 loss to Iowa. The former teammates had agreed to the game the previous winter under the condition that Dorais be the headline coach at the Purdue Football Clinic that April (he also was the headliner at clinics at the University of North Dakota, West Virginia University, and Erie, Pennsylvania). Detroit brought along the University's 72-piece band and over 500 rooters to West Lafayette. The Titans' uniforms were also described as the "most colorful in the pigskin parade," adorned in "blazing cardinal jerseys, gold pants and red and white striped helmets."[17] That wasn't enough, as the Titans suffered a rare opening game loss. The 19–6 setback was the worst defeat since losing by the same margin to Oklahoma A&M in 1934.

Dorais came away pleased in spite of the loss. Sophomore back Al Ghesquiere looked to be the next in line of triple threat backs. According to W.W. Edgar, Ghesquiere booted a punt in the second quarter that traveled 70 yards in the air, going from the Detroit 16-yard line to the Boilermakers' five. He soon became a main cog in the offense and led the team in scoring for the 1938 season. Ghesquiere came to the University of Detroit on a basketball scholarship, from St. Paul's High School in Detroit suburb Grosse Pointe. As a freshman he went out for the football team and caught the eye of Dorais early in the summer practices. On a punt return drill, Ghesquiere, nicknamed "Crazy Buffalo," returned three of five return attempts for touchdowns.

Detroit returned to Dinan Field, which they had to themselves for the first time since 1933. The Lions had switched over to Briggs Stadium, home of the Tigers. The Titans shut out their next two opponents: Western College, 7–0, and Catholic University, 27–0, before going on the road for three difficult games against Boston College, Villanova and Duquesne. During the game against the 20th ranked Dukes, a radio broadcast took place on the 50-yard line at Forbes Field at exactly 10pm, halting play. Dorais spoke about what was taking place on the field—the first occurrence of its kind in sports.

With the abundance of football options in Michigan, Dorais came to the realization that road games were actually more lucrative for the program. Detroit had proven to be quite the drawing card away from Dinan Field. The Titans returned to campus without a victory, suffering three straight losses—all games that could have easily been won. Detroit sat at an embarrassing 2–4, after averaging one-and-a-half losses a year over the past decade. "Somebody will have to pay for the breaks we've been getting," said Dorais after the Duquesne loss. "I hope it's Santa Clara."[18] His words proved to be prophetic.

Superstition crept into the Titans' losing streak. Towards the end of the Boston College game at Fenway Park, when Detroit blew a 6–0 lead to the Eagles with minutes to play, Dorais broke his glasses. The two gut-punch losses followed, and when he was trying to search for a reason for the losing streak, he jokingly brought up his broken spectacles to reporters. The *Detroit Free Press* ran a story about the glasses and later Dorais received a telegram from an optometrist offering to fix them. "I'll supply the glasses, if that's all that's keeping you from victory."[19] Dorais sent them to the doctor, who repaired them, and Detroit's winning ways resumed, counting three in a row to move their record to 5–4.

In the season finale, the Titans traveled west to Sacramento to take on the 19th-ranked Santa Clara University Broncos, winners of the last two Sugar Bowls and up until a few weeks earlier, unbeaten since 1936. They were coached by Buck Shaw, an All-American tackle and placekicker at Notre Dame (1919–1921) and future College Football Hall of Famer. Leading up to the game, Dorais proposed to Shaw that the teams bypass the extra point and instead have the team with the most first downs get the extra point in case of a tie. Shaw initially agreed, but while Detroit was traveling to the game, Dorais received a telegram that Shaw had changed his mind. The decision came back to haunt the Broncos.

Santa Clara dominated the first half, scoring on a 35-yard touchdown pass from halfback Bruno Pellegrini to quarterback Ray McCarthy. The point after failed. Detroit finally broke through in the third quarter, aided by a roughing call on the Broncos and a fluke play. Palumbo launched a pass deep down the field towards end Bill Schauer. The ball bounced off the Santa Clara safety, right into the arms of Schauer, who ran the ball in for a 50-yard touchdown. Ted Pavelec kicked the extra point, which turned out to be the difference in the Titans' 7–6 victory.

Even after the game, Dorais was in favor of doing away with the extra point. "It is not fair to the spectators to have the result of the game hinge on a conversion," Dorais explained. "It is not football to decide a game by the outcome of a try on goal."[20] The Titans were honored by the mayor of San Francisco with a key to the city and were guests of New York Yankees outfielder Joe DiMaggio at Fisherman's Wharf. The team then traveled to Los Angeles for a day, where they were guests of Bing Crosby at Paramount Studios. They were shown around the lot by Larry Crosby and met several actors, having a photo-op with actors Robert Preston and other cast members on the movie set of *Union Pacific*. They finished the day with Bing at the Earl Carroll Vanities Theater for dinner and a show. Dorais stayed behind to watch Notre Dame lose to the University of Southern California (USC), 13–0, on December 3, before traveling up the cost to Spokane to meet with old acquaintances around the city and at Gonzaga.

In the spring, Dorais' name came up in the Detroit political arena. After years of urging Common Council members to allot funds to recreational ventures, he was encouraged to run. In May 1939, Dorais admitted that he was mulling over running. "I can't say anything definite yet," he said. "Naturally, many things must be given consideration. When it was first proposed by some of my friends, I thought it was just a pipe dream. I'm busy at the university, but I understand that being a councilman doesn't prevent a man from continuing his own job as well. I'm thinking it over."[21] Similar to the backing to coach the 1937 All-Star team, a large group of

Trip to Hollywood. In late 1938, Dorais (front row, second from right) and the entire team were guests of Bing Crosby at Paramount Studios following a game in Sacramento. During their visit, the group met actor Robert Preston (front row, center) and other cast members on the movie set of *Union Pacific* (Dorais family photo collection).

supporters came out on Dorais' behalf, particularly University of Detroit students.

On November 7, 1939, Dorais was elected to the Detroit Common Council seat with 172,376 votes. He served four terms, dealing with the good and bad that came from the post–Great Depression recovery resulting from World War I. The defense industry was a boon for the city. Between 1940 and 1943, Detroit's population grew by 350,000. Housing was hard to come by, and tensions ran high between whites and many of the 50,000 blacks who had moved from the South to pursue employment within the defense industry. In early 1942, whites tried to prevent black tenants from moving into the Sojourner Truth Housing Project. Riots erupted as several council members, including Dorais, spoke in favor of white occupancy in the federal housing. Under pressure from protests,

Detroit Mayor Edward Jeffries, and Washington, D.C., Dorais changed his stance. Ultimately, Dorais' legacy on the council would be in Detroit's Recreation Department. In the first few months, $60,000 was allocated to open 40 additional school grounds for outdoor recreational activities.

Dorais spent considerable time during the summer helping design

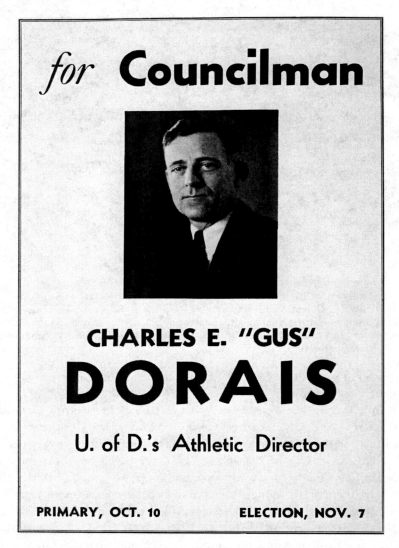

for **Councilman**

CHARLES E. "GUS"

DORAIS

U. of D.'s Athletic Director

PRIMARY, OCT. 10   **ELECTION, NOV. 7**

Poster to elect Dorais to Detroit Common Council in 1939 for his first of four terms (Digital/print image from the University of Detroit Mercy Archive and Special Collections, University of Detroit Mercy).

the family's new 2,600-square-foot house at 18695 Warrington Drive, just a mile from the University. He was an architect at heart. His first year at the University of Notre Dame was spent studying architecture before switching to law. In early June 1939, he was in South Bend for his 25th class reunion. It coincided with the dedication of the of the $600,000 Rockne Memorial Fieldhouse. As the principal speaker, Dorais spoke eloquently:

> We are gathered here, old teammates and friends, to make a feeble gesture in acknowledging a great man. Football coaches as such are not in a position to add much to the world's progress or well-being. But you, Rock, burst all bounds and your memory of what you taught and exemplified made of you a beloved national figure and, better than that, a tremendous power for good among the people of this land.[22]

Detroit went a disappointing 5–3–1 in 1939. The 2–0 Titans were nipped by Catholic University, 14–13, for the first time since 1935. Ghesquiere suffered a right leg injury (initially thought to be a fracture) that hampered him for the remainder of the season. After a pair of wins, Detroit lost two in a row at Dinan Field for the second time in three years. They dropped contests to Villanova, 13–6, for the third year in a row and Boston College, 20–13, for the second straight year. After a convincing 36–13 win over an outmanned Manhattan College Jaspers, the Titans had a few weeks before heading to Pittsburgh to play a December 2 tilt against 6th-ranked Duquesne. It was initially scheduled for Thanksgiving, but President Roosevelt moved the holiday up a week to November 23, in hopes of boosting the economy. It was a hindrance to college football programs, who often played a rivalry game on Thanksgiving, Detroit included. Dorais was already complaining about the situation in August. "I couldn't imagine anything worse than playing that late in Pittsburgh. The field would be under ice, and it's snowy and cold enough on Thanksgiving as it is—or rather, it was," he said, with a few months to stew about the predicament.[23]

The game between the Titans and Dukes had become testy in recent years. Circumstances were heightened with it being homecoming and the 3-to-1 favored Dukes pursuing the first perfect season in school history. Also on Dorais' mind was his son Tom's Greater Detroit High School Football Championship game back in Detroit at Briggs Stadium. Gus sent a telegram of encouragement to his son from Pittsburgh. Tom would quarterback the University of Detroit High to an upset victory over Catholic Central, ending their 34-game winning streak. He enrolled at Notre Dame after graduation in hopes of following in his father's footsteps.

Dorais' family had more activities than ever, effectively coordinated by Vi. Tom and Bill were members of the University of Detroit High School football team of the prep Metropolitan League. Conflicting schedules made it difficult for Dorais to see his sons in action. "They tell me that Tom's a good football player and an outstanding field general," he dejectedly told W.W. Edgar when he couldn't make a key game. "I sure wish I could see him play."[24]

Prior to the game, Dorais noticed that Duquesne's first-year coach, Aldo Donelli, had his players equipped with long spikes, rather than the customary football cleats. Dorais protested, and when Donelli refused to listen, Dorais threatened to pull his team off the field and forfeit the game. "That's up to you," said Donelli in no uncertain terms. "My boys use the equipment they have on now—or there'll be no game."[25] An incensed Dorais begrudgingly went along with the game, rather than disappoint a jam-packed Forbes Field. Dorais enacted some revenge as the Titans nearly upset the Dukes, before a 55-yard touchdown run by back Philip Gonda tied the game at 10–10 in the fourth quarter. The rain-soaked game ended that way and spoiled Duquesne's perfect season.

In the postgame, one of the Dukes grabbed the game ball and ran to their locker room. Dorais had wanted to get it and give it to Titans tackle Bill Neinstedt, who was ill in a Detroit hospital. Team captain Emerson Addison went to the Duquense locker room to explain the situation to the Dukes' team captain, but was kicked out in rude fashion. Dorais was furious from the disrespectful behavior throughout the game, vowing never to play them again.

The 1939 season saw the emergence of Detroit Catholic Central High School graduate Vince Banonis as a center and linebacker. He was big and strong, with surprising speed for his size. Dorais even devised a scoring play for the athletic Banonis, lining him up at the end of the line and throwing a lateral pass to him. In his senior year, 1941, he was team captain, earned All-American honors on Grantland Rice's *Colliers* team and captained the College All-Star Team against the Chicago Bears. In his decade-long NFL career, he was named an All-Pro in 1947 as a member of the Chicago Cardinals.

Dorais continued to be a popular figure on the growing local banquet scene. By the end of the 1930s, he estimated that he had spoken at 1,500 clubs and societies and turned down hundreds of requests over the years. He recalled how on one Sunday the year before, he had two breakfasts, two luncheons and one dinner—all with speeches—and attended church twice. His speeches were short, positive, and informative. He displayed wit and his deep knowledge of football. Of course, there were scheduling errors. There were times where he showed up on the wrong date or at the wrong banquet altogether, which were fodder for his next talk. He regaled one such story at a Coaches Association banquet:

> My confidence in speaking here was not increased a great deal the other night in Michigan when I had the unusual opportunity of speaking at a high school banquet. After I had spoken, the lady in charge of affairs came up and offered me the magnificent sum of five dollars. It was a great chance to be magnanimous, so I said, "It is too much of a pleasure to speak to these football players. I enjoyed it. I don't want any fee."
> "Well, Mr. Dorais," she said, "Thank you. We will put it in our fund."
> I asked, "What fund?"
> She said, "The fund to get better speakers for next year.""[26]

In late December 1939, Dorais was sworn in as a councilman, presiding over the Common Council for the first time towards the end of January 1940. In February, Dorais was in Port Huron attending the premiere of Mickey Rooney's latest feature film, *Young Tom Edison*. At the theater, Dorais was helping Secretary of State Harry Kelly's wife, Anne, out of the car when he lost his footing on the icy sidewalk and fell, hitting his head. Later, when Kelly became governor, the incident was always the subject of humor between the two men, Dorais joking that the governor's wife tripped him.[27] Dorais attended the movie, but his symptoms worsened when he returned home and he was admitted to Henry Ford Hospital for a few days. He was soon back out, continuing his busy off-season routine, but side-effects of the concussion, and head trauma from his playing days, plagued him the rest of his life.

On October 4, *Knute Rockne, All American*, was released. Starring Pat O'Brien as Rockne, the film was a biography of the Notre Dame great. Several other notable University figures were portrayed, including George Gipp by Ronald Reagan. He and O'Brien famously reenacted Gipp's deathbed request to "win one for the Gipper." Dorais was played by Owen Davis, Jr. When the two met a few years later, Dorais was good-natured about Davis. "I found him a very personable and likable fellow," said Dorais, "but he is better looking and a little taller and heavier than I was during my playing days at Notre Dame."[28] When the movie premiered at Notre Dame, Dorais was unable to attend. His son, Tom, a freshman at Notre Dame, was invited to represent his father at the Washington Theater on campus. It was a big thrill, as he got to meet and mingle with the entire cast.

During Tom's freshman year, a controversy arose that required Gus to intervene. Tom's friend, Ed Wilberding asked if Tom would lie in his bed during bed check because Ed was heading off-campus to meet his girlfriend in nearby Michiwaka. Tom agreed because the priest would start on the bottom floor, so Tom had time to lay in Ed's bed and then scramble up to the second floor for his own bed check. For the first time that year, the priest decided to start on the second floor, and Tom was marked absent. However, he did pass bed check for Ed. When Tom was called to the Administration building to face discipline, Ed came with him to tell the truth. Ed was kicked out of Notre Dame, and Tom was suspended for three days. Tom arrived unannounced back home in Detroit. Vi was incensed, saying that Gus would be furious. He was not, perhaps thinking back to the hijinks he and Rockne pulled in college. Gus placed a call to the university, and Tom returned the next day with the suspension lifted.

Detroit was beginning to rebound from the Great Depression, and the University of Detroit felt some of that resurgence. After several years of neglect and patchwork fixes, Dinan Field was added onto, including what Arch Ward described as "the finest press box in the National Football league," which included "hot and cold running water, indirect lighting, steam heat, and a sandwich salon."[29]

Detroit started the 1940 season with a 5–0 record. After allowing seven points to Wayne University in the opener (the first time the two Detroit schools had played since 1904), the Titans' defense shutout the next four opponents.[30] Detroit was in the AP rankings for the first time since 1937, coming in at number 17 in the October 28, week three poll. The fifth win was a satisfying 10–0 victory over Villanova at Shibe Park in Philadelphia. It was the 99th win of Dorais' career and one of the more satisfying of the bunch. Before the game, he said to his team: "Boys, I've been coaching football for 25 years and not one team has ever beaten any of mine five straight times before. I'd hate to see it made six in a row. Villanova has out lucked us for two years, but today we can get even if you carry the battle to them."[31]

When asked by Sam Greene of the *Detroit News* to look back over the 99 wins to date, Dorais listed a few particular games, but said, "We beat some good teams and we won some games that we weren't expected to win. Those always bring the most satisfaction."[32]

It was a perfect scenario for Dorais' 100th win. The Titans were returning to Detroit for a pair of games, allowing all of the necessary acknowledgments to be made in front of a home crowd at Dinan Field. Dorais' patented offense hit a snag beginning with the next game against Tulsa. Ghesquiere, who had gained 100 yards on the ground in each of the first five games, was injured. He stayed in the game but managed just 48 total yards, 39 of them rushing. The Hurricanes scored a touchdown late in the fourth quarter, holding on for a 7–0 win. It was Tulsa's first win in five tries against Detroit. The loss dropped the Titans from the polls, the last time a Dorais team was listed.

Dorais got his 100th win the following week against Texas Christian University, 3–0, on a field goal by Ted Pavelec. Dorais was presented the game ball with the following painted on it: "UofD -3 TCU–0 100th TITAN VICTORY UNDER CHARLES E. DORAIS." Though exact numbers aren't known, Dorais was amongst a handful of coaches to win 100 games at one school, including: Fielding Yost, University of Michigan (165); Bill Anderson, Georgia Tech (134); Bob Zuppke, University of Illinois (131); Howard Jones, University of Southern California (121), and Knute Rockne, Notre Dame (105). Dorais would end his career with 113 victories with the Titans.

Even this far into his tenure, Dorais was still experiencing firsts. It was the first time he won a 3–0 game while coach at Detroit. The other first was that Dorais coached the entire game from the press box, with Boeringer directing from the bench. "A coach can't see any too much of the play from the bench," Dorais explained, "and I believe we can improve our strategy both on offense and defense if I can see just what's going on down on the field."[33]

At the Common Council meeting the following Wednesday, Dorais, President pro tem of the council, was running through procedures when he was interrupted by John Lodge, dean of the council. Lodge gave a resolution in honor Dorais and his 100th victory at the University of Detroit:

> Whereas, The floor members of Detroit's Common Council received the pleasing information that the University of Detroit football team had won fine victory Saturday last, and
> Whereas, This event marked a full "century run" of victories under the direction and leadership of our present presiding officer, now therefore be it
> Resolved, That this expression of pleasure and appreciation be made a matter of permanent record in the Council proceedings, thereby in a small degree conveying to our esteemed associate, Hon. Charles E. Dorais, our City's thanks for a memorable mark in our nation's foot ball history.[34]

Dorais pushed and fiddled with his tie during the reading. After the resolution was unanimously passed, a humbled Dorais said a few words: "As you grow older you have a more intense appreciation of this kind and generous gesture of good will. Memories of this kind make life worthwhile."[35]

The Titans traveled to Spokane the following week. It was Dorais' return to Gonzaga and the Bulldogs' Homecoming game. Gonzaga was

coached by Dorais' former player, John "Puggy" Hunton. Dorais was celebrated with a dinner-dance sponsored by the Gonzaga Alumni Association, scheduled to follow the game. In front of nearly 20 former players,
Dorais' Titans squad lost, 13–7 (the same score he lost to Detroit when
he was coaching the Bulldogs). Gonzaga was led by halfback and team

A rare family photograph. Gus and his mother Malvina, along with his three
sons, Tom, Bill and David, c. 1940. Although they were seldom together,
Gus provided support for his mother his entire life (Dorais family photo collection).

captain Tony Canadeo, who scored all of the Bulldogs' points and would earn AP Little All-American honors at year's end. A future NFL Hall of Famer with the Green Bay Packers, Canadeo credited Dorais with bringing him to the attention of Packers management, who selected him in the seventh round of the 1941 draft. "If it wasn't for Gus, I'm sure Lambeau would never have heard of me or at least not given me much thought, coming from a small school like Gonzaga."[36]

The return of Dorais drew only 6,500 fans and was eventually used as a reason for Gonzaga not resuming football after it was dropped in 1941. At the gala the evening after the game, Dorais was celebrated. He charmed the audience with football anecdotes and stories about his family. He said Spokane was "where Mrs. Dorais and I plan on settling after we have enough of that!"[37]

Detroit finished the season on November 23 by reengaging with Marquette for the first time since 1934. In his final game for the Titans, Ghesquiere opened the scoring with a 37-yard run early in the second quarter. That was all the scoring Detroit needed, emerging victorious, 19–0, to finish the season 7–2. The defense allowed just 27 points. From his left halfback spot, Ghesquiere led the nation in rushing with 957 yards on 146 rushing attempts, a 6.5 average. He also completed 32 passes for 285 more yards. The 1,242 total offensive yards put him among the leaders in total offense. He gained All-Catholic and All-American honors and was named to the College All-Star Game roster along with two linemen: Cass Brovarney and Ted Pavelec.

Following the season, Ghesquiere made a surprising announcement. "I hung up my cleats for the last time, Saturday," he said. "I'm not going to play any more football—unless something awfully important induces me, and I can't see what that would be right now."[38] He held true to that statement, turning down a contract of $1,200 from the Philadelphia Eagles, who drafted him in the fourth round. After being turned down by the military due to football injuries, Ghesquiere began a four-decade career with the Uniroyal Rubber Company, retiring in 1982.

Less than a week after the Titans' 1940 season was over, new Detroit Lions owner Fred Mandel, Jr., was listing Dorais as his number one choice to replace the recently departed Potsy Clark after a 5–5–1 season. Mandel, a Chicago Department store executive, had bought the Lions from George Richards and a group of team investors for $225,000. He failed in luring Dorais, hiring Bill Edwards from Case Western Reserve University in Cleveland instead. The Lions didn't fare any better under his leadership, suffering the franchise's first losing season in Detroit at 4–6–1 in 1941.

A more intriguing job came open in the early 1941. On February 5, Elmer Layden stepped down as athletic director and head football coach at Notre Dame to become the first commissioner of the NFL. Not surprisingly, Dorais' name was among those being considered, along with several other former Notre Dame stars. When asked if he would take the job if offered, Dorais laughed, "Not so long as the voters of Detroit have confidence in me."[39] The Irish vacancy eventually went to Frank Leahy.

Dorais looked to change a few things in 1941. First, he tried to schedule Sunday games. This wouldn't come to fruition until 1942. Secondly, he looked to drop the two-team system, which he had used for the last half-dozen seasons, deciding to focus instead on one strong unit. This, too, wouldn't stick. One thing he didn't do was implement the popular T formation that was being integrated at all levels of play. That style of offense was nothing new. Dorais had used a similar set of plays for years, before abandoning it in the mid–30s. However, Dorais did return to a pass-first game plan in 1941. Behind 15 returning letterman and strong-armed sophomore halfback Elmer "Tippy" Madarik, who had quarterbacked the freshman team the year before, the Titans set a school record with 1,307 passing yards. Madarik had 874 of them, completing 64-of-128 passes, with seven interceptions. He was also the team's main ground gainer, with 667 yards on 171 carries for a 3.9 average—nearly triple the work load of the second-closest ball carrier. The yardage total was fourth in the nation.

For the third straight year, the Titans began the season 4–0. The highwater mark included a 14–7 win over Big Ten team, Indiana University, in the opener at Bloomington, Indiana. It was Detroit's first win over a school from the conference. Blowout wins against instate schools followed: Wayne, 54–0, and Central St. Teachers, 45–0, followed by a hard fought 20–14 win over Oklahoma A&M in Stillwater, Oklahoma. Dorais was surprised at his team's success. Madarik was off to a strong start, and end Howard Keating was one of the leading receivers in the country, thanks in part to a six-catch game against Central. His play earned him a spot on the roster for the College All-Star Game in Chicago the following summer. Captain Vince Bannois, a lineman, was doing everything, including a 44-yard run on a lateral to set up the first touchdown against Indiana.

That fall, Dorais found himself in some political turmoil when he was accused of posting promotional posters for reelection to the city council at Dinan Field. Fellow councilman James Garlick accused him of this unethical practice, which Dorais denied. The two exchanged heated words at a Dorais-led council meeting, with nether backing down. The ethics questions did little to deter voters from casting their ballots for Dorais, who was reelected on November 4.

There were visions of an undefeated season. Dorais had his players studying game tape in a makeshift film room in the gym leading up to the October 24 game at Dinan Field against the strong air attack of the University of Arkansas. The Titans kept the Razorbacks' passing game in check, but lost, 9–6, on a field goal in the waning seconds. Winners of their next two, Detroit shut out Manhattan, 15–0, and won a mud-filled game against Marquette, 7–6, on Homecoming, doubling as a celebration of Dad Butler. The Titans split their last two games of the season. The first was another tough 7–6 loss in Philadelphia at Shibe Park against Villanova, thanks to a missed extra point in the fourth quarter, and then a 28–0 shutout win over Creighton in Omaha, Nebraska. Detroit finished 7–2 for the second consecutive season.

A few weeks after the season, on December 7, Japanese military bombed an American fleet in Pearl Harbor, Hawaii. Shortly thereafter, the United States became engaged in World War II. In the war years, many alumni enlisted in the military. Dorais lost several players to the draft or enlistment. Athletics at all levels were hampered, and the Detroit School Superintendent, Warren Bow, called to end interscholastic sports, which Dorais called "war hysteria."[40] On April 22, 1942, at age 50, Dorais, a veteran of World War I, registered as part of the fourth registration group, known as the "Old Man's Registration," or "Old Man's Draft."

That spring, Dorais tinkered with the T formation and contemplated what his team would look like in the fall, as more players either enlisted in the military or were drafted. To makeup for this, incoming freshman were eligible to play on the varsity squad. The 1942 season would be Dorais' 18th and final campaign at the University of Detroit. With Bob Zuppke stepping down from his post at the University of Illinois after 29 seasons, Dorais was now the longest-tenured coach of Western universities.

Perhaps the most difficult obstacle for Dorais in 1942 was coaching his son, Tom. His eldest son returned home to Detroit in 1941 after his year-long stint at Notre Dame. Tom's dream of following in his father's footsteps at Notre Dame was dashed when he had to compete for the quarterback position with another freshman, Angelo Bertelli. Bertelli went on to become one of the all-time great Irish quarterbacks. His senior year, 1943, Bertelli led the Irish to a National Championship and was named All-American, *Sporting News* "Player of the Year," and took home the Heisman Trophy.

Tom played well for the Titans, quarterbacking the freshman team. Now eligible for the varsity, team members signed a petition for Gus to play Tom more often. It didn't sway Dorais' opinion, keeping his son at third string. When Georgetown played Detroit on October 24, Vi invited her sister and family and a few other out-of-town guests for the weekend—specifically to see Gus coach and Tom play. According to Tom, he "wasn't a starter and it was a close game. Well, I never got in the game. It was a really close game and we won. I got into the car with my Dad to go home. He said, 'You know I really wanted to put you in the game, but they were throwing a lot of passes, Tom.' I really wasn't good at pass defense and I wouldn't have put me in either." His father said, "I think I'm in trouble when we get home." Sure enough, Vi was waiting. "How could you, Charles?" she asked incredulously. "How could you not put Tom in the game?" It was so embarrassing. Gus didn't say anything as he went and poured himself a drink.[41]

Detroit once again started out 4–0, outscoring opponents, 70–7. The final five games were a disaster. The offense went feeble, scoring a meager

"Skull sessions" were an integral part of Dorais' coaching methodology. Here he is in 1942, running through a game situation in front of the team with his star player, Elmer "Tippy" Madarik (Dorais family photo collection).

22 points, the lowest output over a five-game span since Dorais' early years at the University. The Titans suffered their first loss of the season in Milwaukee against Marquette. A muddy Hilltop Stadium surface kept both teams scoreless in the first half, before the Golden Avalanche scored on a one-yard plunge by Hal Eigner in the third quarter and a field goal in the fourth by Bobby Dams. The 10–0 affair was the first time Marquette defeated a Dorais-led Detroit team.

The Titans rebounded with a satisfying 9–0 shutout of Villanova, before an embarrassing three-game slide to finish out Dorais' University of Detroit career with a 5–4 record. It started with a 14–7 loss to Arkansas on "Bud Boeringer Day." One of the Razorbacks touchdowns was a defensive fumble recovery in the end zone. The score was indicative of Boeringer's defenses. In the 146 games since he took over in 1927, opponents scored more than two touchdowns only six times (five of these were three-touchdown games). Detroit's defense posted 69 shutouts in that time and allowed one touchdown on 37 occasions.

A snow-filled Homecoming game dedicated to servicemen followed, and on some accounts, the worst defeat of Dorais' tenure. Fewer than 5,000 fans watched the Titans throw 10 interceptions in a demoralizing 33–6 loss to Oklahoma A & M. The final game was in San Francisco, a 2–0 muted effort against Santa Clara on December 6. After the fast start, Detroit finished the season 5–4. Charles Weber of the *Varsity News* called it the "most disastrous year in Titan gridiron annals since 1926," Dorais' second at the university.[42]

Signs during the season pointed towards no football at the University in 1943. Dorais contemplated a move to the professional ranks, and there was an opportunity right there in Detroit. Lions owner, Fred Mandel, Jr., was looking to replace John Karcis, who took over for Bill Edwards three games into the 1942 season. Neither was successful, as the War took away several players, including Byron "Whizzer" White, the first member of the Lions to lead the league in rushing with 514 yards in 1940. Detroit went 0–11 in 1942, scoring a total of 38 points. They were shut out five times and failed to score more than seven points in a game.

Mandel seized the opportunity, openly courting Dorais with a five-year offer that included paying him a salary even if the NFL season was suspended due to the war. Dorais was bordering on accepting. He felt he had taken the Titans as far as they could go under his leadership, and in war time his salary would put a financial strain on the university if they suspended football. He also knew after the war they would have a very capable replacement in Lloyd Brazil. Around Christmas, rumors of Dorais going to the Lions intensified. He and Mandel were meeting almost daily. In addition, it was looking more like the University of Detroit would suspend the entire varsity sports program. Mandel was in Detroit the first full week of January, and within a few days of his arrival was making an offer to Dorais to not only coach the Lions, but serve as general manager, part owner and Athletic Director—the first time that a NFL team appointed such a job. His responsibilities included hiring his own assistants, scouting, scheduling, travel and drafts. Mandel reserved contract signings as his own responsibility, a problem that would hinder the franchise in the years that followed.

The Lions job was an opportunity that Dorais couldn't ignore like he had in the past. He could have remained at the University of Detroit indefinitely, but wanted to test his abilities at the professional level. In his 18 seasons as head coach of the Titans, Dorais went 113–48–7, a .693 winning percentage. At home he was 84–25–3, on the road, 29–23–4. His teams outscored opponents at nearly a three-to-one clip, 2,889–1,053, and recorded 69 shutouts. He would be the longest tenured of the 16 coaches in the nearly six decades the university had a football program, which ceased after the 1964 season.

On January 9, Dorais accepted Mandel's overwhelming offer. The next day, the announcement was made public, leaving many stunned. The yearly overtures were expected for Dorais, as were his annual mulling over and eventual rejections. The move was applauded by fellow NFL owners, including the defending champion Washington Redskins' George Marshall, who called it "a contribution to the entire league as well as to Detroit."[43] Much like at the college level, there was a heavy Notre Dame influence in the NFL. Elmer Layden became commissioner in 1941. Beside Dorais, Art "Dutch" Bergman took over head coaching duties of the Washington Redskins. Curley Lambeau led the Green Bay Packers, and Hunk Anderson the Chicago Bears.

Dorais put out a heartfelt statement to the University of Detroit:

> The University of Detroit, its friends and followers have been good to me. I would like them to know that the University authorities and myself are in complete agreement that the best interests of both the school and myself can best be served by my acceptance of Fred Mandel's generous offer to take me into his foot ball club. I leave the school with their best wishes.
>
> I leave the old job and approach the new with mixed emotions. You can't laugh off a pleasant association of many years. And you can't laugh off an opportunity to direct and have a part interest in a major league foot ball club, located in a great sports town.
>
> I am enthusiastic about the future of major league foot ball and will bend every

effort to see that the Detroit Lions take their rightful place in the foot ball world.[44]

"I gave the problem a lot of study before I joined the professionals. And I joined them because I know their foot ball is going to become a far more important part of American sports life than it ever has, yet," Dorais said.[45]

CHAPTER 10

The Professional Game, 1943–1947

The roots of the Detroit Lions can be traced to the pre–National Football League days in the Midwest in the beginning of the 20th century. Ohio was the hotbed of the developing professional game, Dorais himself playing professionally with the Massillon Tigers from 1915–1916 and 1919 and Indiana's Fort Wayne Friars in 1916 and 1917. Many teams came and went in the first decade of the NFL. Through the 1920s, Detroit fielded four different pro clubs, most lasting only one or two seasons.

In 1929, the team that became the Detroit Lions, the Portsmouth Spartans (Portsmouth, Ohio), was established. In 1930 Portsmouth was granted a franchise by the NFL after completing construction of a new stadium. The Spartans lasted four years. Portsmouth was a small city and wasn't able to generate the revenue necessary to keep up with other teams in the league. In 1934 the Portsmouth Spartans were purchased by a group led by George Richards, owner of Detroit radio station WJR. They bought the team, moved them to Detroit, and renamed the team the Lions as a complement to the Detroit Tigers.

The Lions were a solid football team throughout the 1930s, winning the NFL championship in their second year, 1935. Those early successes firmly established pro football in the city. Detroit made their lasting mark by scheduling a Thanksgiving Day game in their first season, 1934, and, except for a six-year gap between 1939 and 1944, continue the tradition to present day. Attendance grew, and by 1937 the Lions were averaging 19,000 fans a game. A deal was struck the following year to move from Dinan Field at the University of Detroit into the Tigers' home of Briggs Stadium, which could seat 55,000 and was available during the fall football season.

Dorais immediately jumped headlong into his Lions duties. He received a portfolio of information of players with 4-F status. He also wrote letters to college coaches all over the country, asking that they consider playing pro ball if their school was planning on dropping football in the coming year. Those efforts ceased in March 1943, when Dorais suffered another severe head injury. He was at the Detroit Athletic Club for a function when he began to feel dizzy. He went to the washroom to compose himself, but passed out, hitting his head on the floor. He was taken home, but later moved to the Henry Ford Hospital for treatment. X-rays showed that he had suffered a linear fracture, and a six- to-eight-week recovery period was recommended. He remained hospitalized for two weeks, but didn't lose his interest or sense of humor. "I've just thought of a swell punt return play, but nobody in this place will give [me] a pencil and paper to diagram it," he told Bob Latshaw of the *Detroit Free Press*.[1]

The NFL draft was postponed to April 8 as a result of Dorais' fall. He planned to travel to Chicago for the draft and relay picks from his bed at the Palmer Hotel to Lions owner Fred Mandel, but Dorais was too sick to do even that. There was no mistaking whom the Lions would take with the first pick in the draft. It was University of Georgia running back Frank Sinkwich, who capped off his All-American senior season by winning the Heisman Trophy. During that campaign, he set the NCAA single-season total offense record of 2,187 total yards. He joined the U.S. Marine Corps after graduating, but received a medical discharge due to flat feet, a heart murmur and high blood pressure. He signed a $1,000 a game contract. As a member of the Lions, he was named NFL MVP in 1944. He was the first Lions player to win the award, and he earned All-Pro recognition in 1943 and 1944. He injured his knee playing for an Air Force service team in 1945, and was never the same when he returned to the NFL.

Dorais was transitioning into the professional game during an uncertain time. There were conversations about shutting down the whole league in 1943, but upon the urging of President Roosevelt, plans for the season continued. Nearly 400 former players who appeared on rosters in the early 1940s were in military uniform by the start of the 1943 season. Over 600 served during the war—twice the number needed to fill the 10 teams' rosters. To ensure that a full season took place, concessions were made. Rosters were trimmed from 33 to 28, free substitutions were allowed, and helmets were required. The schedule was also pared down to ten games, one fewer than the year before. The league was trimmed to eight teams, four in each division. The Cleveland Rams withdrew from the league for a year due to their owners'—Fred Levy and Dan Reeves—military obligations. In Pennsylvania, there was a co-oped effort by the Steagles (Steelers and Eagles). Players unable to serve in the military flourished, and the dominant teams before the War continued their success: the Eastern Divi-

After a few years of pursuit, Detroit Lions owner Fred Mandel finally got his man. Here Dorais signs his contract with the Lions (Dorais family photo collection).

sion's Redskins and New York Giants, and the Western's Packers and Bears. Fewer teams brought about parity, and despite the reduced schedule, the league drew over one million fans, just a few thousand less than the record set the year before.

Feeling somewhat better by the summer, Dorais began working tirelessly to prepare for training camp. He hired former Notre Dame tackle Joe Bach as an assistant. Bach, who was the head coach for the Pittsburgh Steelers for two years, 1935–1936, remained Dorais' assistant throughout his tenure with the Lions. In June, Dorais traveled to Chicago to attend the NFL meeting at the Blackstone Hotel. The main talk was a merger, about which Dorais quipped, "I suggest that the Lions merger with every other club."[2] He was confident in the upcoming season, and Detroit went forward with the slogan, "Gus Dorais' New Lions Will Show You Football at Its Best."[3]

Despite the setback with the head injury and the Lions' lowly status of late, Dorais was rejuvenated by the challenge ahead. Detroit's fans looked forward to seeing what he could do, too, evident by the spike of 255 season tickets by midsummer. There were three weeks to trim the roster from 55 prospects to 28 at West Shore Golf Club in Grosse Ile. "We will use plenty of razzle-dazzle, which will include forward and lateral passes," said Dorais. "The basic formation will be the T and the main-in-motion will be a prominent feature. However, the offense will be as compact and as simple as we can make it."[4]

The collection of players harkened back to the pre–NFL years with factory workers, ex-high school players, rugby players from Canada, and older, former players. A few Lions veterans returned, most notably future Hall of Fame center Alex Wojciehowicz and fullback Harry Hopp. There was also newcomer Chuck Fenenbock, a single wing specialist from UCLA, where he was known for both his breakaway speed and throwing abilities. For the last two seasons, he had played in the Pacific Coast Professional Football League (PCPFL), first for the in 1941 San Diego Bombers and the 1942 season with the Los Angeles Bulldogs. He was voted the MVP of the PCPFL All-Star Game in 1942.

Dorais found himself in political turmoil in September, when he defended five members of the team who received temporary war-housing. He claimed that these men were eligible because they worked at the Ford plant during the day and went through all the proper channels. There was public outcry of preferential treatment, but it didn't hurt Dorais, who was re-elected to the Common Council in November.

On September 11, 1943, Sinkwich received a medical discharge because of flat feet. A few days later, he was in Lions' camp. Detroit started the season at Briggs Stadium against the Chicago Cardinals, who finished in front of the Lions in 1942 with a 3–8 record. The much-anticipated debut of Sinkwich (he threw eight passes—four of them interceptions) was overshadowed by Fenenbock's day. The halfback completed four of seven passes for 71 yards and a pair of touchdowns to Hopp, who had three touchdowns on the day. In the win—Detroit's first in two seasons—the Lions scored more points than they had during the entire 1942 campaign. After a 27–0 shutout of the Brooklyn Dodgers, Dorais prepared his team for the first test of the season—the Chicago Bears. "We've done alright in the second division, but you never know what you have in this league until you meet the Bears. We'll soon find out," said Dorais.[5]

By his own admission, the pro game was much more complex than the one that Dorais played in decades earlier. "In my day we always used the same system—a seven-man line and a diamond. And we all had the same offense and defense at all times," he told W.W. Edgar early in the season. "Today the fellows have to master such things as the three systems we are using."[6]

Dorais was hampered by his players' work schedules, many of them in the defense industries. Practices were limited to just a few hours a week and didn't begin until after 5pm. He got the most out of them, though, incorporating his ever-calm, encouraging style. It was a stark change from Edwards' penchant to jump on any infraction and charge a fine. "Every player on this squad respects Dorais," said a veteran at midseason, adding that they were "ready to break their necks" to please him."[7] Fenenbock was even more sure of Dorais' influence, saying that "90 percent of our team is our coach."[8]

A crowd in excess of 48,000 saw the Lions battle the Bears—over twice as big a group as had seen any game professional game in Detroit over the past two seasons. Fans were standing in the aisles and around the playing field. They showered Chicago with beer bottles and their Jewish quarterback, Sid Luckman, with racial epithets. The teams went into the half tied. The eventual NFL champions found their groove in the second half, running behind the great Bronko Nagurski, escaping the hostile environment with a 27–21 win. The Bears' head coach and Dorais' rival, Hunk Anderson, was impressed by his fellow Notre Dame alum's game plan, saying "he comes into our league and he tries everything—man in motion, spreads, punt formation."[9]

Lions star player and Heisman Trophy winner Frankie Sinkwich with Gus Dorais on the practice field at the West Shore Golf and Country Club, September 16, 1943 (Dorais family photo collection).

A 35–14 defeat in Green Bay followed for

the Lions, before once again beating the Cardinals, 7–0, in Chicago. It was the last win of the season for Detroit. A return home on October 24, brought a 27–6 loss to the Packers, during which the Lions set a team record by tossing nine interceptions. Sinkwich alone had seven. The next week at Wrigley Field, Dorais coached from the press box, phoning down instructions to Bach. It didn't help as the Bears won, 35–14. Sinkwich finally got his first rushing touchdown in the game. The press was starting to be critical of the Heisman winner, but Dorais stuck up for the rookie, saying the Lions "aren't in the position to keep those hard-rushing pro lineman away long enough to give Frankie a chance."[10]

On November 7, Detroit and the New York Giants played the last 0–0 tie in NFL history. The teams combined for just nine first downs, and the Lions forced 14 punts. In a 42–20 loss to Washington the next week, Redskins back Sammy Baugh, in the midst of one of the greatest all-around NFL seasons, tossed four touchdown passes, intercepted four passes and booted an 81-yard punt.

Detroit finished the season third in the Western Division, 3–6–1. It was the first financially successful season under Mandel's ownership, thanks in large part to the 160,241 attendance mark, doubling the previous year's total in two fewer games. Sinkwich, though closely critiqued, was one of the few rookies that had any impact in the league. He led the team in rushing with 266 yards and passing with 699 (seven touchdowns and 20 interceptions). Hopp was the team's top receiver (17 catches for 229 yards), and his 54 points scored was among the league leaders. As a team, the Lions paced the league in the bygone statistic, laterals.

During the 1944 off-season, the Lions moved their offices from the Book Building to Park Avenue. The war was still on, and NFL-caliber talent remained hard to come by. The Lions lost two key components from the previous year to the military: Hopp and Fenenbock. In April, Dorais served on the rules committee at the three-day NFL meetings, pushing for one set of rules for all levels: high school, college and professional teams. At the draft he chose Otto Graham, a quarterback from Northwestern, with the fourth overall pick. The future Hall of Famer never played a down with Detroit, after being called to service by the Navy. The Lions still had Sinkwich (who signed a contract late) and Wojciechowicz. Detroit added wingback Art VanTone and end Dave Diehl.

The most heralded addition was fullback Bob Westfall. A former All-American at the University of Michigan, he led the Big Ten in rushing in 1941 and was the Lions' first-round pick in 1942, but was in the Army by the summer. In December 1943, he received a medical discharge from the

Army Air Corps (bronchitis and asthma). He returned to Ann Arbor to finish his degree and work at the B-4 bomber plant in nearby Willow Run. He was able to resume his playing career at Michigan under wartime rules, but concerns arose that he would play for the Wolverines early in the fall and finish with the Lions. Dorais made his thoughts clear about what "Bullet Bob" should do: "He's 25 years old now, and we believe that if he going to cash in on his football, now's the time."[11] Westfall signed on August 12, prompting Sinkwich to finally commit.

The league returned to 10 teams in 1944 when the Cleveland Rams resumed play and the expansion Boston Yanks joined. The Dodgers changed their name to the Tigers. The Eagles returned to a solo operation and the Steelers remained in a co-op situation, this time with the Chicago Cardinals. The Lions dropped their 1944 opener, 27–6, in Green Bay, and injuries led to a bleak outlook after a 1–3–1 start. The season took a turn in November, starting with a pair of wins in a home-and-home series with the abysmal Card-Pitt co-op.[12] It was the first of five wins to finish the season for Detroit, landing them in second place in the Western Division with a 6–3–1 record. Dorais coached a handful of games from the press box. The five victories was the club's longest string since the 1934 season. The high point was a November 19 victory at Briggs Stadium over the Bears, the Lions' first defeat of Chicago in eight games. Sinkwich tossed a club record four touchdowns.

Mandel was looking ahead to the post-war years, so he and Dorais created a new position—associate coach. They hired Pete Cawthon, the former head coach at Texas Tech. He had recently resigned from his head coaching duties for the Brooklyn Tigers after they dropped the first five games of the season. Cawthon's focus was on scouting and personnel. Detroit's success would focus around Westfall and Sinkwich. The latter did it all for the Lions, despite a battery of injuries, including a reported attack of appendicitis early in the season. He was among the leaders in several categories: rushing (563 yards), passing (58-for-148, 1060 yards, 12 touchdowns, 20 interceptions), scoring (66 points on six touchdowns, 24 PAT and 2 field goals), and punting (41-yard average). He won the Joe E. Carr Trophy, the early NFL MVP award, the first Lion to do so. He was also all-league for the second straight season. Wojciechowicz made his second All-Pro team (1939), setting a then-club record with seven interceptions.

Dorais moved the 1945 training camp up a week and to Assumption College in Ontario, Canada, a place where he frequently held football clinics during his days at the University of Detroit. Located just 15 minutes from downtown Detroit, it was the first time that a professional football team trained out of the country. Absent was Sinkwich, who joined the Merchant Marines—a huge loss for the Lions. Chuck Fenenbock returned after a medical discharge from the Marines. He showed no rust after playing for the El Toro Marine Corps team in 1944. Dorais also drafted his son, Tom Dorais, in the 32nd and last round with the 330th pick. A former Marine lieutenant who served in the Battle of Okinanwa, Tom practiced with the team, but failed to make the final cut. He went on to organize and quarterback one of the top semi-pro teams in the city—the Detroit All-Stars. He also coached St. Mary's High School of Royal Oak. The team was winless the previous year, but using his father's playbook, Tom led the team to an undefeated season and won the Catholic League's Second Division title in 1946. He scouted for the Lions that fall and was officially hired in December. He worked for Detroit through 1947 before serving as a Labor Relations representative at the Detroit Forge plant.

Dorais wasn't convinced that his backfield was complete, so he traded

The Lions drafted Tom Dorais with the 330th pick in the 32nd and last round. He didn't make the team, but went onto to serve as a scout and advisor to his father. Here, the two are discussing a football matter (Dorais family photo collection).

for Andy Farkas, his former star at the University of Detroit. The one-time Washington Redskins star and fan favorite was past his prime, never the same after suffering a knee injury in an exhibition game in 1941. He had a strong pro résumé, though, and Dorais hoped a return to Detroit could revitalize Farkas' career. It didn't, as the first man to wear eye black in the NFL retired after the season. In 1955 he helped found the Gus Dorais Foundation, shortly after Dorais passed away.

The Lions and Dorais earned praise for finishing the 1944 season strong. Attendance was up, and the franchise appeared to be poised for the future. There were 10 starters returning, but for Sinkwich. Dating back to the previous season, Detroit had their best streak in franchise history, winning 11 of 12 games. Known for his offensive innovations, Dorais was being lauded for his defensive success against the T formation. The Lions were the league's number one rated defense by the end of October, allowing just 456 yards rushing through six games. At 6–1, Detroit looked like contenders for the championship midway through the season. Westfall was at the top of his game, filling Sinkwich's void nicely and earning a spot on the *Associated Press'* All-Pro team at season's end. Guard Bill Radovich earned All-League honors, too, following three years of military service.

After a powerful 35–28 win in Chicago over the Bears, the Lions stumbled at the Polo Grounds, losing 35–14 to the Giants, who snapped a four-game losing streak. Dorais was furious, cutting four players, including back Cotton Price, who had sparked the club against Chicago. "You can't beat one ball club when you're thinking about another," said Dorais. "Most of the boys overlooked the Giants and were caught spending their time thinking about the Rams and the league championship."[13] Dorais signed his former back at the University of Detroit, Tippy Madarik, recently out of the Army, for backfield insurance.

On November 22, four days after the Giants stunner, the Lions were back at Briggs Stadium entertaining the 6–1 Rams, in front of a season-high 40,017 spectators. It was the first Thanksgiving Day game since 1938 and a must-win game for Detroit. A Lions victory would have tied the two teams for first in the conference, but Cleveland won, 28–21, dooming Detroit's playoff hopes for the tenth straight season. The Lions finished the season in Green Bay with a 14–3 win behind 219 yards passing from Fenenbock. It was Detroit's first victory over the Packers in 11 games dating back to October 10, 1940. And it was the first time they held them without a touchdown since 1934. Detroit finished with a 7–3 record, the high mark of Dorais' pro tenure.

The post-war years proved unkind to Dorais and the Lions. There were players who didn't return to the game, or, like in Sinkwich's case, came back a different player, having injured his knee while playing for the Second Air Force team. However, the biggest change in 1946 was the emergence of the upstart All-America Football Conference (AAFC). Dorais was more familiar than most with the AAFC, its having been created by his old friend, Arch Ward. The eight-team league was broken into two divisions: In the East were the New York Yankees, Brooklyn Dodgers, Buffalo Bisons and Miami Seahawks. The West was comprised of the Cleveland Browns, Chicago Rockets, Los Angeles Dons and San Francisco 49ers.

The AAFC was formed on June 4, 1944, with the intent of not beginning until the end of World War II. Ward felt that the return of soldiers would provide football with enough quality players to form another league. His job at the *Chicago Tribune* kept the league in the news. In December 1945, Dorais said that the NFL's negotiating tactics couldn't continue if they wanted to compete with the upstart AAFC. He warned that the NFL "will realize that it can't monopolize players any more and assume a take-it-or-leave-it attitude in the matter of contracts.[14] Both leagues held a secret draft, as the two teams would be competing for players.

By the summer of 1946, it was apparent that the AAFC was going to impact the NFL. Over 100 former NFL players signed with AAFC teams, as did 40 of the 66 participants in the College All-Star Game. The Lions lost their 1943 backfield to the rival league. Sinkwich signed with New York, Fenenbock with Los Angeles, and Hopp with Buffalo. Detroit made a point of locking in Westfall to a two-year contract in January, 1946.

A problem keeping the Lions from competing with other NFL teams and the AAFC clubs for players was financial constraints. Although attendance was up, it wasn't enough. Mandel was struggling to meet expenses. This came to the surface behind the scenes near the end of training camp. Tom Dorais, now a scout with the Lions, worked with his father. He explained the problem in a 1995 interview:

> I think it was probably due to Mandel. It got to the point the team was not getting enough support through the turnstiles playing at Briggs Stadium. And the payroll was getting out of hand as far as the owner was concerned. So he would have two players at one position. They would get to the point of cutting before the season started. He'd say there are two centers, the guy we are paying the most is the better center, but the other guy isn't too bad. Cut the higher salary guy and keep the lower salary guy. He really interfered from the standpoint of personnel.[15]

Detroit was simply not competitive in 1946. On top of this, training camp, now held at Alma College, was disastrous. Four players suffered bone fractures, and several highly-touted rookies failed to live up to their expectations. The team's third-round pick was Russ Thomas, a tackle from Ohio State. He'd play four years with the Lions before a knee injury cut his career short. He served as the team's general manager from 1967–1989.

Following an embarrassing 34–14 loss to the Chicago Cardinals to begin the 1946 season, Dorais tried to make a rare, hardline statement by cutting four linemen, including nine-year veteran Wojciechowicz. The former first-round pick from Fordham was claimed a few days later by the Philadelphia Eagles and went on to play five more seasons, winning two NFL championships and eventually a place in the Pro Football Hall of Fame.

The Lions lost a week later, 17–16. to the Redskins. There were rumors of the Detroit All-Stars, an amateur team. joining the AAFC. The team's secretary was star quarterback Tom Dorais, who would soon be hired by the Lions as a scout. In a surprising vote of confidence, Mandel gave Gus Dorais a new five-year contract through the 1951 season. "His teams have shown constant improvement and have finished second in the league's western division the last two seasons. I have every confidence in his ability to turn out a champion."[16]

Dorais' new contract did nothing for the Lions, losers of their next three games. The closest game was a 10–7 contest against the Packers at State Fair Park on the State Fair Grounds in West Allis outside Milwaukee. Dorais was honored by a group from his hometown, Chippewa Falls, with amongst other gifts, a full hunting outfit from the Chippewa Woolen Mill. Detroit finally won a game on November 10, a 17–7 victory over the Steelers, who were no longer co-oped. Success was short-lived, and the Lions lost the last four games of the season to finish 1–10, last in the Western Division. At season's end, Dorais said, "I guess I'll have to retreat into my den and lick my wounds and hope for a break on material next year."[17]

In December 1946, the Lions chose Heisman Trophy winner Glenn Davis with the second overall pick. Over three collegiate seasons, the back from Army won numerous awards, and though he had military service obligations, Detroit chose him. "We couldn't afford to pass up a player of Davis' caliber," explained Dorais. "He may not become available for two, three or even four years. When he does, we'll have prior rights in conducting negotiations."[18] Otherwise, Dorais adopted a Michigan-heavy draft, picking several players from within the state.

The following year, 1947, saw many changes for Dorais. He resigned from the Detroit Common Council in late May, after four terms. The pressures of coaching peaked in the 1946 season when the Lions went 1–10. He missed several council meetings in a row and was called out by the papers. He knew it would be impossible to keep up both commitments. Despite being one of the few popular councilmen and some urging to stay on the council, Gus finally resigned, citing pressures of other duties.

Tom and his wife, Mary Catherine, were in a head-on collision in March. Mary Catherine, who was pregnant, was in serious condition, but recovered and gave birth to a daughter, Diane, in early April.

On July 10, tragedy struck when 13-year-old David Dorais drowned on Tecon Lake near Gaylord, Michigan. At that time, there were only two homes on the lake, one owned by the Durant family, one of the founders of General Motors, and Gus' summer home. The Dorais family had gathered there with cousins from Iowa for a summer family reunion. Gus, who was an avid fisherman, and the older men set out in a boat to the opposite end of the lake to enjoy a few hours of fishing.

Prior to leaving, David, who did not know how to swim, promised his father he would be swimming by the time he returned. David and his 15-year-old cousin, William McCabe, began practicing swimming and venturing out further from shore towards a raft nearby. As David practiced, he became more adventurous and decided to head out on his own. Nearing the raft, he began to struggle and started going under. William got to David and started to pull him up on the raft, but David slipped out of William's grip and sank in the water. The boys' mothers watched helplessly from shore, before going to find Gus and Tom. The pair assisted in the recovery of David's body and for two hours watched the attempts to resuscitate the boy. The next day, Gus, along with sons Tom and Bill, drove David's body back to Detroit.[19]

Dorais was never the same after losing his youngest. His health was already in decline and worsened following David's death. Bob Murphy, a good friend of Gus and Sports Editor at the *Detroit Times*, was with him the following day after David drowned. "I saw a man go from middle age to old age overnight. That was how tough he took it."[20]

For the 1947 season, Dorais committed the Lions' offense to the T formation, abandoning the single wing. He dubbed his new offense the "D-T" or "Detroit T," a slight variation on the standard T featuring an unusual line alignment. For all the changes, the Lions had another lackluster season, finishing last in the division at 3–9. One of the few bright spots on the team was "Bullet" Bill Dudley. The reigning NFL MVP and a two-way player, he won a rare Triple Crown in 1946 (rushing, interception and punt return titles), but abruptly stepped away from the game following the season. The future Hall of Famer had suffered a knee injury during the last game of the season and was worn down by playing nearly every down for demanding coach Jock Sutherland. Dudley was put on waivers by the Steelers, and Detroit went after him. He returned to his alma mater, the University of Virginia, to coach the backs, but Dorais traveled to Charlottesville to talk him into playing for the Lions. Dudley was hesitant, as his knee had yet to heal. Detroit said they'd pay for him and his soon-to-be wife to go out to California to see a knee specialist. Dudley was given the okay to play, and Mandel offered him a three-year, no-cut contract at $20,000 a season, the highest per-season contract since Red Grange in 1925.

The Lions began 1–3 and had won of just two of their last 15 games. Dorais was feeling pressure to produce. Mandel was threatening his job in the papers by midseason. It didn't get any easier, as the team traveled to Chicago to take on the 2–1 defending NFL champion Bears. In a brief pre-game address, Dorais showed his frustration with the situation. Dudley recalled the talk. "We're here to play the big, bad Bears," said Dorais, "and we're going to get the hell kicked out of us, get on the train, get drunk, go home, and get fired. Now let's go out there and have some fun!"[21] The Lions lost, 33–24.

Dorais remained coach, and Detroit won two of their last seven games, going just 1–5 on the road. After seven seasons without a title, Fred Mandel was weighing his options for selling the team and buying Dorais out of his contract. In mid–December, the owner purchased the remaining four years of Dorais' contract, estimated to be $50,000–$75,000. They had a secrecy agreement regarding the terms of the settlement, but Dorais was described as "well satisfied" with the payment. Tom Dorais was also let go. Gus Dorais' record over the five seasons and 53-game tenure with the Lions was, 20 wins, 31 losses and two ties, for a .396 winning percentage.

Looking back on his five years with the Lions, Dorais gave some insight into his successes and failures:

> Player strength faded until an all-time low was reached in 1942 when the Detroit club lost every game of an 11-game schedule and scored only 38 points against its opponents' 263.
>
>   Then came the wartime teams when it was mostly catch-as-catch-can for material. This helped to equalize personnel and the record improved. In 1944 they tied for second place, and in 1945 they took second place alone. At one point going 12 of 15 between the two seasons.
>
>   By 1946 all the clubs began to get their good players back from the services, but the Lions had no such reserve to draw from and another dismal year developed.... There have been great players here since [1942]—but a supporting cast to provide proper help has been missing....[22]

Dorais with his youngest son, David, at the Lions training camp. In July 1947, David drowned while swimming. The tragedy would cast a pall on Gus Dorais for the rest of his life (Detroit Lions Archives).

"I'm going to continue living in Detroit," Dorais said. "My roots run deep in Detroit."[23]

Soon after settling with Dorais, Mandel sold the team for $165,000 to a group of Detroit area businessmen, led by D. Lyle Fife, head of an electrical products firm, and Edwin J. Anderson, president of Goebel Brewing Co. Mandel could have paid less to Dorais if he sold the club first, due to a contract clause, but it was likely that he needed to clear up the Dorais situation prior to entertaining offers for the club sale. Dorais said his ties with the Lions were severed and that he had no plans for the future, but would rest for a while. "Maybe I'll get out of football and into private business," he said.[24] In another interview, he stated, "Football is my business and I intend to stay in it."[25]

CHAPTER 11

A Football Man to the End

After leaving the Detroit Lions, Dorais temporarily retired from the public spotlight and settled in to his home in Detroit. He kept up his connections in the city and the world of football. By the summer of 1948, he was again back in football—this time in a different capacity. He was hired by the New York Yankees of the All-America Football Conference as a scout. One of his former players at Gonzaga, Ray Flaherty, was now the head coach of the squad. A proponent of the forward pass, he is credited with inventing the screen pass in 1937 while coaching the Washington Redskins. When Dorais was let go by the Lions, Flaherty jumped at the opportunity to have his mentor scout the Midwest for him. Gus remained a scout with the Yankees through mid–September 1948, when Flaherty was let go.

Dorais had lived in Detroit since 1925, becoming a popular sports and political figure. He established many connections in the community and was a regular at the Detroit Athletic Club, as were many prominent Detroiters. One such connection was with the executives of General Motors. After his scouting job with the Yankees had ended in September, Dorais started to look seriously for a private business opportunity—a notion he'd had since graduating from Notre Dame. He now had a sizable nest egg from his contract buyout with the Lions and selling his home on Tecon Lake. He had been approached by Ford once before in the late 30s to start a dealership in Spokane. The timing wasn't right, but the idea intrigued him. Now he had the time and the money, and both his sons were in the automobile business. Bill had been working the last three years as a salesman in Hamtramck at Dick Connell Chevrolet, and Tom had just begun the job at the Detroit Forge plant. Gus' idea was to start a business with his sons that they would take over and run as a family business. Tom quickly passed on the idea, having secured an executive position with General Motors.

In late 1948, Gus and Bill arranged a meeting at the GM building to talk with Gus' close friend and fellow Notre Dame alumnus, Hugh Dean, Vice President and General Manager of Chevrolet, about the possibilities of obtaining a dealership. Dean was very keen on the idea because the Dorais name would be popular and identifiable and would likely lead to a very successful dealership. Soon after the first meeting, Chevrolet contacted Gus and informed him there was a dealership available in Ohio along Lake Erie. Gus and Bill agreed to go take a look. They arrived on a Thursday and met with the Regional Manager. At the end of the day, Chevrolet wanted them to accept and sign on the spot. Both Gus and Bill said they had to get back to Detroit and discuss the move with their spouses, Vi and Helen, and would give them an answer after the weekend. On Monday, they had decided to take the dealership. However, Chevrolet informed them that the dealership was no longer available. They were very disappointed but hopeful another opportunity would present itself.

In early January 1949, Hugh Dean called to say that a dealership had become available in Wabash, Indiana. Vere E. Bromley, owner of Bromley Chevrolet in Wabash, had passed away on Christmas Day. His family was not interested in continuing the dealership. Gus and Bill jumped on the opportunity and went to Wabash as soon as they were given the news. They signed the agreement for the dealership and began working right away. They lived in a hotel near the dealership for the first two months before moving their families from Detroit to Wabash. In March, Vi and daughter, Joan, along with Bill's wife, Helen, and their two small children moved to Wabash, Indiana. Gus, Vi and Joan moved to a house on the Wabash River near Rich Valley, a home they dearly loved during their time there.

The dealership was renamed "Gus Dorais Chevrolet." Gus was the face of the dealership, but for all intents and purposes Bill Dorais ran the franchise from the beginning. Gus had no experience in business or with cars. Bill Dorais had the dealership experience and quickly got the business on track and moving. Today, Dorais Chevrolet is successfully run by Gus' grandson, Dave Dorais. Gus and Vi stayed in Wabash until June 1953, before moving back to the Detroit area.

In spring, 1949, Dorais was invited back to Detroit by the Michigan Football Writers' Association to give him the thank you they had failed to when he left the city in haste. Not surprisingly, the affair turned into a huge event as the party sponsors were deluged with ticket requests. Over 100 coaches, writers and radiomen showed up at the Fort Shelby Hotel on June 9. The party was forced to move from the Sky Room to the much larger Coral Room. Even then, accommodations were tight. When comparing running his dealership to coaching, Dorais quipped, "At least I can sleeps nights... ..so far."[1]

Dorais slipped into life at the dealership in Wabash and made the rounds as a public speaker, but it was impossible for him to completely step away from football. In July, he was announced as the head scout and talent scout for the All-America Football Conference's Chicago Hornets, now coached by Flaherty. The 1949 season would be the last in the league's existence. Dorais' duties included scouting conference opponents and college teams for future prospects. "I guess football is like a germ you can't shake off," Dorais once said. "I just can't seem to be happy out of it."[2]

While living in Wabash, Dorais was a member of the

In early 1949, Gus along with his son, Bill, opened the "Gus" Dorais Chevrolet Automobile Agency in Wabash, Indiana (The Indiana Album: Johnson Bros. Sign Company Collection).

Elks Lodge and Rotary Club. He was also an active member of the St. Bernard Catholic Church. He was often found on the practice fields of the local high schools—Wabash High, Southwood High and Northfield High— serving as an unofficial assistant coach. All the high schools instituted Gus Dorais Awards in football and basketball, voted on by the teams.

On September 1, Dorais helped unveil a bronze plaque dedicated to Knute Rockne at Cedar Point Beach in Sandusky, Ohio. It read:

> To Knute Rockne.... In grateful memory of the man whose standards of fair play are an immortal inspiration to the youth of America. And whose many contributions to the great sport of football will never be forgotten.... He developed the forward pass on this strip of beach at Cedar Point.
>
> Memories flooded back as he spoke of the summer he and Rockne worked on the forward pass. Dorais held no animosity towards not being mentioned on the plaque, saying "it is the proudest moment of my life when I can do something in honor of Rockne."[3]

Yet another tribute for Rockne took place in late October, this one in Chicago. Dorais was one of the speakers for the dedication of Rockne Stadium at Roosevelt Road and Central Avenue. The program was televised on television—WGN-TV—in its second year of existence.

Dorais' health had been declining for years. During much of 1950, he received treatment for a gallstone ailment. When pain persisted, he traveled to Rochester, Minnesota, for exploratory surgery at world-renowned Mayo Clinic. The operation was deemed a success when no cancer was found, and he returned to football. In the fall, he did some freelance scouting for the Chicago Bears and Washington Redskins. Dorais also appeared on several football radio programs. He stayed active on the banquet circuit up until 1952, speaking before various football groups and associations around the Midwest. In 1951, he was a television analyst before and after college games under a National Collegiate experimental program called "Foot Ball Scoreboard." Before games on WWJ-TV, Dorais analyzed games and picked the winners of a big national slate. He then

Chicago's Rockne Stadium was dedicated in October 1949. Dorais served as one of the speakers (Dorais family photo collection).

reviewed the highlights of the televised games and checked his selections in a postgame program.[4]

In February 1952, Gus and Vi set out on an adventure aboard a cruise ship. They took a two-week cruise from New York to the Panama Canal. The trip was the first time Gus had been outside the United States. He remained an active member of the Notre Dame community. In June 1952

In 1952, Dorais was hired by the Pittsburgh Steelers as an assistant coach to help head coach Joe Bach implement the T formation. Bach, a fellow Notre Dame alum, had served as an assistant coach for Dorais' entire time as head coach of the Detroit Lions (Dorais family photo collection).

he was named one of the directors of the Notre Dame National Monogram Club.

That summer, Dorais was hired as the backfield coach for the Pittsburgh Steelers. His longtime assistant coach with the Detroit Lions, Joe Bach, was beginning his second stint as head coach of the Steelers. Pittsburgh was the last pro team running the single wing, and Bach was brought in to implement the T formation. He turned to Dorais to aid in the process. "Dorais does me a great honor to accept this position" he declared. "He is the most pass-minded coach in the country and will help us greatly in Pittsburgh."[5] Also called into help was Keith Molesworth, a former quarterback for the Bears, where he ran the T and won back-to-back NFL titles (1932 and 1933).

The Steelers went 5–7 in 1952, finishing fourth in the American Division. Dorais' influence was very noticeable as Pittsburgh's passing game was near the top of the league, statistically. This was a big improvement over the previous year, when they were near the bottom. The Steelers went from a top defense in 1951 to one of the worst in 1952. At the end of the season, Gus wrote in a letter, "At the present time I am not planning to return to the Steelers. However, I have high hopes for the Pittsburgh Club next season, if it can sharpen up its pass defense. The Steelers made enough points last season [1952] to be in the running if they could have held down the scoring of the opposition a bit more."[6]

During that season, Dorais was approached by longtime friend, Sam Greene, a sports columnist in Detroit, requesting an all-time team. Dorais reluctantly agreed, but said he would only name a team of players that either he had seen on the field or whose careers preceded the free substitution rule of the early 1940s:

Quarterback—Dutch Clark (Colorado College and Detroit Lions): Nobody could top the Dutchman in football instinct or in ability to run the team. Few topped him in mechanical skill.
Halfback: Jim Thorpe (Carlisle and Canton Bulldogs): A one-man team.
Halfback: George Gipp (Notre Dame): Maybe I'm prejudiced having coached the Gipper when I was Rock's assistant, but I'd have to pick him over any other halfback, except Thorpe.
Fullback: Bronko Nagurski (Minnesota and Chicago Bears): Some people prefer Ernie Nevers (Stanford), but I thought the Bronk a better all-around man.
Center—Mel Hein: Washington State and New York Giants): I'd

give him an edge over Bulldog Turner (Hardin-Simmons University and Chicago Bears).

Guard—Clarence Spears (Dartmouth and Canton): More than a guard, Doc was half a line in himself.

Guard—Danny Fortmann: (Colgate and Bears): The best in the modern pro league.

Tackle: Wilbur Henry: (Washington & Jefferson and early Ohio pro teams): Closest to Doc Spears among the lineman to come under my observation.

Tackle: Ed Healy (Dartmouth and Bears): He could do everything.

End: Harold Muller (University of California—Berkeley): Remembered best for his long passes but outstanding in all other phases, too.

End: Don Hutson (Alabama and Green Bay Packers): A pass receiver who drove defensive coaches to distraction. I doubt that we'll ever again see his equal.[7]

It was clear that Dorais had limited time. He looked 82, not 62. Interviews increased, pushing him to recall his greatest moments. About a year before his death, he was interviewed as a part of the series "My Greatest Day" that the *Detroit News* did with famous personalities:

Memories come trooping out of the past—

Of the day on the plains of West Point when unsung, low rated Notre Dame introduced to the east a team out of the west that decisively defeated a great Army team with a barrage of passes to Knute Rockne in the big upset of the year.... Being on the throwing end of the passes made a day I'll never forget—

Of the day I saw my name on an All-American football selection—

Of the day I was put into my first game to play with the Notre Dame varsity—

Of getting five drop kicks over the bar to bring victory to an unbeaten Notre Dame team over unbeaten Texas in one of the first great intersectional games—

Of a day as a coach at Gonzaga U., when we, always the chopping block in the opener against Washington State, rose up and beat them for the first time.... And of getting a ride back to the locker rooms on the shoulders of my players—

The day my underdog University of Detroit team came up at Sacramento, Calif., and beat Santa Clara, the "Wonder Team of the West," by a 7–6 score—

The night the College All-Stars, I coaching, beat Green Bay for the first All-Star victory over the pros—

And, as another flashback, the championship game between Canton and Massillon when I put two drop kicks over and threw a final clinching pass to Rockne for a victory over Jim Thorpe's great Canton team.

But, summing and assaying everything, I believe my greatest day was as a high school boy at Chippewa Falls, Wis., when we outpassed and outscored an unbeaten Marinette high team for the state championship in a postseason game between our two unbeaten squads and returned home to be met at the depot by the entire town and the welcoming band, behind which we marched right up the main street. I believe that day remains the greenest and the greatest in my memory.[8]

In March 1953, Dorais was diagnosed with arteriosclerosis. As his health concerns became dire, he and Vi moved back to the Detroit area in June to be near doctors. They moved into a residence at 19050 Middlesex Avenue in Southfield, Michigan. Confined to his home, Dorais spent a lot of time entertaining visitors, whom he liked to tell: "I've have seen more football on television this season than in any season before in my life—all I miss is the depth of play, but I guess I qualify as a TV expert."[9]

The last press statement Dorais ever gave was in December 1953, when he provided his opinion on the two-point conversion plan proposed by Fritz Crisler. Dorais was against any point after touchdown. "I have never been against ties when they occur between teams of equal strength, but I never believed a specialist's foot should tilt the scales one way or another."[10]

As Dorais' illness worsened, the television was moved to his bedside. He was dropping weight rapidly—at the time of his death he weighed a mere 67 pounds. On New Year's Day, 1954, he watched parts of the early games and all of the Rose Bowl. The next evening he watched the annual East-West Shrine Game. A few hours afterwards, he took a turn for the worse and the family physician was called to the house. When death seemed imminent, a priest was called, and Dorais was given communion and the sacrament of Extreme Unction. With his wife of 36 years and four children by his side, Dorais passed away at 5:50 am, Monday, January 3, 1954, at the age of 62. He was further survived by his mother, siblings and 13 grandchildren.

Later that morning, Dorais' body was removed from his home. The news of his death flashed across the wire services and radio. Soon his small home was flooded with phone calls. More than 75 telegrams of condolence were delivered from sports personalities from around the country.[11] The next day, countless headlines and articles across the nation recounted Dorais' playing days and his coaching career.

On Tuesday, a viewing for Dorais was held in Detroit at the Ted C. Sullivan Funeral Home. The funeral service was held at Gesu Church on Wednesday, with hundreds of people gathered, including several prominent sports figures in Detroit and from around the country. Dozens of his former players and staff crowded in to the church. The six pallbearers were former University of Detroit football players who played for Dorais, including his first star player and captain from the undefeated 1928 team,

Tom Connell. The others included Alex Chesney, John Hackett, Ed Kukurowski, Art Masucci and John Shada, all now local high school coaches. Charles Emile "Gus" Dorais was laid to rest on January 6, 1954, at Holy Sepulcher cemetery. He was interred in the mausoleum next to his son David, who tragically passed away in 1947.

Sports figures from around the country weighed in on Dorais' passing:

Fr. John Cavanaugh, former president of Notre Dame: "For all time he is solidly in the foundation of football at Notre Dame."[12]

Michael "Dad" Butler, Dorais' longtime trainer at the University of Detroit: "Tell them how I feel—I—I can't. Why, he was my boy, my son. You know he brought me here—tell them—I can't talk.... God bless Gus."[13]

Art Rooney, Pittsburgh Steelers owner: "Gus did as much as any man that ever lived for the game of football."[14]

Fred Gushurst, teammate and starting end on the 1913 Notre Dame team: "Dorais was a tremendous football player. He not only developed the forward pass, but he was as good an open field runner as football has ever had and he could punt with the best."[15]

Thomas D. Leadbetter, Detroit City Clerk: "He was the only councilman in my memory who approached his civic job with complete humility."[16]

Lloyd Brazil, University of Detroit Athletic Board Chairman and former player and coach: "Gus was a wonderful man to work for both as a player and a coach. Athletics at the University of Detroit would have never reached the high pinnacle it now enjoys without his guidance and influence."[17]

A few weeks later, the Gus Dorais Memorial Award was created by the Detroit Sports Guild. For years it was given at the Detroit Sports Guild Awards banquet. Shortly thereafter, an ordinance was proposed to name a playfield at the northwest corner of Mound Road and East Outer Drive as the "Charles E. Dorais Playfield," which would later be shortened to Dorais Park. It had one of the few hills in town, became a spot for sledding, and held the *Detroit News* Soap Box Derby races over the years. It also was home to a velodrome that was completed in July 21, 1969, and was part of the U.S. National Track Championships. Although in disrepair, the Dorais Velodrome is still in use today.

In 1955, the Gus Dorais Memorial Foundation was organized. Funds were used to defray the cost of athletic scholarships. The first president was Andy Farkas. Numerous former players of Dorais served in various capacities. On November 11, 1955, the Metropolitan Alumni Club dedicated a plaque to Dorais' memory outside the main entrance to Calihan Hall by the athletic offices.

Though he never made it back to Chippewa Falls to live, Dorais' hometown put his name on a permanent structure in 1976. On September 17, Dorais Field was dedicated. Since then, it has turned into a multipurpose sports facility for two high schools and the community: football,

Vi Dorais at the unveiling of Gus' Wisconsin Sports Hall of Fame plaque in 1955 (Dorais family photo collection).

soccer, and band competitions are a few of the events that are held there throughout the year. In 2007, the field underwent a $2 million renovation, with a synthetic turf field being the central piece, along with new bleachers, press box and concession stand. Continued upgrades are scheduled.

In June 1981, Gus Dorais Memorial Drive was dedicated on the University of Detroit's McNichols Campus, along with a park in his name. Both were adjacent to the field house where he trained his teams. Over 300 friends and members of the Dorais family gathered at the University of Detroit's Football Alumni Association Annual Dinner for a "We Remember Gus" program at the downtown Roostertail Restaurant.

Dorais was posthumously named to numerous Halls of Fame:

College Football Hall of Fame (1954) (Coach)
National Football Foundation Hall of Fame (1954)
Wisconsin Sports Hall of Fame (1955)
Michigan Sports Hall of Fame (1958)
Helms Foundation Hall of Fame (1960)
Inland Island Sports Hall of Fame (1963)
Cardinals Hall of Fame (Chippewa Falls High School, Inaugural
     Class of 1981)
Loras College Athletics Hall of Fame (Inaugural Class of 1983)
University of Detroit Mercy Athletics Hall of Fame (1987)
Gonzaga Athletic Hall of Fame (Inaugural Class of 1988)

Dorais earned many nicknames during his football career: Will O' Wisp, Mighty Mite, Little General and the Livernois Fox, to name a few. They all were feeble attempts by writers to describe a diminutive kid from a broken home in the northwoods of Wisconsin, who had an immeasurable impact on football. He grew up with the game and had a strong influence on and off the field. Held in the highest regard by his peers and players, Dorais was an innovator and a pioneer, always looking for a new angle and often succeeding. He played with and coached against most of the legends of his era and was a friend to everybody. One of the greatest football minds of his time, large schools wouldn't dare schedule a game with him. He toiled at smaller schools and made these teams play beyond their means. Not a yeller, but rather an even tempered, soft-spoken man, he instilled not only football knowledge in his players but taught them to play at their best, to act like men, to handle the challenge, to keep going after failure, and to be humble in victory. Dorais' good friend Arch Ward may have said it best: "Hundreds of men are better citizens because of their association with one of the noblest characters American sport has produced."[18]

APPENDIX I

Year-by-Year Playing Record

High School

School	Year	Win	Loss	Tie	Home	Away	Points For	Points Against	Shutouts
Notre Dame High School	1906	—	—	—	—	—	—	—	—
	1907	—	—	—	—	—	—	—	—
	1908	4	1		—	—	—	—	—
Total		4	1		4–1–1				
Chippewa Falls High School	1909	6	0	1	4–0–1	2–0	171	5	5
Total		6	0	1	4–0–1	2–0	171	5	5
Career Total		10	1	1	8–0–1	2–0	171	5	5

College

School	Year	Win	Loss	Tie	Home	Away	Points For	Points Against	Shutouts
University of Notre Dame	1910	4	1	1	3–0–0	1–1–1	192	25	3
	1911	6	0	2	5–0–0	1–0–2	222	9	4
	1912	7	0	0	4–0–0	3–0–0	389	27	3
	1913	7	0	0	3–0–0	4–0–0	268	41	2
Career Total		24	1	3	15–0–0	9–1–3	1,242	102	12

Professional

Only games Dorais played in

Team	Year	Win	Loss	Tie	Home	Away	Points For	Points Against	Shutouts
Massillon Tigers	1915	2	1	0	1–0	1–1	19	6	2
	1916	1	0	1	1–0–1	—	54	0	1
	1919	5	2	1	1–0	4–2–1	69	38	3
Total		8	3	2	3–0–1	5–3–1	142	44	6
Ft. Wayne Friars	1916	5	0	0	5–0	—	154	20	3
	1917	5	3	1	5–2–1	0–1	179	64	3
Total		10	3	1	10–2–1	0–1	333	84	6
Career Total		18	6	3	13–2–2	5–4–1	475	128	12

APPENDIX II

Coaching Record

College

School	Year	Win	Loss	Tie	Home	Away	Points For	Points Against	Shutouts
Dubuque College	1914	2	4	1	2–3	0–1–1	50	119	0
	1915	7	1		5–1	2–0	168	39	3
	1916	7	0	1	4–0–1	3–0	64	33	2
	1917	3	4		3–1	0–3	59	104	1
Total		19	9	2	14–5–1	5–4–1	441	295	6
Gonzaga Univ.	1920	4	3		2–2	2–1	164	55	3
	1921	3	4	1	2–2–1	1–2	70	93	2
	1922	5	3		3–1	2–2	215	79	2
	1923	4	3		3–0	1–3	119	64	
	1924	5	0	2	2–0–2	3–0	138	26	3
Total		21	13	3	12–5–3	9–8	706	317	10
Univ. of Detroit	1925	5	4		4–3	1–1	70	80	3
	1926	3	6	1	3–4–1	0–2	62	132	1
	1927	7	2		4–1	3–1	235	54	3
	1928	9	0		6–0	3–0	267	27	7
	1929	7	1	1	5–1–1	2–0	174	52	3
	1930	5	3	2	5–2	0–1–2	198	32	4
	1931	7	2	1	6–1–1	1–1	113	71	5
	1932	8	2		6–0	2–2	136	66	3
	1933	7	1		6–0	1–1	157	20	6
	1934	5	3	1	4–2	1–1–1	112	52	3
	1935	6	3		5–1	1–2	187	60	4

School	Year	Win	Loss	Tie	Home	Away	Points For	Points Against	Shutouts
	1936	7	3		4–2	3–1	194	58	4
	1937	7	3		4–2	3–1	252	42	5
	1938	6	4		4–0	2–4	149	81	3
	1939	5	3	1	4–2	1–1–1	149	90	1
	1940	7	2		5–1	2–1	147	27	6
	1941	7	2		5–1	2–1	195	43	4
	1942	5	4		4–2	1–2	92	66	4
Total		113	48	7	84–25–3	29–23–4	2,889	1,053	69
Career Total		153	70	12	110–35–7	43–35–5	4,036	1,665	85

Professional Record

Team	Year	Win	Loss	Tie	Home	Away	Points For	Points Against	Shutouts	Place in Western Division
Detroit Lions	1943	3	6	1	2–2-1	1–4	178	217	2	3rd
	1944	6	3	1	5–2	1–1–1	216	151		2nd
	1945	7	3		4–1	3–2	188	194	2	2nd
	1946	1	10		1–5	0–5	142	310		5th
	1947	3	9		2–4	1–5	231	305		5th
Total		20	31	2	14–14–1	6–17–1	955	1,178	4	

Combined Lifetime Record All Games

Team	Win	Loss	Tie	Home	Away	Points For	Points Against	Shutouts
High School Player	10	0	1	8–0–1	2–0	171	5	5
College Player	24	1	3	15–0–0	9–1–3	1,242	102	12
Professional Player	18	6	3	13–2–2	5–4–1	475	128	12
College Coach	153	70	12	110–35–7	43–35–5	4,036	1,665	85
Professional Coach	20	31	2	14–14–1	6–17–1	955	1,178	4
Career Total	225	108	21	160–51–11	65–57–10	6879	3078	118

Chapter Notes

Preface

1. *Detroit Times*, April 1, 1931, 6.
2. *Detroit News*, January 5, 1954, 2.

Introduction

1. Max Loeb (February 1949), "Wonderful Eddie Cochems," *Wisconsin Alumnus* 50, no. 5), 9.
2. Charles E. "Gus" Dorais, *The Forward Pass And Its Defense* (Chicago: The Athletic Book Co., 1931), 8.
3. *Athletic Journal* , March 1932, 35.
4. Dorais Family Clippings File.

Chapter 1

1. *Notre Dame Scholastic* (University of Notre Dame), June 14, 1913, 573–574.
2. Tom Dorais interview, September 23, 1995.
3. *Notre Dame Scholastic*, June 14, 1913, 574.
4. Tom Dorais interview, September 23, 1995.
5. *Daily Independent* (Chippewa Falls, WI), November 15, 1908, 1.
6. *Wisconsin State Journal* (Madison, WI), January 31, 1957, sec. 3, 1.
7. *Wisconsin State Journal*, November 21, 1907, 5.
8. *Daily Independent*, September 19, 1909, 3.
9. *Eau Claire Leader* (Eau Claire, WI), September 30, 1909, 2.
10. *Daily Independent*, October 3, 1909, 3.
11. *The Monocle* (Chippewa Falls High School Yearbook), 1909–1910 school year, 36.
12. *Daily Independent*, October 10, 1909, 3.
13. *Ibid.*, October 17, 1909, 3.
14. *Ibid.*, November 21, 1909, 3.

15. *Ibid.*, November 28, 1909, 3.
16. *La Crosse Tribune* (La Crosse, WI), November 30, 1909, 2.
17. *Madison State Journal* (Madison, WI), May 24, 1953, sec. 3, 1.
18. *La Crosse Tribune*, November 30, 1909, 2.
19. *Ibid.*
20. *Chippewa Herald-Telegram* (Chippewa Falls, WI), April 2, 1931, 1.
21. *The Monocle*, 1909–1910 school year, 41.
22. *Ibid.*, 12.
23. *Detroit Free Press*, February 3, 1935, 47.
24. *Ibid.*
25. *Varsity News* (University of Detroit), September 25, 1940, 3.
26. *Detroit Free Press*, January 16, 1936, 14.
27. *Ibid.*
28. *Chicago Tribune*, January, 5, 1954, C1.

Chapter 2

1. *Collier's*, October 18, 1930, 9.
2. *Collier's*, October 18, 1930, 72.
3. *Street & Smith's Sport Story Magazine*, December 1, 1938, 37.
4. Arthur J. Hope, *Notre Dame: One Hundred Years* (South Bend, IN: Notre Dame University Press, 1943), 241.
5. *Indianapolis News*, November 23, 1901, 6.
6. *Street & Smith's Sport Story Magazine*, December 1, 1938, 43.
7. *South Bend Tribune*, September 5, 1910, 10.
8. *Detroit Free Press*, January 16, 1936, 14.
9. *Athletic Journal*, March 1932, 35.
10. Karen Croake Heisler, *Fighting Irish: Legends, Lists and Lore* (Champaign, IL: Sports Publishing, 2006), 40.

11. *Street & Smith's Sport Story Magazine*, December 1, 1938, 45.
12. *South Bend Tribune*, October 21, 1910, 12.
13. *Collier's*, October 18, 1930, 73.
14. *Detroit Free Press*, January 16, 1936, 14.
15. *South Bend Tribune*, October 24, 1910, 9.
16. *Ibid.*, October 13, 1911, 14.
17. *Street & Smith's Sport Story Magazine*, December 2, 1938, 105.
18. Ken Rappoport, *Wake Up the Echoes: Notre Dame Football* (Huntsville, AL: Strode Publishers, 1975), 42.
19. *Notre Dame Scholastic*, November 26, 1910, 176.
20. *Ibid.*, December 3, 1910, 192.
21. *Ibid.*, 182.
22. *Street & Smith's Sport Story Magazine*, December 2, 1938, 103.
23. Dorais family clippings file.
24. *Street & Smith's Sport Story Magazine*, December 2, 1938, 42.
25. *Ibid.*, 41.
26. Dorais Family Clippings File.
27. *Ibid.*
28. *Madison Capital Times* (Madison, WI) April 2, 1931, 5.
29. *Detroit Free Press*, January 16, 1936, 14.
30. *The Dome: The Yearbook of the University of Notre Dame* (South Bend, IN: University of Notre Dame Press, 1914), 25.
31. *Street & Smith's Sport Story Magazine*, December 2, 1938, 103.
32. *Sandusky Register Star-News* (Sandusky, OH), September 2, 1949, 1.
33. *Street & Smith's Sport Story Magazine*, December 2, 1938, 104.
34. *Spokesman-Review* (Spokane, WA), February 15, 1925, 15
35. *Spokesman-Review* (Spokane, WA), February 15, 1925, page unknown.
36. *Notre Dame Scholastic*, November 15, 1913, 126.
37. Chris Willis, *Old Leather: An Oral History of Early Pro Football in Ohio, 1920–1935* (Lanham, MD: Scarecrow, 2005), 34.
38. *Chicago Daily Tribune*, April 4, 1931, 21.
39. Ken Rappoport, *Wake Up the Echoes: Notre Dame Football* (Huntsville, AL: Strode Publishers, 1975), 44.
40. *Street & Smith's Sport Story Magazine*, December 2, 1938, 105.
41. James Beach and Daniel Moore, *Army vs. Notre Dame: The Big Game, 1913–1947* (New York: Random House, 1948), xiv.
42. *Collier's*, October 25, 1930, 20.
43. *Ibid.*
44. *Anaconda Standard* (Anaconda, Montana), November 24, 1911, 7.
45. James Beach and Daniel Moore, *Army vs. Notre Dame: The Big Game, 1913–1947* (New York: Random House, 1948), xii.
46. *Street & Smith's Sport Story Magazine*, December 2, 1938, 108.
47. *Milwaukee Journal*, January 6, 1935, 12.
48. *Ibid.*
49. *South Bend Tribune*, October 28, 1912, 10.
50. *Street & Smith's Sport Story Magazine*, December 2, 1938, 108.
51. *Chicago Daily News*, November 3, 1942, 16.
52. *Ibid.*
53. *Ibid.*
54. *Ibid.*
55. *Milwaukee Sentinel*, November 29, 1912, 8.
56. *Chicago Daily Tribune*, November 29, 1929, 16
57. *Ibid.*

Chapter 3

1. *Street & Smith's Sport Story Magazine*, December 2, 1938, 110.
2. *South Bend Tribune*, September 17, 1913, 10.
3. *Blue and Gold Illustrated* (Durham, NC), November 9, 1998, 23.
4. Charles E. "Gus" Dorais, *The Forward Pass and Its Defense* (Chicago: The Athletic Book Co., 1931), 8–9.
5. *Athletic Journal*, September, 1931, 16.
6. *South Bend Tribune*, October 15, 1913, 14.
7. *Varsity News* (University of Detroit), March 25, 1931, 3.
8. *South Bend News-Times*, October 30, 1913, 8.
9. *Ibid.*, 10.
10. *Wisconsin State Journal* (Madison, WI), August 12, 1937, 15.
11. *Chicago Daily Tribune*, December 30, 1933, 13.
12. *Street & Smith's Sport Story Magazine*, January, 1, 1939, 88.
13. *Ibid.*, 89.
14. *New York Times*, November 2, 1913, 33.
15. *Street & Smith's Sport Story Magazine*, January, 1, 1939, 90.
16. *Detroit Free Press*, October 4, 1936, 57.
17. *Notre Dame Scholastic* (University of Notre Dame, South Bend, IN), November 15, 1913, 126.

18. *Ibid.*,159.

19. *Detroit Free Press*, June 9, 1949, 22.

20. *Ibid.*

21. *Dress & Vanity Fair* (New York, NY), January, 1914, 55.

22. *Detroit Free Press*, October 4, 1936, 57.

23. *Morning Oregonian* (Portland, OR), January 21, 1914, 14.

24. *South Bend Tribune*, December 3, 1913, 14.

25. *South Bend Tribune*, December 18, 1913, 18.

26. *Notre Dame Scholastic*, April, 18, 1914, 599.

27. *Notre Dame Alumnus*, November 1928, 91.

28. Dorais Family Clippings File.

29. *Cedar Rapids Evening Gazette* (Cedar Rapids, IA), June 20, 1914, 8.

30. *Ibid.*

Chapter 4

1. Mathias Martin Hoffmann, *The Story of Loras College, 1839–1939, The Oldest College in Iowa* (Dubuque, IA: Loras College Press, 1939), 181.

2. *Dubuque Telegram-Herald*, January 1, 1915, sec. 2, 1.

3. *Dubuque Telegram-Herald*, September 13, 1914, 20.

4. *Detroit Saturday Times*, April 4, 1925, page unknown. Dorais Family Clippings File.

5. *Spokesman-Review* (Spokane, WA), January 4, 1954, 9.

6. *Chicago Tribune*, October 14, 1932, 28.

7. *Dubuque Telegram-Herald*, September 5, 1954, 19.

8. Maurice Sheehy, *The Dubuque Football Review* (Dubuque, IA: Dubuque College, 1917), 14.

9. *Dubuque Telegram-Herald*, September 26, 1915, 20.

10. *Dubuque Telegram-Herald*, September 27, 1914, 21.

11. Maurice Sheehy, *The Dubuque Football Review* (Dubuque, IA: Dubuque College, 1917), 15.

12. Professional Football Research Association, "Thorpe Arrives, 1915."

13. *Detroit Free Press*, September 4, 1943, 12.

14. *Evening Independent* (Massillon, OH), November 15, 1928, 11.

15. *Detroit Free Press*, December 20, 1934, 21.

16. *The Witness* (Archdiocese of Dubuque, Dubuque, IA), February 21, 1974, 10.

17. *Dubuque Telegram-Herald*, September 5, 1954, 19.

18. *The Witness* (Archdiocese of Dubuque, Dubuque, IA), February 21, 1974, 10.

19. Jack Cusack, *Pioneer in Pro Football: Jack Cusack's Own Story of the period from 1912 to 1917 Inclusive, and the year 1921* (Fort Worth, TX: privately published, 1963), 16.

20. *Ibid.*, 17.

21. *Waterloo Evening Courier* (Waterloo, IA), January 24, 1916, 10.

22. *Dubuque Telegram-Herald*, September 5, 1954, 19.

23. *Dubuque Telegram-Herald*, November 20, 1916, 7.

24. *Evening Independent* (Massillon, OH), November 27, 1916, 10.

25. *Ibid.*

26. *Fort Wayne Journal-Gazette* (Fort Wayne, IN), December 21, 1916, 14.

27. Maurice Sheehy, *The Dubuque Football Review* (Dubuque, IA: Dubuque College, 1917), 30–31.

Chapter 5

1. *Spalding's Official Football Guide* (New York: American Sports Publishing, 1917), 3.

2. *Detroit Free Press*, November 25, 1936, 20.

3. *Dubuque Telegram-Herald*, December 2, 1917, 24.

4. *Fort Wayne Journal-Gazette* (Fort Wayne, IN), October 3, 1917, 6.

5. *Massillon Evening Independent* (Massillon, OH), October 6, 1917, page unknown.

6. *Notre Dame Scholastic*, February 16, 1918, 280.

7. *Notre Dame Scholastic*, November 2, 1918, 61.

8. *Detroit News*, 1940, date unknown. Taken from Dorais Family Scrapbook.

9. *Dubuque Telegram-Herald*, December 4, 1918, 10.

10. *Street & Smith's Sport Story Magazine*, December 1, 1938, 42.

11. *South Bend News-Times*, December 29, 1918, 6.

12. *South Bend News-Times*, January 5, 1919, 8.

13. *Street & Smith's Sport Story Magazine*, January 1, 1939, 93.

14. *Ibid.*, 92.

15. *Ibid.*, 93.

16. *South Bend News-Times*, March 6, 1919, 10.

17. Francis Wallace, *Knute Rockne: The Story of the Greatest Football Coach Who Ever Lived* (Garden City, NY: Doubleday, 1960), 78.

18. *South Bend News-Times*, June 4, 1920, 10.

19. Gonzaga University, Athletic Department: Football Newsclippings, 1920–1935, University Archives and Special Collections.

20. *Athletic Journal*, March 1932, 35.

21. Emil Klosinski, "Inflation of 1920: A Tale of two Cities," *The Coffin Corner* 14, no. 3, 1992.

22. *Detroit News*, November 14, 1951, 55, 57.

23. Clark Shaughnessy, *Football in War & Peace* (Clinton, SC: Jacobs Press, 1943), 85–86.

24. *Detroit News*, November 13, 1951, 39.

25. *Ibid.*, 40.

26. *Street & Smith's Sport Story Magazine*, January 1, 1939, 96.

Chapter 6

1. Walter Camp, *Spalding's Official Foot Ball Guide: Foot Ball Rules as Recommended by the Rules Committee* (New York, New York: American Sports Publishing Company, 1921), 8.

2. William Schoenberg, *Gonzaga University: Seventy-Five Years, 1887–1962*. (Spokane, WA: Gonzaga University, 1963), 268.

3. *Spokane Daily Chronicle*, August 28, 1920, 2.

4. *The Gonzaga*, October, 1920, 27.

5. *Spokesman-Review* (Spokane, WA), January 4, 1954, 9.

6. Tom Dorais interview, September 23, 1995.

7. *The Evergreen* (Washington State University newspaper), November 15, 1920, 4.

8. *Detroit Free Press*, November 16, 1941, 116.

9. *The Argonaut* (University of Idaho newspaper), September 30, 1924, 1.

10. *Athens Messenger* (Athens, OH), December 20, 1922, 10.

11. *Jacksonville Daily Journal* (Jacksonville, FL), December 24, 1922, 6.

12. *Spokane Daily Chronicle*, December 22, 1922, 23.

13. William Schoenberg, *Gonzaga University: Seventy-Five Years, 1887–1962* (Spokane, WA: Gonzaga University, 1963), 269.

14. Publications in the era had Mohardt with a total of 1,159 passing yards over 11 games for 105 yards per game. That number has since dropped to 995, for an average of just 90.

15. Pecarovich eventually became one of three Dorais protégés to become head football coach at their alma mater. He coached form 1931–1938. Ray Flaherty, 1930, and John

"Puggy Hunton," 1939–1941, were the other two.

16. *Spokesman-Review* (Spokane, WA), January 4, 1954, 9.

17. *Detroit News*, January 4, 1954, 22.

18. Schoenberg, *Gonzaga University*, 270.

19. *Ibid.*

20. *Detroit Free Press*, February 14, 1932, 40.

21. *Spokesman Review* clippings file, January 20, 1924.

22. *Spokesman Review* clippings file, January 4, 1925.

23. *Spokesman-Review*, January 4, 1954, 9.

24. *Ibid.*

25. *Spokane Daily Chronicle*, November 28, 1924, 10.

26. *Spokesman-Review*, April 30, 1967, sec. 2, 1.

27. *Spokesman Review* clippings file. December 3, 1924.

28. *Detroit Free Press*, February 8, 1925, 20.

29. *Ibid.*

30. *Spokesman-Review*, January 4, 1954, 9.

Chapter 7

1. *Varsity News* (University of Detroit), April, 1, 1925, 2.

2. *Varsity News*, May, 1925, 6, 20.

3. *Varsity News*, March 2, 1932, 3.

4. *Varsity News*, March, 26, 1926, 1.

5. *The Monocle* (Chippewa Falls High School Yearbook), 1925, 14.

6. *Varsity News*, October 21, 1925, 7.

7. *The Tower* (University of Detroit), 1927, 163.

8. *Varsity News*, November 18, 1925, 3.

9. *Varsity News*, November 25, 1925, 2.

10. *Chippewa Herald-Telegram* (Chippewa Falls, WI), September 15, 1976, 15.

11. *Varsity News*, November 16, 1926, 2.

12. *Varsity News*, October 26, 1926, 38.

13. University of Detroit Football Program, September 27, 1946, 39.

14. *Varsity News*, October 26, 1926, 18.

15. *Ibid.*, 42.

16. *Escanaba Daily News* (Escanaba, MI), February 17, 1926, 5.

17. *The Red and White* (University of Detroit), 1926, 161.

18. *Varsity News*, January 20, 1927, 1.

19. *Ibid.*, 2.

20. *Detroit Free Press*, October 2, 1927, 22.

21. Raymond Schmidt, *Shaping College Football: The Transformation of an American Sport, 1919–1930* (Syracuse, NY: Syracuse University Press, 2007), 125–126.

22. Tom Dorais interview, September 23, 1995.

23. *Notre Dame Alumnus* March 1927, 209.

24. *Detroit Free Press*, March 24, 1950, 26.

25. *Athletic Journal*, March 1932, 36.

26. *Ibid.*, 35.

27. Tom Dorais interview, September 23, 1995.

28. *Detroit Free Press*, November 20, 1942, 26.

29. *Chippewa Herald-Telegram* (Chippewa Falls, WI), September 15, 1976, 15.

30. *Ibid.*

31. *Detroit Free Press*, February 10, 1938, 16.

32. Letter from Dorais to Rockne, November 4, 1928, Records of the Director of Athletics 1908–1931 (UADR), box 10, folder 193, University of Notre Dame Ar-chives.

33. *Ibid.*

34. *Detroit Free Press*, April 7, 1965, 27.

35. *Detroit Free Press*, March 24, 1950, 26.

36. *Detroit Free Press*, February 11, 1947, 10.

37. *Detroit Free Press*, October 5, 1936, 15.

38. *College Football Historical Society Newsletter*, November 2016, 16.

39. *Chicago Tribune*, November 20, 1929, 22.

40. *Detroit Free Press*, April 4, 1964, 46.

41. *Detroit Free Press*, April 7, 1965, 27.

42. *Detroit Free Press*, December 8, 1930, 15.

43. *Detroit Free Press*, September 24, 1940, 15.

44. *Detroit Free Press*, August 12, 1938, 16.

45. *Detroit Free Press*, December 26, 1930, 13.

Chapter 8

1. *Notre Dame Alumnus*, May, 1931, 307.

2. *Reading Eagle* (Reading, PA), December 27, 1937, 13.

3. *Street & Smith's Sport Story Magazine*, January, 1, 1939, 97.

4. *Chippewa Herald-Telegram* (Chippewa Falls, WI), September 16, 1976, 11.

5. In 1930, the Xi chapter of Alpha Epsilon Pi established the Smead Trophy in hon-or of former Michigan State captain and center Harold Smead, who lost his leg following a motorcycle accident that summer.

6. The Georgetown Club of Detroit sponsored the Georgetown Trophy, to be given to the winner of three consecutive games between the two schools.

7. *Detroit Free Press*, April 28, 1932, 3.

8. *Detroit Free Press*, September 18, 1932, 15.

9. *Detroit Free Press*, January 6, 1937, 17.

10. *Detroit Free Press*, April 23, 1936, 19.

11. *Detroit Free Press*, February 10, 1938, 16.

12. *Varsity News*, March 27, 1935, 3.

13. *Ibid.*

14. Tom Dorais interview, September 23, 1995.

15. *Varsity News*, May 3, 1933, 3.

16. *Detroit Free Press*, October 25, 1937, 12.

17. University of Detroit Archives. Letter to Dorais from "Some of the Professors," April 24, 1933.

18. *Chicago Tribune*, November 12, 1931, 21.

19. *Detroit Free Press*, April 24, 1933, 16.

20. Tom Dorais interview, September 23, 1995.

21. *Detroit News*, January 11, 1933, 17.

22. *Varsity News*, April 6, 1933, 4.

23. *Detroit Free Press*, September 12, 1933, 15.

24. In the program for the Holy Cross game, Detroit took out a full-page advertisement for Nott as an All-American candidate.

25. *Detroit Free Press*, November 13, 1933, 15.

26. *Detroit News*, November 25, 1937, 27.

27. Vi Dorais interview, 1988.

28. Murray A. Sperber, *Shake Down the Thunder: The Creation of Notre Dame Football* (Bloomington, IN: Indiana University Press, 2002), 411.

29. *Chicago Tribune*, April 21, 1934, 23.

30. *Chicago Tribune*, April 23, 1934, 21.

31. *Ibid.*

32. *Chicago Tribune*, September 4, 1934, 21.

33. *Detroit Free Press*, January 4, 1954, 31.

34. *Ibid.*

35. *Chicago Tribune*, October 20, 1934, 19.

36. *Chippewa Herald-Telegram* (Chippewa Falls, WI), November 26, 1934, 3.

37. *Varsity News*, December 5, 1934, 1.

38. *Varsity News*, December 19, 1934, 1.

39. *Detroit News*, December 17, 1934, 25.

40. *The Day* (New London, CT), May 16, 1935, 16.

41. *Detroit Free Press*, October 17, 1935, 17.

42. *Detroit Free Press*, October 20, 1935, 42.

43. *Detroit Free Press*, October 28, 1936, 21.

44. *Detroit News*, October 29, 1940, 22.

45. *Chicago Tribune*, December 29, 1935, A1.

46. *Detroit News*, December 29, 1935, sec. 2, 1–2.

47. *Detroit News*, April 22, 1936, 21.
48. There is no record of the trip ever taking place.
49. *Detroit Free Press*, November 3, 1936, 17.
50. *Detroit News*, October 31, 1936, 15.
51. *Detroit News*, December 31, 1936, 13.
52. *Ibid.*
53. *Ibid.*

Chapter 9

1. *Detroit Free Press*, July 21, 1927, 15.
2. *Chicago Tribune*, August 13, 1937, 23.
3. *Ludington Daily News* (Ludington, MI), August 21, 1937, 6.
4. *Detroit Free Press*, August 20, 1937, 17.
5. *Detroit Times*, September 21, 1937, page unknown. Dorais Family Clippings File.
6. *Chicago Tribune*, December 15, 1937, 27.
7. *Chicago Tribune*, July 21, 1941, page unknown. Dorais Family Clippings File.
8. *Detroit News*, September 21, 1937, 26.
9. Tom Dorais interview, September 23, 1995.
10. *Chicago Tribune*, July 30, 1987, 2.
11. *Chicago Tribune*, November 2, 1937, 17.
12. *Detroit Free Press*, November 4, 1937, 19.
13. *Detroit Free Press*, November 9, 1937, 16.
14. *Ibid.*
15. *Detroit Free Press*, December 10, 1937, 21.
16. *Detroit Free Press*, February 19, 1939, 15.
17. *Evening Independent* (St. Petersburg, FL), October 5, 1938, 11.
18. Dorais Family Clippings File.
19. *Detroit Free Press*, November 23, 1938, 16.
20. *Spokesman Review* (Spokane, WA), November 28, 1938, 37.
21. *Detroit Free Press*, May 28, 1939, 7.
22. *Notre Dame Scholastic*, September 22, 1939, 3.
23. *Detroit Free Press*, August 15, 1939, 14.
24. *Detroit Free Press*, November 2, 1939, 18.
25. *Detroit Free Press*, September 22, 1943, 16.
26. *Athletic Journal*, March 1932, 36.
27. Tom Dorais interview, September 23, 1995.
28. *Varsity News*, October 15, 1941, 1.
29. *Chicago Tribune*, October 15, 1940, 23.
30. The game spawned the Motor City Trophy—an automobile painted in the colors of the Titans and Tartars.

31. *College Football Historical Society* (Ventura, CA), November 1996, 3.
32. *Detroit News*, October 29, 1940, 21.
33. *Detroit Free Press*, November 8, 1940, 15.
34. *Detroit News*, November 13, 1940, 27.
35. *Ibid.*
36. Richard Whittingham, *What a Game They Played: Stories of the Early Days of Pro Football by Those Who Were There* (New York: Harper & Row, 1984), 212.
37. *Gonzaga Bulletin*, November 27, 1940, 6.
38. *Varsity News*, November 27, 1940, 3.
39. *Detroit Free Press*, February 4, 1941, 13.
40. *Detroit Free Press*, October 13, 1942, 14.
41. Tom Dorais interview, September 23, 1995.
42. *Varsity News*, December 9, 1942, 3.
43. *Chicago Tribune*, January 30, 1943, 15.
44. *Detroit News*, January 10, 1943, page unknown. Dorais Family Clippings File.
45. *Detroit Times*, February 14, 1944, page unknown. Dorais Family Clippings File.

Chapter 10

1. *Detroit Free Press*, April 2, 1943, 24.
2. *Chicago Daily Tribune*, June 24, 1943, 23.
3. *Detroit Free Press*, July 11, 1943, 19.
4. *Detroit Free Press*, August 19, 1943, 14.
5. *Milwaukee Journal*, September 30, 1943, 8.
6. *Detroit Free Press*, September 4, 1943, 12.
7. *Detroit Free Press*, October 16, 1943, 11.
8. *Ibid.*
9. *Chicago Daily Tribune*, October 28, 1943, 25.
10. *Detroit Free Press*, November 5, 1943, 22.
11. *Charleston Gazette* (Charleston, WV), May 21, 1944, 10.
12. The Card-Pitt team and the Tigers both went winless—the last time there were two teams that did so in one season.
13. *Detroit Free Press*, November 20, 1945, 12.
14. *Detroit Free Press*, December 8, 1945, 11.
15. Tom Dorais interview, September 23, 1995.
16. *Detroit Times*, October 9, 1946. Dorais family clippings file.
17. *Detroit Free Press*, December 7, 1946. Dorais family clippings file.

18. *Detroit Free Press*, December 17, 1946, 20.

19. Mary Kay Dorais interview, 2005.

20. *Detroit Times*, January 4, 1954. Dorais family clippings file.

21. Richard Whittingham, *What a Game They Played: Stories of the Early Days of Pro Football by Those Who Were There* (New York: Harper & Row, 1984), 232.

22. *Detroit News*, February 14, 1948. Dorais Family Clippings File.

23. *Detroit Free Press*, January 4, 1954, 31.

24. *News-Palladium* (Benton Harbor, MI), January 9, 1948. Dorais Family Clippings File.

25. *Detroit News*, January 8, 1948. Dorais Family Clippings File.

Chapter 11

1. *Detroit Free Press*, June 12, 1949, 13.

2. *Wisconsin State Journal* (Madison, WI), January 4, 1954, sec. 2, 2.

3. *Sandusky Register Star-News* (Sandusky, OH), September 2, 1949, 1.

4. *Detroit News*, September 25, 1951, page unknown. Dorais Family Clippings File.

5. *Detroit Free Press*, June 22, 1952, 30.

6. *Pittsburgh Sun-Telegraph*, January 18, 1953, page unknown. Dorais Family Clippings File.

7. *Detroit News*, January 9, 1954, page unknown.

8. *Wisconsin State Journal* (Madison, WI), May 24, 1953, sec. 3, 1.

9. *Detroit News*, January 5, 1954, 1.

10. Dorais Family Clippings File.

11. *Birmingham Eccentric* (Birmingham, MI), January 7, 1954, 1.

12. *Detroit News*, January 4, 1954, 22.

13. *Ibid.*

14. *Ibid.*, January 6, 1954. Dorais Family Clippings File.

15. *Denver Post*, January 4, 1954, Dorais Family Clippings File.

16. *Detroit News*, January 6, 1954, 32.

17. *Detroit Free Press*. Dorais Family Clippings File.

18. *Chicago Tribune*, January 5, 1954. Dorais Family Clippings File.

Bibliography

Books

Beach, Jim, and Daniel Moore. *Army Vs. Notre Dame: The Big Game, 1913–1947.* New York: Random House, 1948.

Camp, Walter. *Spalding's Official Foot Ball Guide: Foot Ball Rules as Recommended by the Rules Committee.* New York: American Sports Publishing, 1921.

Cusack, Jack. *Pioneer in Pro Football: Jack Cusack's Own Story of the Period from 1912 to 1917 Inclusive, and the Year 1921.* Fort Worth, TX: privately published, 1963.

Dorais, Charles E. *The Forward Pass and Its Defense.* Chicago: Athletic Book Company, 1931.

Heisler, Karen Croake. *Fighting Irish: Legends, Lists and Lore.* Champaign, IL: Sports Publishing, 2006.

Hoffmann, Mathias Martin. *The Story of Loras College, 1839–1939, the Oldest College in Iowa.* Dubuque, IA: Loras College Press, 1939.

Hope, Arthur, J. *Notre Dame: One Hundred Years.* South Bend, IN: Notre Dame University Press, 1943.

Rappoport, Ken. *Wake Up the Echoes: Notre Dame Football.* Huntsville, AL: Strode, 1975.

Schmidt, Raymond. *Shaping College Football: The Transformation of an American Sport, 1919–1930.* Syracuse, NY: Syracuse University Press, 2007.

Schoenberg, William P. *Gonzaga University: Seventy-Five Years, 1887–1962.* Spokane, WA: Gonzaga University, 1963.

Shaughnessy, Clark. *Football in War & Peace.* Clinton, SC: Jacobs Press, 1943.

Sperber, Murray A. *Shake Down the Thunder: The Creation of Notre Dame Football.* Bloomington: Indiana University Press, 2002.

Wallace, Francis. *Knute Rockne: The Story of the Greatest Football Coach Who Ever Lived.* Garden City, NY: Doubleday, 1960.

Whittingham, Richard. *What a Game They Played: An Inside Look at the Golden Age of Pro Football.* New York: Simon & Schuster, 1987.

Willis, Chris. *Old Leather: An Oral History of Early Pro Football in Ohio, 1920–1935.* Lanham, MD: Scarecrow, 2005.

Newspapers

Anaconda Standard (Anaconda, MT)
Athens Messenger (Athens, OH)
Birmingham Eccentric (Birmingham, MI)
Capital Times (Madison, WI)
Cedar Rapids Evening Gazette (Cedar Rapids, IA)
Chicago Daily News
Chicago Tribune
Chippewa Herald-Telegram (Chippewa Falls, WI)
Daily Independent (Chippewa Falls, WI)
The Day (New London, CT)
Denver Post
Detroit Free Press
Detroit News
Detroit Saturday Times
Detroit Times

Dubuque Telegram-Herald (Dubuque, IA)
Eau Claire Leader (Eau Claire, WI)
Escanaba Daily News (Escanaba, MI)
Evening Independent (Massillon, OH)
Evening Independent (St. Petersburg, FL)
Fort Wayne Journal-Gazette (Fort Wayne, IN)
Indianapolis News
Jacksonville Daily Journal (Jacksonville, FL)
La Crosse Tribune (La Crosse, WI)
Ludington Daily News (Ludington, MI)
Milwaukee Journal
Milwaukee Sentinel
Morning Oregonian (Portland, OR)
Pittsburgh Post-Gazette
Pittsburgh Sun-Gazette
Reading Eagle (Reading, PA)
Sandusky Register Star-News (Sandusky, OH)
South Bend News-Times (South Bend, IN),
South Bend Tribune (South Bend, IN)
Spokane Daily Chronicle (Spokane, WA)
Spokesman-Review (Spokane, WA)
Waterloo Evening And Reporter (Waterloo, IA),
Wisconsin State Journal (Madison, WI)

Magazines/Journals/ Newsletters

Athletic Journal
Blue and Gold Illustrated
Coffin Corner
College Football Historical Society Newsletter
Collier's
Dress & Vanity Fair

The Dubuque Football Review
Notre Dame Alumnus
Wisconsin Alumnus
The Witness (Archdiocese of Dubuque, IA)
Street & Smith's Sport Story Magazine

Yearbooks

The Dome (University of Notre Dame)
The Monocle (Chippewa Falls High School, Chippewa Falls, WI)
The Red and White (University of Detroit)
The Tower (University of Detroit)

School Newspapers

The Argonaut (University of Idaho)
The Evergreen (Washington State University)
Gonzaga Bulletin (Gonzaga University)
Notre Dame Scholastic (University of Notre Dame)
Varsity News (University of Detroit)

Archival Research

Gonzaga University clippings file
Dorais family clippings file
Spokesman Review clippings file

Interviews

Tom Dorais, September 23, 1995
Mary Kay Dorais, 2005
Vi Dorais, 1988

Websites

https://www.pro-football-reference.com
http://www.profootballresearchers.org/

Index